A Book I Value

Samuel Taylor Coleridge

A Book I Value

Selected Marginalia

EDITED BY

H. J. Jackson

PRINCETON UNIVERSITY PRESS
PRINCETON AND OXFORD

Library of Congress Cataloging-in-Publication Data
Coleridge, Samuel Taylor, 1772–1834.
A book I value : selected marginalia / Samuel Taylor Coleridge ;
edited by H. J. Jackson.
p. cm.
Includes index.
ISBN 0-691-11351-3 (alk. paper) —
ISBN 0-691-11317-3 (pbk. : alk. paper)
1. Coleridge, Samuel Taylor, 1772–1834—Books and reading.
2. Books and reading.   3. Marginalia.   I. Jackson, H. J.
II. Title.
PR4472 .J28 2003
821′.7—dc21   2002074981

British Library Cataloging-in-Publication Data is available

This book has been composed in Times New Roman
with Perpetua display
Printed on acid-free paper. ∞
www.pupress.princeton.edu
Printed in the United States of America
1 3 5 7 9 10 8 6 4 2

FOR ELIZABETH WHALLEY

CONTENTS

Contents

Contents

INTRODUCTION

This selection is intended as a sampler for readers who are interested in Coleridge, curious about the way his mind worked, and ready to venture beyond the few canonical poems and essays into uncharted territory—but perhaps not yet ready for the collected works, which amount now to about fifty volumes in the standard scholarly editions, including six volumes of marginalia. Even advanced students feel the need of a guide to such a labyrinth, and those whose main concerns lie elsewhere may find that the guide itself gives them all they want. The marginalia are a good place to start, because they represent an informal, unintimidating kind of writing that Coleridge practiced with pleasure for most of his working life, and because the topics broached in them cover pretty well the whole range of his very extensive interests—literature, philosophy, politics, biology, psychology, religious controversy, social justice, ethnography, education—in *their* full range from the workings of divine creation to the stubbornness of fruit stains in muslin. Sometimes aphoristic, sometimes rude, often surprising, they are at least the equal of Coleridge's letters and notebooks in conveying those distinctive qualities of mind and character that we tend to sum up as his individual "voice." Aphoristic? "The Spirit is an Island harbourless, and every way inaccessible" (# 23); "If Necessity and Freedom are not different Points of View of the same Thing, the one the *Form*, the other the Substance, farewell to all Philosophy and to all Ethics" (# 61); "I would not give a groat for a man, whose Heart does not sometimes betray his Judgement" (# 235). Rude? "And thus the Book impressed me, to wit, as being Rant, abuse, drunken Self-conceit that kicking and sprawling in the 6 inch-deep Gutter of muddy Philosophism from the drainings of a hundred Sculleries dreams that he is swimming in an ocean of the Translucent & the Profound" (# 7); ". . . the Barrister might as rationally expect to blow up Windsor Castle by breaking wind in one of its Cellars, as hope to demolish Calvinism by such arguments as his" (# 45); "The Pope in his Conclave had about the same influence on Charles's Fate as the Pope's Eye in a Leg of Mutton" (# 159). Distinctive in voice? Informal as they are, relatively speaking, in language and structure, the marginalia are far from languid and lazy; they crackle with energy and with a sense of urgency that reflects both Coleridge's serious attention to the book at hand and his excitement over ideas just emerging in his mind as he reads it. Often the urgency takes the shape of questions, rhetorical or otherwise. "Is Germany the ruling Influence of Europe?" he wonders (# 220). Or "what do not *Women* owe to Christianity!" (# 263). Or he rises to the bait of the author who placidly describes the Bible as accessible to all, a plain and easy book: "What if I were to call Newton's 'Principia' a *plain*, easy Book, because certain detached passages were axiomatic, & because the results were evident to common-sense?—What? The Pentateuch? the Solomon's Song? The Prophets in general, & Ezekiel in particular? What? the Ecclesiastes? The praise of Jael? of Ehud? of David?—What? St John's Gospel, & his Revelations? the *apparent* Discordances of the Evangelists in the most important narration, that of the Resurrection? What? St Paul's Epistles, declared by a contemporary Apostle, dark & hard?—are these parts of a plain & easy Book?" (# 70). Or he puzzles over the fact that Kant's early work went unnoticed, while his *Critique of Pure Reason* produced an intellectual revolution:

> What was the cause of this difference? Is it, that the same Thoughts appeared less strange, less paradoxical, in Latin than in the vernacular Tongue? Or that the ordinary proofs of the higher psychology are exposed more openly & expressly in the Crit. d. r. V. than in the former work?—Or lastly, that one's mother tongue however philosophized and technical still produces on us a liveliness of impression which a dead Language cannot produce? (# 47)

In remarks such as these Coleridge is not questioning the book only, as annotators commonly do; he is running with the question to see where it might lead him. "A book, I value," he declared, "I reason & quarrel with as with myself when I am reasoning."

OCCASIONS FOR ANNOTATION

"People aren't supposed to write in our books": that was the indignant reaction of a librarian when I proudly showed off previously unrecognized annotations made by Coleridge 160 years earlier. It is an understandable response, particularly from the custodian of a public collection who has to consider the interests of future users. Concerns about property, aesthetics, and the privacy of the reading experience all argue against marginal annotations, which are taboo in the librarian's world. Book dealers think differently, at least if the notes can be attributed to a certified celebrity. Scholars and critics point out that marginalia are sometimes more interesting than the books in which they appear—the annotator outshining the author—and that in any case marginal notes may be of historical value no matter who wrote them, if they tell us something about the way readers used to read, or about the reputation of a particular work at a given moment. The consensus nowadays appears to be that it's all right to put notes in books so long as they are your own books. It is thought to be modest and seemly to do it in pencil. It is more excusable if you have something really worthwhile to say or if you are a very important person.

Coleridge, however, usually wrote his notes in ink, and more often than not in other people's books, to judge by the 450 or so of his annotated books still extant. To understand why, we must consider briefly both his particular situation with regard to books and the history of readers' notes in general.

Coleridge's education equipped him to be a scholar, but his religious convictions at a critical point of his life prevented him from pursuing a career in the church or the university. He left Cambridge without a degree. He tried instead to live by his pen or by his gifted tongue, being in turn teacher, lay preacher, private secretary, playwright, journalist, and lecturer. He published miscellaneously. He was not, in worldly terms, a great success: for most of his life he had no settled occupation and no financial security. Before he moved into the household of a surgeon, James Gillman, in 1816, he led a nomadic existence, and there was no guarantee even after 1816 that the stability would last. In Coleridge's experience, books came and went: some were library copies in the first place, some had to be pawned, some were lost at sea or on the road. His attitude toward books was rather casual, perhaps because he could never count on keeping them. He used to borrow books for years on end; inscribe them to give away as gifts but hang onto them after all; and lend them out even when they didn't belong to him. (His long-suffering friend Charles Lamb, who *did* like to keep track of his books, once described a fine collection of German books belonging to a mutual acquaintance as "pant[ing] for that free circulation which thy custody is sure to give them.") But Coleridge managed at practically all times to have access to books—other people's libraries if not his own—and the very circumstances that withheld conventional success made him an ideal reader. Books were his bread and butter and his recreation as well; he had, most of the time, nothing to do but to read. In a letter written to his brother-in-law Robert Southey in 1805, he measures perfect contentment in terms of love and books:

> O had I domestic Happiness, and an Assurance even of the Health,
> I now possess, continuing to me in England, what a blessed Crea-
> ture should I be, tho' I found it necessary to feed me and mine on
> roast Potatoes for 2 days in each week in order to make ends meet,
> and to awake my Beloved with a Kiss on the first of every Janry—
> Well, my best Darling! we owe nobody a farthing!—and I have you,
> my children, two or three friends, and a thousand Books!

Coleridge read widely, depending on what was available and what his current projects and obligations were. He read Latin, Greek, German, and
Italian easily, and French if he had to; he had some Hebrew. By the time
he began to be serious about writing notes in books, he had a great range
of experience to draw on.

Although toward the end of his life, when he was so well known as an
annotator that even strangers sent him their books to write in, Coleridge
himself put it about that he had always been a compulsive scribbler in
books, the evidence of the surviving annotated books suggests otherwise.
Rather, it seems that it was not until he was in his thirties that he began
writing extensive comments in books, and that he did so then in order
to share those books with a few very close friends—initially William
Wordsworth, Robert Southey, Sara Hutchinson, Thomas Poole, and
Charles Lamb; later, James and Anne Gillman and Joseph Henry Green.
This social use of books was not something he undertook out of constitutional habit or professional necessity: these were people with whom he
talked about books, and when they were apart he could in a sense continue the conversation by commenting on the books he had borrowed
from them or would be lending to them. On occasion, however, professional necessity played a part, as when he annotated books to help
Southey, who had them to review. Rapidly, the practice did become a
habit, a harmless habit "indulged by the partiality of my friends," as he
wrote in one of his German books. It also became a decided professional
asset. When he had to deliver a set of lectures on Shakespeare in 1818–
19, he took an interleaved, annotated copy of the plays into the lecture hall
(# 102–12). As time went on and the mass of marginalia grew steadily,
he began to see the notes in his books as a resource susceptible of infinite
reconfiguration and hence a way of beating writer's block. Several of the
projects that Coleridge proposed to publishers in the 1820s include references to marginalia that, as he truthfully said, needed only to be sorted
and transcribed to form the basis of a new book; some of the projects realized in that decade, notably his *Aids to Reflection*, did exploit the marginalia and the note-writing mentality.

This personal history helps to account for the complex status of Coleridge's marginal notes, which might serve any one of several functions, or several at once. At the most elementary level, writing in books was a practical method for assimilating the contents and filing them for future use. While he was working on an essay or lecture, for instance, rather than setting down an argument at length, Coleridge could refer himself to such-and-such a book, where he had done it already. Like other professional writers, he put his books to work. But annotating a book for a friend imposed other requirements, since it made the book a permanent token of friendship and made the act of annotation a more or less deliberate performance, like a letter. Yet again, in the process of reading and annotating for these conscious purposes, Coleridge was likely to find himself involuntarily enmeshed in debate with the author—so that his notes became the record of a fantasy dialogue in the imagined presence of the absent friend. For example, he expresses his gratitude to Southey's *Life of Wesley*, a source of comfort to him in times of sickness and distress:

> How many and many an hour of Self-oblivion do I owe to this Life of Wesley—how often have I argued with it, questioned, remonstrated, been peevish & asked pardon—then again listened & cried, Right! Excellent!—& in yet heavier hours intreated it, as it were, to continue talking to me—for that I heard & listened & was soothed even tho' I could make no reply. (# 148)

In this case the author and the imagined friend were one and the same, but Coleridge clearly articulates the impression of personal contact that he and other intense readers experience with books. Finally, we can see that under the spell of the book Coleridge sometimes forgot the author, the friend, and the ostensible purpose of reading altogether, and became engaged in a deeply personal struggle, his notes then an effort to come to terms with his own demons, especially his addiction to opium and fears for his moral and spiritual welfare. The marginalia were an outlet for Coleridge, but in various and occasionally conflicting ways.

TRADITION AND THE INDIVIDUAL TALENT

In making his books work for him by writing marginalia, Coleridge was himself working creatively within a well-established tradition. For centuries, students had been trained to copy approved explanatory glosses and eventually to add their own, in printed books just as previously in manuscripts. In the century before Coleridge became a celebrated annotator, the great expansion of publishing in Britain meant that more people had opportunities to own books and to make them their own with appropriate manuscript supplements. So scholars collated their copies of classical works with other editions, and children put the translations of hard words directly into their textbooks. Lawyers kept records of new statutes and significant judgments that affected the law by entering them in their Coke upon Littleton and other handbooks. Amateur naturalists made notes in their field guides about the incidence of species of birds, butterflies, and plants in their own areas. Readers exercised their wits and displayed their knowingness, as they were meant to do, by filling in the blanks in satires and poems *à clef* with the proper names of the subjects, so that D—— of B——ck——m, for example, became "Duke of Buckingham." Those who were engaged in controversy carried their arguments over into the margins and endpapers of their opponents' works. The devout enriched their Bibles and prayer books with learned commentary and pious meditations. Such usage was continuous with earlier practice. These notes were usually made in ink because they were expected to be preserved as long as the book itself remained in use.

The eighteenth century, however, also saw significant changes in the practice of annotation. The introduction of the footnote as a supplement to or substitute for the printed marginal gloss in books gave readers a new model to imitate. The footnote had more latitude than the old marginal gloss both in terms of its functions and in terms of the space it might be permitted to occupy. Readers encountered it especially in the great editions in the vernacular for which the period is famous—Pope's Homer, Percy's *Reliques*, several Shakespeares. Emulating the editors, readers began to write critical notes in their books. They also began, in a way that is characteristic of the period, to share their annotated books with friends. The one development reinforced the other: you might not comment on the work at all without an anticipated audience; with such an audience you would want to make the commentary worth having. It should appear as value added to the book, not as mere self-indulgence or vandalism.

Coleridge was not anomalous, then, in using books as he did. He was, however, exceptional and could be said to have transformed the tradition single-handedly. His notes struck his contemporaries as they strike us today (when we have the marginalia of Blake and Keats available in print for comparison), that is, as uncommonly subtle and searching. They ratcheted up the standard for critical commentary—and they did so publicly, for Coleridge saw to it as early as 1819 that the pick of his "marginalia," as he called them, were published as freestanding essays, not simply as footnotes to somebody else's text. In compliance with his known wishes, his executors included large quantities of marginalia in his posthumous *Literary Remains* and other collections.

Coleridge's great innovation was, as these things often are, wonderfully simple. Traditionally, the virtues of the marginal note are accuracy (as it improves or illuminates the text) and compression. If it lends itself to aphorism, that may be because it has to fit into the nutshell of the margin. But Coleridge did not trade in nutshells. He turned the page. If he had more to say than would fit into the margin, he turned the page and carried on—and on and on, until he was through. He refused to apologize for the length of the results: "On a subject of such infinite importance I fear prolixity less than obscurity" (# 24). His legacy to the tradition of the marginal note is therefore twofold, the addition of a new kind of note, the extended personal reflection; and the example of a sustained body of such material.

MODEL MARGINALIA

Coleridge remains the exemplary model for the sort of marginal note that he invented and publicized, a hybrid resembling but distinct from its three closest relations, the traditional marginal comment, the familiar letter, and the personal essay. I do not mean to suggest that his marginalia should be considered mainly as formal curiosities, far from it. They owe their strength to Coleridge's real power as a thinker and reader—a particularly subtle thinker, an unusually charitable reader. But the unorthodox form of the notes contributes to their fascination. Readers tend to react to them very much as Coleridge's contemporaries reacted to his conversation, some automatically turned off by what they see as self-indulgent rambling but others, more patient or more attentive or fond of Coleridge already, completely charmed. When I read through the Princeton edition again to put together this selection, I experienced both kinds of reaction, but with an overwhelming balance of admiration. In the marginal note as tailored to his own mental frame, Coleridge found an ideal vehicle for his thoughts and his *way* of thinking. How so?

The marginal note, in the first place, is by definition dependent on a prior text. It is responsive, that is, analytical and critical, in the neutral (not necessarily negative) sense of the word "critical." It takes what is given and explores it, sounds it, fixes it if there is something seriously wrong. In Coleridge's hands, the exploration is likely to be thorough; but because the note is only a manuscript note, not a public pronouncement, it remains tentative and provisional. This feature must have been a great liberation to Coleridge: it not only suited his inquiring habit of mind but also deferred commitment and thereby left him free to say what he thought at the time of writing. Many of the notes are dated. He could come back to the book if he changed his mind or could comment later on the notes themselves, as in his second look at Luther's position on justification by faith: "I should not have written the above Note in my present state of Light. Not that I find it false; but that it may have the effect of falsehood by not going deep enough" (# 132). This same provisional quality makes the notes more attractive and more stimulating to the reader than they would be if they were firm and dogmatic.

Then there is the spontaneity of the marginal note, with its unpredictable development. Coleridge appears to ramble or rather to vault from one subject to another. Weren't we talking about waltzing in Germany? Then how did we get on to the education of women (# 193)? The unexpected twists and turns of the note prove that it is an uninhibited outpouring of ideas. So it seems, and so to some extent it may really be. But Coleridge cultivated the dazzling leap, especially in conversation. One of his late poems refers to the art of the *improvisatore*, the one who makes up extempore verses at a party. He was himself an intellectual improvisor: give him a topic and he could play with it for hours, generally to the delight of the company. In his case, however, the primary goal was not to entertain with metaphysical wit in which "the most heterogeneous ideas are yoked by violence together" (as Johnson crushingly described it), but to trace the real but hidden connectedness of things. Coleridge loved a joke but was himself constitutionally serious. And this fact leads to the aspect of his thinking that is perhaps the most difficult for a modern reader to grasp sympathetically, his bedrock of belief.

In response to a remark in Samuel Parr's *Spital Sermon* to the effect that atheism is naturally alien to the human mind, Coleridge produces a riff on atheism that begins with his own spiritual experience but soon passes on to consider the reasoned defense of religion, the French Revolution, the Inquisition in South America, and the rise of modern experimental science, before ending with a call for the revival of Plato and *Jack the Giant Killer* (# 83). Here he is sketching out what he saw as deep and important links between individual (and mass) behavior and the spirit of the age. All the marginalia belong to Coleridge's maturity, when he had worked out the fundamental convictions that formed the basis of a constant system of values. He read widely to test those convictions but also to extract from the work of other minds materials with which he might construct a vision of the universe to compete with the popular but in his view fatally flawed materialism stemming from Descartes, Locke, and Newton. He welcomed scientific evidence and philosophic arguments that appeared to lend support to his faith in a dynamic universe driven by energy, not matter, and to his hard-won Trinitarianism. His position was profoundly counter-Enlightenment. Therefore he was prepared to lend an ear to voices that had been effectively silenced by the fashions of the day—to foreigners, mystics, and the out of date—and we honor him for it. But the schools of Locke and Newton have prevailed, and it is hard for most of us to imagine the world in any way but theirs. So there is much that is profoundly alien to us in the marginalia, and though they may be often entertaining and quotable, they are not *easy* reading.

On the other hand, we can still learn from Coleridge's example a lesson of sympathy that makes it hard to dismiss out of hand even the most seemingly preposterous views. Most writers who express their opinions in marginalia exercise their power over the author by focusing on points of disagreement and making it their business to put the author straight. Though criticism is their raison d'être, in Coleridge's notes as a general rule charity trumps criticism. Much as he is given to questioning and challenging, he understands—and perhaps it came easily to him because he had found himself, as an author, much in need of such understanding— that his job as a critic is first of all to make an effort to see things from the writer's point of view. Hence his repeated injunctions to readers to exercise historical imagination, to put themselves in the writer's place, to see how it must unavoidably come about, under those circumstances, that the writer should make mistakes, and how amazing it is really that the writer should get so many things right. Hence the length and complexity of his own notes, which are only incidentally aphoristic or rude, their main aim being to do the author justice. "Read then in meekness—lest to read him at all, which might be thy folly, should prove thy Sin" (# 28).

PRESENTATION

The selection that follows is based on the six-volume *Marginalia* in the Bollingen Edition of Coleridge's *Collected Works* (Princeton UP, 1980–2001). I have tried to make it a warts-and-all representative sample reflecting Coleridge's preoccupations, not our own, though it was tempting to focus on those aspects of his life and character that at the moment we find most interesting—his mercuriality, his complicated relations with Wordsworth, his various weaknesses and the torment they brought him.

The chronological arrangement, an experiment here, is also part of the effort to minimize subjectivity and what historians call "presentism." The obvious alternatives would be the similarly impersonal alphabetical arrangement of the standard edition (but I wanted to try something new) and an arrangement by topic (but that would be not only subjective but doomed). There is no easy solution. If the organization is by author, readers will be disappointed when they find the content of the notes frustratingly remote from the contents of the book; Coleridge once wrote a note about fever-hospitals in a rhyming dictionary. If by topic, what are the headings to be: Religion, Daily Life, Childhood, Law, Dreams, Friendship? There might be almost as many topics as there are notes. And given Coleridge's familiar bridging of realms of experience, would the 1817 note on Shakespeare (# 102) go under Literary Criticism as a note about dramatic illusion, or under Psychology as an observation about dreams? The marginalia are desperately hard to pigeonhole. (Readers who prefer the topic option may find the index a helpful way of reconstituting the collection.) A chronological arrangement naturally has its own problems. Sometimes there is no internal or external record of when the reading took place and therefore no way to date the notes. Dating is often speculative. Sometimes Coleridge returned to a book, writing new notes among and on top of the old; in that case I have left the whole set of notes at the time of the first or main reading, but use the headnote to give warning of the actual range of likely dates.

This selection consists of approximately 5 percent of the extant marginalia. It therefore necessarily excludes many titles and, even for the titles chosen, the majority of the notes. The section on John Reynolds (# 94–100), however, as a sample, contains all the notes from that volume. It incidentally illustrates a technical point in that it shows how the first note in a book, written on a flyleaf or title page, is often a summary composed after the commentary as an introduction both to the book and to the notes in it.

Though every note is given in full and the sequence of the notes follows the front-to-back sequence (from the flyleaves to the endpapers of the original volume) of the Bollingen Edition, texts have been somewhat simplified and editorial interference has been kept to a minimum. Coleridge's notes are reproduced faithfully as far as spelling, punctuation, and capitalization are concerned, but ligatures are expanded; the possessive "it's" is regularized to "its"; cancelled words and letters are silently omitted; inserted passages are silently incorporated; the page numbers by which Coleridge sometimes located his note, and the signatures or initials with which he sometimes closed, are generally left out. Points of ellipsis in square brackets within Coleridge's notes mean that the note at that point is damaged or for other reasons illegible. In two or three cases I have used square brackets for an editorial insertion in order to clarify the meaning of a word, but normally Coleridge's slips of the pen—"chocate" for "chocolate," for example—are allowed to stand, as signs of haste but authentic and not impenetrable. Foreign-language titles are translated unless the work is actually in English with a self-explanatory English subtitle. Foreign words in Coleridge's notes are translated in square brackets unless Coleridge himself goes on to translate them.

The headnote for each title, given in italics, provides information about the circumstances under which Coleridge wrote his notes—for example, the name of the owner of the book or the project to which the notes were designed to contribute. If it is necessary to print the passage annotated, it is given in smaller type than Coleridge's note itself; if the original language was not English, the translation only is provided, in braces. Underlining represents Coleridge's underlining in the book. Since footnotes are often an unwelcome distraction, all the more so in a collection composed of notes, I have avoided them and have instead provided what seemed to be essential information in the headnotes. (Much fuller annotation is of course available in the complete edition.) To save space, notes are not usually repeated: once persons have been identified and words defined, the reader should use the index to find them again.

MARGINALIA

1801

Immanuel Kant, *Critik der reinen Vernunft* *[Critique of Pure Reason]*, Leipzig, 1799.

The works of Kant were of the profoundest influence upon Coleridge, who memorably described them as having taken possession of him "as with a giant's hand" when he was a young man; he goes on to say, in Biographia Literaria, *that "after fifteen years familiarity with them, I still read these and all his other productions with undiminished delight and increasing admiration." The following notes from Coleridge's first reading of the* Critique of Pure Reason *date from about 1801.*

An aeolian or eolian harp is a stringed box that is left out of doors or in a window to make music as the wind passes over the strings. "Linley" is a reference to Thomas Linley the Younger, a celebrated violinist; "mind's eye" is a phrase from Hamlet *1.2.185; Fichte was one of the two or three most important successors to Kant in the next generation.*

[# 1] Doubts during a first perusal—i.e. Struggles felt, not arguments objected.

1. How can that be called ein mannigfaltiges ὑλὴ [a confused manifold], which yet contains in itself the ground, why I apply one category to it rather than another? one mathematical form and not another? The mind does not resemble an Eolian Harp, nor even a barrel-organ turned by a stream of water, conceive as many tunes mechanized in it as you like— but rather, as far as Objects are concerned, a violin, or other instrument of few strings yet vast compass, played on by a musician of Genius. The Breeze that blows across the Eolian Harp, the streams that turned the handle of the Barrel Organ, might be called ein mannigfaltiges [a manifold], a mere sylva incondita [unformed matter], but who would call the muscles and purpose of Linley a confused Manifold?

[# 2] The perpetual and unmoving Cloud of Darkness, that hangs over this Work to my "mind's eye", is the absence of any clear account of—was ist Erfahrung [what is experience]? What do you mean by a *fact*, an empiric Reality, which alone can give solidity (inhalt [content]) to our Concep-

3

tions?—It seems from many passages, that this indispensible Test is itself previously manufactured by this very conceptive Power—and that the whole not of our own making is the mere sensation of a mere Manifold—in short, mere influx of motion, to use a physical metaphor.—I apply the Categoric forms to a Tree—well! but first *what* is this tree? How do I come by this Tree?—Fichte I understand very well—only I cannot believe his System. But Kant I do not understand—i.e. I have not discovered what he proposes for my Belief.—Is it Dogmatism?—Why then make the opposition between Phaenomena and Things in themselves—τα οντως οντα [things that really exist]? Is it Idealism? What Test then can I find in the different modifications of my Being to verify and substantiate each other? What other distinction between Schein and Erscheinung, Illusion and Appearance more than the old one of—in one I dream to myself, and in the other I dream in common: The Man in a fever is only *outvoted* by his Attendants—He does not see their Dream, and they do not see his.

1803

Robert Anderson, ed., *The Works of the British Poets*, Edinburgh and London, 1792–95.

Coleridge wrote notes in three different sets of Anderson's popular anthology. This set is unusual in containing notes by William Wordsworth as well; in fact, in the example given, Coleridge's note begins as a comment on an earlier note by Wordsworth, written at the end of the section devoted to Shakespeare's sonnets. The book belonged to Coleridge, but he expected that his brother-in-law and housemate Robert Southey, whom he mentions, would be reading his notes, and that his own son Hartley, whom he addresses directly, would one day inherit the set.

"Potter's Antiquities" was a common schoolbook, John Potter's Archaeologia Graeca: or the Antiquities of Greece; *Coleridge mentions specifically a chapter about the Greeks' "Love of Boys" which maintains that there was nothing sexual about it. "Johnson" means the playwright Ben Jonson, whom Coleridge frequently uses, as here, along with Beaumont and Fletcher and Massinger, as a more or less contemporary point of comparison with Shakespeare.*

[# 3]

[Wordsworth's note:] These sonnets, beginning at 127, to his Mistress, are worse than a puzzle-peg. They are abominably harsh obscure & worthless. The others are for the most part much better, have many fine lines very fine lines & passages. They are also in many places warm with passion. Their chief faults, and heavy ones they are, are sameness, tediousness, quaintness, & elaborate obscurity.—

With exception of the Sonnets to his Mistress (& even of these the expressions are unjustly harsh) I can by no means subscribe to the above pencil mark of W. Wordsworth; which however, it is my wish, should never be erased. It is *his*: & grievously am I mistaken, & deplorably will Englishmen have degenerated, if the being *his* will not, in times to come, give it a Value, as of a little reverential Relict—the rude mark of his Hand left by the Sweat of Haste in a St Veronica Handkerchief! And Robert

5

Southey! My sweet Hartley! if thou livest, thou wilt not part with this Book without sad necessity & a pang at Heart. O be never weary of reperusing the four first Volumes of this Collection, my eldest born!—To day thou art to be christened, being more than 7 years of age, o with what reluctance & *distaste* have I permitted this unchristian, & in its spirit & consequences anti-christian, Foolery to be performed upon *thee*, Child of free Nature. On thy Brother Derwent, & thy Sister Sara, somewhat; but chiefly on thee. These Sonnets then, I trust, if God preserve thy Life, Hartley! thou wilt read with a deep Interest, having learnt to love the Plays of Shakespere, co-ordinate with Milton, and subordinate only to thy Bible. To thee, I trust, they will help to explain the mind of Shakespere, & if thou wouldst understand these Sonnets, thou must read the Chapter in Potter's Antiquities on the Greek Lovers—of whom were that Theban Band of Brothers, over whom Philip, their victor, stood weeping; & surveying their dead bodies, each with his Shield over the Body of his Friend, all dead in the place where they fought, solemnly cursed those, whose base, fleshly, & most calumnious Fancies had suspected their Love of Desires against Nature. This pure Love Shakespere appears to have felt—to have been no way ashamed of it—or even to have suspected that others could have suspected it/ yet at the same time he knew that so strong a Love would have been made more compleatly a Thing of Permanence & Reality, & have been blessed more by Nature & taken under her more especial protection, if this Object of his Love had been at the same Time a possible Object of Desire/ for Nature is not bad only—in this Feeling, he must have written the 20th Sonnet, but its possibility seems never to have entered even his Imagination. It is noticeable, that not even an Allusion to that very worst of all possible *Vices* (for it is wise to think of the Disposition, as a *Vice*, not of the absurd & despicable Act, as a *crime*) not even any allusion to it in all his numerous Plays—whereas Johnson, Beaumont & Fletcher, & Massinger are full of them. O my Son! I pray fervently that thou may'st know inwardly how impossible it was for a Shakespere not to have been in his heart's heart chaste. I see no elaborate obscurity & very little quaintness—nor do I know any Sonnets that will bear such frequent reperusal: so rich in metre, so full of Thought & *exquisitest* Diction.

S. T. Coleridge, Greta Hall, Keswick, Wed. morning,
½ past 3, Nov. 2. 1803.

1804

Marcus Aurelius Antoninus, *The Emperor Marcus Antoninus*
His Conversation with Himself . . . To which is added
The Mythological Picture of Cebes the Theban,
trans. Jeremy Collier, London, 1701.

The earliest notes in this volume appear to have been written aboard the
ship Speedwell *when Coleridge went to Malta in the spring of 1804, but*
he returned to the book later—in 1808, 1811, 1818–19, and 1826.

[# 4]

> That Remedies were prescrib'd me in a Dream, against Giddiness, and Spit-
> ting of Blood; As I remember, it happen'd both at *Cajeta*, and *Chrysa*. . . .

I am not convinced that this is mere Superstition. Providence is at once
general & particular/ there is doubtless a sort of *divining* power in man/
Sensations awaken Thoughts congruous to them. I could say much on this
Subject. A Gentleman told Dr Beddoes a remarkable Dream: the Dr immediately examined his pulse, &c &c, bled him &c—and it was evident
that in a day or two he would otherwise have had an apoplectic Fit. My
Father had a similar Dream 3 nights together before his Death, while he
appeared to himself in full & perfect Health—He was blest by God with
sudden Death. That was the only part of our Liturgy, which he objected
to/ the prayer against sudden Death.

[# 5]

> Therefore don't forget the Saying of *Heraclitus*; *That the Earth dies into Water,*
> *Water into Air, Air into Fire, and so Backward.*

Expressed in the present chemical nomenclature/ Solids by increased repulsion of their parts become fluids, by a still greater repulsion aeriform
Gasses, and it is possible that these may all be resolvible into imponderable & igniform natures, Light, Electricity, Magnetism, Heat—& that all
these four may be but detachments of one & same substance—the plas-
tic Fire of the ancients—in different proportions of repulsion & attrac-

7

tion in se [in itself], acting on other proportions—Then to comprehend attraction & Repulsion as one power is perhaps the point of the Pyramid of physical Science.

[# 6]

[From "The Picture of Cebes":] *Resumptions* are very common with this Lady [Fortune], and there's no depending upon her Favour; And therefore the *Genius* advises People to be loose and indifferent with her, and neither be transported when she gives, nor dejected when she takes away. For she never acts upon Reason, but throws out every thing at Peradventure. Therefore the Rule is never to be surpriz'd at any of her Proceedings. . . .

This is the most defective Passage of the whole Treatise. It is not true, and it is of pernicious consequence, to represent Fortune as *wholly* mad, blind, deaf, and drunk. On the *average* each man receives what he pays for— the miser gives care & self-torment, and receives increase of Gold—the vain give clamour, & bustle, pretensions & flattery, & receive a *Buz*—the Wise man Self-conquest & neighbourly Love, and receives sense of Dignity, of Harmony, and Content. Each is paid in sort—Virtue is not rewarded by Wealth, nor is the Eye affected by Sound.

Johann Gottfried Herder, *Kalligone*, Leipzig, 1800.

This work on aesthetics attacks Kant's analysis of the sublime in the Critique of Judgment; *the other works that Coleridge refers to also attack aspects of Kant's philosophy to a greater or lesser extent. "Philosophism," merging "philosophy" and "sophism," could be applied to any false system of thought but was commonly applied especially to eighteenth-century French rationalism by its enemies.*

[# 7] Dec. 19. 1804. Malta.—And thus the Book impressed me, to wit, as being Rant, abuse, drunken Self-conceit that kicking and sprawling in the 6 inch-deep Gutter of muddy Philosophism from the drainings of a hundred Sculleries dreams that he is swimming in an ocean of the Translucent & the Profound/—I never read a more disgusting Work, scarcely so disgusting a one except the Meta-critik [*Metacritique of the Critique of Pure Reason*] of the same Author. I always even in the perusal of his better works, the Verm. Blätter, the Briefe das Stud. Theol. betreffends and the Ideen zur Gesch. der Mensch. [*Miscellaneous Papers, Let-*

ters Concerning the Study of Theology, and *Ideas Towards a Philosophy of the History of Mankind*] thought him a painted Mist with no sharp outline—but this is mere Steam from a Heap of Mans dung.—

[# 8] Herder mistakes for the SUBLIME sometimes the GRAND, sometimes the MAJESTIC, and sometimes the INTENSE: in which last sense we must render a [. . .] or magnificent, but as a *Whole*, (a visual Whole, I mean) it cannot be sublime. A mountain in a cloudless sky, its summit smit with the Sunset is a beautiful, a magnificent Object—the same with its Summit hidden by Clouds, & seemingly blended with the Sky, while mists & floating Vapors of [. . .]

1807

Aulus Persius Flaccus, *Satirarum liber [Book of Satires]*, ed. I. Casaubon, London, 1647.

[# 9] 616 pages in this Volume, of which 22 are text; and 594 Commentary and introductory matter. Yet when I recollect, that I have the whole works of Cicero, of Livy, and Quintilian, with many others, the whole works of each in a single Volume, either thick Quarto with thin paper & small yet distinct print, or thick Octavo or duodecimo of the same character & that they cost me in the proportion of a Shilling to a Guinea for the same quantity of worse matter in modern Books, or Editions, I a poor man yet one whom "βιβλίων κτήσεως ἐκ παιδαρίου δεινὸς εκτέτηκε πόθος" [I from childhood have been penetrated by a passionate longing to acquire books] feel the liveliest Gratitude for the Age, which produced such Editions, and for the Education, which by enabling me to understand and taste the Greek and Latin Writers, has thus put it in my power to collect on my own Shelves for my actual use almost all the best Books in spite of my so small Income. Somewhat too I am indebted to the ostentation of expense among the Rich, which has occasioned these cheap editions to become so disproportionately cheap.

Andrew Fuller, *The Calvinistic and Socinian Systems Examined and Compared, as to their Moral Tendency*, Market-Harborough, 1793.

Coleridge spent part of the summer of 1807 visiting his old friend Thomas Poole, a prosperous tanner, in Nether Stowey, Somersetshire. Poole gave him the run of his library and invited him to write notes in his books—the first of many book owners who actively solicited his marginalia. This book, probably Poole's copy, takes up contemporary religious issues raised especially by the success of the Socinians, who deny the divinity of Christ. The leader of the late-eighteenth-century resurgence of this move-

10

*ment and founder of the Unitarian sect (in 1791) was Joseph Priestley,
the discoverer of oxygen. Coleridge had considered himself a Unitarian
as a university student and for a few years afterward, until a conversion
experience in 1804 brought him back to orthodox Trinitarianism.*

*In the passage first commented on, Fuller quotes from Priestley's writ-
ings on necessity; as Coleridge points out, he also drew on the American
theologian Jonathan Edwards's* Careful and Strict Enquiry into the Modern Prevailing Notions of that Freedom of the Will which is supposed
to be Essential to Moral Agency *(1754). Coleridge's second note alludes
to Baruch (or "Benedict") Spinoza (1632–77), whose theological and
philosophical writings he greatly admired in spite of their alleged atheism.*

[# 10]

> As to our being *passive* in regeneration, if Dr. Priestley would only admit that
> any one character could be found that is so depraved as to be destitute of all
> true virtue, the same thing would follow from his own Necessarian principles.
> According to those principles, every man that is under the dominion of a vi-
> cious habit of mind, will continue to chuse vice, till such time as that habit is
> changed, and that by some influence from without himself. "If says he, I make
> any particular choice to day, I should have done the same yesterday, and should
> do the same to morrow, provided there be no change in the state of my mind
> respecting the object of the choice." [*On Necessity*] p. 7. Nor can any person
> in such a state of mind be supposed to be active in the changing of it; for such
> activity must imply an inclination to have it changed, which is a contradiction;
> as it supposes him at the same time under the dominion of evil, and yet in-
> clined to goodness.

I have hitherto made no objection to, no remark on, any one part of this
Letter; for I object to the whole—not as Calvinism, but—as what Calvin
would have recoiled from. How was it that so good and shrewd a man as
Andrew Fuller should not have seen, that the difference between a Calvinist and a Priestleyan Materialist-Necessitarian consists in this:—The
former not only believes a will, but that it is equivalent to the *ego ipse* [I
itself], to the actual self, in every moral agent; though he believes that in
human nature it is an enslaved, because a corrupt, will. In denying free
will to the unregenerate he no more denies will, than in asserting the
poor negroes in the West Indies to be slaves I deny them to be men. Now
the latter, the Priestleyan, uses the word will,—not for any real, distinct,

correspondent power, but,—for the mere result and aggregate of fibres, motions, and sensations; in short, it is a mere generic term with him, just as when we say, the main current in a river. Now by not adverting to this, and alas! misled by Jonathan Edward's book, Fuller has hidden from himself and his readers the damnable nature of the doctrine—not of necessity (for that in its highest sense is identical with perfect freedom; they are definitions each of the other); but—of extraneous compulsion. O! even this is not adequate to the monstrosity of the thought. A denial of all agency;—or an assertion of a world of agents that never act, but are always acted upon, and yet without any one being that acts;—this is the hybrid of Death and Sin, which throughout this letter is treated so amicably! Another fearful mistake, and which is the ground of the former, lies in conceding to the Materialist, *explicite et implicite* [explicitly and implicitly], that the νούμενον [*noumenon*; object of purely intellectual intuition], the *intelligibile* [that which can be apprehended by the mind], the *ipseitas supersensibilis* [supersensible selfness], of guilt is in time, and of time, and, consequently, a mechanism of cause and effect;—in other words, in confounding the φαινόμενα, τὰ ῥέοντα, τὰ μὴ ὄντως ὄντα [phenomena, things in flux, things that have no real being]—all which belong to time, and cannot be even thought of except as effects necessarily predetermined by the precedent causes, (themselves in their turn effects of other causes),—with the transsensual ground or actual power.

After such admissions, no other possible defence can be made for Calvinism or any other *ism* than the wretched recrimination: "Why, yours, Dr. Priestley, is just as bad!"—Yea, and no wonder:—for in essentials both are the same. But there was no reason for Fuller's meddling with the subject at all,—metaphysically, I mean.

[# 11]

> Secondly, If the unconditionality of election render it unfriendly to virtue, it must be upon the supposition of that view of things, "which ascribes more to God, and less to man," having such a tendency; which is the very reverse of what Dr. Priestley elsewhere teaches, and that in the same performance.

But in both systems, as Fuller has erroneously stated his own, man is annihilated. There is neither more nor less; it is all God; all, all are but *Deus infinite modificatus* [God infinitely modified]—in brief, both systems are not Spinosism, for no other reason than that the logic and logical consequency of 10 Fullers + 10 × 10 Dr. Priestleys, piled on each other, would not reach the calf of Spinoza's leg. Both systems of necessity lead to Spinosism, nay, to all the horrible consequences attributed to it by Spinoza's enemies. O, why did Andrew Fuller quit the high vantage ground of notorious facts, plain durable common sense, and express Scripture, to delve in the dark in order to countermine mines under a spot, on which he had no business to have wall, tent, temple, or even standing-ground!

Patrick Colquhoun, *A Treatise on Indigence*, London, 1806.

This book was certainly in Poole's library when Coleridge annotated it. The lines that Coleridge refers to at the end of his note, in Milton's Comus, have to do with the just distribution of wealth.

[# 12]

> *Poverty* is . . . the state of every one who must labour for subsistence. *Poverty* is therefore a most necessary and indispensable ingredient in society, without which nations and communities could not exist in a state of civilization. It is the lot of man—it is the source of *wealth*, since without poverty there would be *no labour*, and without labour there could be no *riches*, no *refinement*, no *comfort*, and no *benefit* to those who may be possessed of wealth—inasmuch as without a large proportion of poverty surplus labour could never be rendered productive in procuring either the conveniences or luxuries of life.

Certainly! if the present state of general Intellect and morals be supposed a fair average of the capabilities of society. Otherwise I can not see why without this *Poverty* (even as here contra-distinguished from Indigence) A. might not agree to make Shoes, B. Cloth, C. Breeches, &c: and the whole Alphabet of Labor carry on a similar Barter to the present, even tho' one third of Society were *not* devoted to the production of useless & *debasing* Luxuries for those who are privileged to live in Idleness.—For mark, the definition of Poverty is invidious—he is not a poor man whose subsistence depends on constant Industry, but he whose bare wants can not be supplied without such unceasing bodily Labor from the hour of waking to that of sleeping, as precludes all improvement of mind—& makes the intellectual Faculties to the majority of mankind as useless a boon as pictures to the Blind. Such a man is poor indeed: for he has been robbed by his unnatural Guardians of the very house-loom of his *human nature*, stripped of the furniture of his Soul.
See Milton's Comus. line 765 to 779.

William Hayley, *Life of Milton*, London, 1796.

Another of Poole's books. In the first note, Coleridge speaks up for Milton's Paradise Regained *while regretting a few lines in which Milton has Christ reject imaginative literature, like Pope Gregory the Great, who was said to have gone about burning copies of Livy and Cicero. "Martyrworshippers" is Coleridge's contemptuous phrase for those who participated in the annual church service, held on January 30 from 1662 to 1859, in honor of "Charles the Martyr." "Mrs. Hutchinson" is Lucy Hutchinson, author of* Memoirs of Colonel Hutchinson—*her husband John, one of those who signed the king's death warrant. The Latin* qui cum victus erat *etc. is from Ovid,* Metamorphoses *13.20. Samuel Butler's* Hudibras *(1662–78) is a burlesque poem attacking the Puritans. Coleridge's last note considers charges of plagiarism, such as were later leveled at him.*

[# 13]

[Hayley quotes from *The Reason of Church Government* as illustrating] the mental character of Milton, with a mild energy, a solemn splendor of sentiment and expression peculiar to himself.

"Time serves not now, and, perhaps, I might seem too profuse to give any certain account of what the mind at home, in the spacious circuits of her musing, hath liberty to propose to herself, though of highest hope and hardest attempting; whether that epic form, whereof the two poems of Homer, and those other two of Virgil and Tasso, are a diffuse, and the book of Job a brief, model; or whether the rules of Aristotle herein are strictly to be kept, or nature to be followed. . . ."

These words deserve particular notice. I do not doubt, that Milton intended his Paradise lost as an Epic of the first class, and that the poetic Dialogue of Job was his model for the general Scheme of his Paradise Regained.

Readers would not have been disappointed in this latter poem, if they had proceeded to it with a proper preconception of *the kind* of interest intended to be excited in that admirable work. In its kind it is the most *perfect* poem extant; tho' its *kind* may be inferior Interest, being in its essence didactic, to that other sort, in which Instruction is conveyed more effectively because more indirectly, in connection with stronger & more pleasurable Emotions, & thereby in a closer affinity with *action*. But might we not as rationally object to an accomplished Woman's conversing, however agreeably, because it has happened that we have received a keener pleasure from her singing to the Harp? Si genus sit probo et sapienti homine haud indignum, et si poema sit in suo genere perfectum, satis est! quod si hoc autor idem altioribus numeris et carmini diviniori ipsum pene divinum superadderit, mehercule, satis est, et plusquam satis [If the kind be not unworthy of a good and wise man, and if the poem be perfect in its kind, that is enough. But if the same author shall have superadded this, itself almost divine, to heightened numbers and still more divine song, that by heaven is enough and more than enough]. I cannot however but wish, that the answer of Jesus to Satan in the fourth book, 1. 285 et sequentia [following], had breathed the spirit of this noble quotation rather than the narrow bigotry of Gregory the Great. The passage indeed is excellent, & is partially true; but partial Truth is the worse mode of conveying falsehood.

[# 14]

> The sincerest friends of Milton may here agree with Johnson, who speaks of his controversial merriment as disgusting. . . .

The man who reads a work meant for immediate effect on one age, with the notions & feelings of another, may be a refined gentleman, but must be a sorry Critic. He who possesses imagination enough to *live* with his forefathers, and leaving comparative reflection for an after moment, to give himself *up* during the first perusal to the feelings of a contemporary if not a partizan, will, I dare aver, rarely find any part of M.'s prose works *disgusting*.

[# 15]

> [Hayley refers to John Bradshaw, president of the parliamentary commission that tried and condemned Charles I.] The odium which the president justly incurred in the trial of Charles seems to have prevented even our liberal historians from recording with candour the great qualities he possessed: he was undoubtedly not only an intrepid but a sincere enthusiast in the cause of the commonwealth.

Why *justly*? What would the contemptible Martyr-worshippers, (who yearly apply to this fraudulent would-be-despot the most aweful phrases of holy writ concerning the Saviour of Mankind, concerning the Incarnate *Word* that is with *God* & *is God*, in a cento of ingenious blasphemy, that has no parallel in the annals of impious Adulation) what would even these men have? Can they, as men, expect that Bradshaw & his Peers *should* give sentence against the Parliament & Armies of England, as guilty of all the blood that had been shed—as Rebels and Murderers! Yet there was no other alternative. That he or his peers were influenced by Cromwell is a gross Calumny, sufficiently confuted by their after lives & by their death-hour—& has been amply falsified by Mrs Hutchinson in her incomparable Life of her Incomparable Husband, Colonel Hutchinson. O that I might have such an action to remember on my Death-bed! The only enviable part of Charles's Fate & Life is that his name is connected with the greatest names of ancient or modern times—Qui cum victus erat, *tantis* certâsse feretur [Who, when conquered, will be famed for having fought against *such great men*].

[# 16]

[Referring to Milton's answer to *Eikon Basilike,* an account of the sufferings and prayers of Charles I before his execution, allegedly composed by the king himself:] Milton himself may be also urged as an example to enforce the same caution [against prejudice]; for although he was certainly no impostor in imputing the prayer in question to the king, yet his considering the king's use of it as an offence against heaven, is a pitiable absurdity; an absurdity as glaring as it would be to affirm, that the divine poet is himself profane in assigning to a speech of the Almighty, in his poem, the two following verses:

Son of my bosom, son who art alone
My word, my wisdom, and effectual might—

Because they are partly borrowed from a line in Virgil, addressed by a heathen goddess to her child:

"Nate, meae vires, mea magna potentia solus."
[Son, my strength, my great power alone.]

Assuredly, I regret that Milton should have written the passage alluded to/ and yet the adoption of a prayer from a Romance on such an occasion does not evince a delicate or deeply sincere Mind. We are the creatures of association—there are some excellent moral & even serious Lines in Hudibras/ but what if a Clergyman should adorn his Sermon with a quotation from that Poem? Would the abstract propriety of the Lines leave him "*honorably acquitted?*" The Xtian Baptism of a Line of Virgil is so far from being a parallel, that it is ridiculously inappropriate—"an absurdity as glaring" as that of the bigotted puritans, who objected to some of the noblest & most scriptural prayers ever dictated by wisdom & piety simply because the Catholics had used them.

[# 17]

In the course of this discussion we may find, perhaps, a mode of accounting for the inconsistency both of Dryden and Voltaire; let us attend at present to what the latter has said of Andreini!—If the Adamo of this author really gave birth to the divine poem of Milton, the Italian dramatist, whatever rank he might hold in his own country, has a singular claim to our attention and regard.

If Milton borrowed a hint from any writer, it was more probably from Strada's Prolusiones, in which the fall of the Angels &c is pointed out as the noblest subject for a Christian Poet. The more dissimilar the detailed images are, the more likely it is that a great genius should catch the general idea.

Robert Percival, *An Account of the Island of Ceylon*, London, 1803.

Another of Poole's books, Percival's Ceylon was especially interesting to Coleridge for its account of the use of the drug called "bhang" or "bang" or "bangue," which, like hashish, is made from the dried leaves of Indian hemp. In 1803, Coleridge and his patron Thomas Wedgwood had themselves experimentally taken bhang that they obtained from the president of the Royal Society, Sir Joseph Banks, with the help of another of Poole's friends, Samuel Purkis. Tippoo Sahib (1751–99) was the sultan of Mysore.

[# 18]

All day long they chew the betel or penang, and smoke *bang*. From this last herb a species of opium is prepared, which they chew in great quantities, as Europeans use strong drinks, to exhilarate their spirits. Too much of it, however, entirely deadens their senses, and reduces them to a state of complete stupefaction. I have frequently seen these people, after having chewed too large a portion of this noxious drug, lying speechless on the ground with their eyes fixed in a ghastly stare. Yet, such is the effect of habit, that they get completely infatuated with fondness for this drug, and absolutely cannot do without it.

The Bang is the powder from the dried Leaves of the Cannabis Indica, or Indian Hemp/ It is commonly blended with opium; & in Turkey and Barbary with Saffron & Spices. It is either chewed in large Pills, or smoked in the Powder. I have both smoked & taken the powder/ so did my ever-honoured ever-lamented Benefactor, T. Wedgewood: the effects in both were the same, merely narcotic, with a painful weight from the flatulence or stifled gas, occasioned by the morbid action on the coats of the Stomach. In others however it had produced, as we were informed by Sir J. Banks, almost frantic exhilaration. We took it in the powder, and as much as would lie on a Shilling. Probably, if we had combined it with opium and some of the most powerful essential Oils, to stimulate & heat the stomach, it might have acted more pleasantly. On the coast of Barbary the charitable Mahometans give it to poor Criminals, previous to the amputation of their Limbs; and it inspires a complete insensibility to suffering, and in these circumstances does not commonly disturb the understanding. Tippoo Saib gave to each of his Horse soldiers a pipe immediately before the engagement—likewise to those sent to storm forts.

[# 19]

> Before entering upon any desperate enterprise, it is customary with the Malays to take opium, or, as they term it, to *bang* themselves. This plant, the bang, which is used among the natives of India as an instrument of intoxication, is found over all that continent as well as in Ceylon. It is a small shrub, with a leaf in shape and texture resembling that of the tobacco, but not larger than the leaf of the sage. From this plant a species of opium is extracted, and being made into balls, is taken internally, and operates in the same manner as a dram of spirits among the European nations. The leaf of the bang is also dried and smoked like tobacco, with a still stronger intoxicating effect than the opium.

See p. 152.—The account there given I received from Sir J. Banks thro' Mr Purkis with a Bottle of the Powder—which I after gave to Mr Ridout, a truly respectable medical practitioner, in Paternoster Row. Sir J. B. had made the most exact inquiries—whether he or Mr Percival was misinformed, or whether the Bang of Ceylon is different from that of Turkey & the Barbary Coast, I have no means to conjecture.

Edward Stillingfleet, *Origines Sacrae, or a Rational Account of the Grounds of Christian Faith*, London, 1675.

Another of Poole's books. Henry More, the Cambridge Platonist whose Theological Works *Coleridge warmly advocates in a later note (# 186), argued in* An Antidote Against Atheism *(1653) that belief in the powers of evil spirits is itself a test of faith, since it implies "the presence of some free subtile understanding essence distinct from the brute Matter, and ordinary power of Nature."*

[# 20]

> The *Devil* no question may, and doth often deceive the world, and may by the *subtility* and *agility* of his *nature*, perform such things as may amuse the *minds* of *men*, and sometimes put *them* to it, to find a *difference* between *them* and real miracles, if they only make their *senses* judges of them.

If Satan, as an invisible Spirit, should lift a man up to the Clouds surrounding him with Light by his power as a Spirit, or God effect the same by his power as God, how are the Laws of Nature suspended more or less in one instance or the other? I speak it with reverence—Yet how many most learned & pious men have declared it impious to doubt the former fact. See Dr Hen. More on Atheism.—

It is a perilous and painful task for a man to find himself engaged by conscience & a zeal for Christian Truth in the confutation of an error when the error is of such a kind that it cannot be confuted but by adopting language & using arguments, which have been or may be used by an acute Infidel—altho' it is the Error which gives to the Infidel's arguments all their strength, & to his general system its sole plausibility.

[# 21]

> *Lactantius* excellently manifests that *Philosophy* could never do so much *good* in the world as *Christianity* did, because that was not suited at all to *common capacities*, and did require so much *skill* in the *Arts* to prepare *men* for it, which it is impossible all should be well *skilled* in, which yet are as capable of being *happy*, as any others are. And how *inefficacious* the *precepts* of *Philosophy* were, appears by the *Philosophers* themselves, who were *far* from having *command* by them over their *Masterless passions*, and were fain sometimes to *confess* that *nature* was too *headstrong* to be kept in by such weak *reins* as the *precepts* of *Philosophy* were. . . .

Cannot the Philosophers quote as many instances as can reasonably be expected from men who did not make plebeian Sects? And are not the lives of nominal Xtians as offensive to Xtnty, as those of nominal Philosophers to Philosophy? And is not the number in each proportionate to that of the Professors? Nay! are there not more bad Christians in proportion?—Why? because the very habits of Speculation remove men farther from Temptation, or disarm it. This is not meant as an argument in favour of Philos. against Xtñty; but to overthrow its dangerous enemy, false Reasoning in its favor. And why is Philosophy for ever to be set up as the Rival rather than as the Friend & natural Companion, of Christianity? What is Xtianity but divine & pre-eminent Philosophy? a stream, in whose depths the Elephant must *swim*, and in whose practical & saving Truths the Lamb may *ford*?—Besides, who shall dare say of yon river, such & such a wave came from such a fountain? What Scholar (& by scholars the vulgar are taught) shall say—Such a conviction, such a moral feeling, I received from St John/ such & such from Seneca, or Epictetus?—

[# 22]

. . . though *God* be *essentially* and *necessarily good*, yet the *communications* of this *goodness* are the effect of his *Will*, and not meerly of his *nature*. . . .

Well! but is not the *Will* of God identical with his Nature? Is it not naturally good or beneficient? Is there in Eternity a distinguishable moment, that one moment should possibly be preferred to another?—And where is the danger to Religion, if we make preservation a perpetual creation, & interpret the first words of Genesis as we must do (if not Socinians) the first words of St John—From all eternity God created the Universe—And the Earth became waste & void &c. It might have been a Comet—it might have been, as to its whole surface, ruined by a Comet. It is a rule of infinite importance that the Scriptures always speak not ad rem in se ipsâ, sed quoad *hominem* [to the subject in itself, but as far as *humankind* is concerned]. It is a moral & religious, not a physical, revelation, & in order to render us good moral agents, not accurate natural speculators, to make us know ourselves & our relations both present & future, not to make us knowing in nature—without industry or intellectual exercitation.

Robert Anderson, ed., *The Works of the British Poets*, Edinburgh and London, 1793–95.

This second annotated set of Anderson is associated with Coleridge's friend John James Morgan, a Bristol lawyer, later an unsuccessful businessman. In the note printed here, Coleridge outlines a fundamental principle of a system of thought that he developed in his maturity, according to which there is ultimately only one substance, and that is spirit, from which matter is derived secondarily. *The Kantian distinction between reason and understanding as mental faculties that are different in kind and not merely in degree is one that Coleridge proposed and elaborated in his own work.*

[# 23]

[Milton *Paradise Lost* 5.469–74]

> O Adam, one Almighty is, from whom
> All things proceed, and up to him return,
> If not deprav'd from good, created all
> Such to perfection, one first matter all,
> Indued with various forms, various degrees
> Of substance, and in things that live, of life;

There is nothing wanting to render this a perfect enunciation of the only true System of Physics, but to declare the "*one first matter all*" to be a one Act or Power consisting in two Forces or opposite Tendencies, φυσις διπλοειδης potentialiter sensitiva [a two-formed nature potentially sensitive]; and all that follows, the same in different Potencies. For matter can neither be *ground* or distilled into spirit. The Spirit is an Island harbourless, and every way inaccessible. All its contents are its products: all its denizens indigenous. Ergo, as matter could exist only for the Spirit, and as for the Spirit it cannot exist, Matter as a *principle* does not exist at all—; but as a mode of Spirit, and derivatively, it may and does exist: it being indeed the intelligential act in its first Potency.

The most doubtful position in Milton's ascending Series is the Derivation of Reason from the Understanding—without a medium.

Thomas Adam, *Private Thoughts on Religion*, York, 1795.

Another of Poole's books. Coleridge's notes return many times to the great divisive theological issue of the means of salvation, and specifically to the debate about the relative merits of faith and good works.

[# 24]

Why then are works to be the great subject of inquiry at the day of judgment? Because they are the visible effects of faith, and only good as springing from a root of faith, so that the want of them proves of course the want of faith.

Explain it thus: God will judge each man before all men; consequently, he must judge relatively to man. But man knoweth not the heart of man, scarcely each knoweth his own; there must therefore be outward & visible signs by which man may be enabled to judge of the inward state, & thereby justify the ways of God to man. Now good works are these; and as such & only as such become *necessary*. In short, there are two parties, God & the human Race—and both are to be satisfied: God, who seeth the root & knoweth the heart—therefore there must be Faith/ Man, who can judge only by the Fruits—therefore that Faith must bear fruits of Righteousness. But that, which God seeth, that alone justifieth/ what man seeth doth, in this LIFE, shew that justifying Faith *may* be the root of the things seen—in the life to come, will shew that it actually *is* & *was* the root. *Here* a good life presumes justification, as its only possible tho' still ambiguous Revelation; the absence of a good life not only presumes, but proves, the contrary. Good works may exist without saving principles, therefore cannot contain in themselves the principle of Salvation; but saving principles never did, never can, exist without good works. On a subject of such infinite importance I fear prolixity less than obscurity. Men often talk against Faith, yet themselves judge by the same principle: for what is Love without kind offices? and yet what noble mind values the offices except as *signs* of Love?

George Lyttelton, *The History of the Life of King Henry the Second*, London, 1769.

The dating of the notes is not certain in this case and might be almost any time between 1804 and 1814, though 1807–9 seems most probable. The "elder Brutus" is the one who assassinated Julius Caesar.

[# 25]

[Henry I of England had given over the son of the governor of one of his castles in France as a hostage; when the boy returned blinded to his father, Henry allowed the father to mutilate in a similar fashion *his* two hostages, the two daughters of Henry's own illegitimate daughter.] Ancient Rome would perhaps have admired him for this action, and the history of England has no other that comes up to the force of it: but, though the principle on which it was done demands veneration, and no ordinary mind could be capable of it, the deed raises horror; and one could wish, for Henry's honor, that he had found less direful methods to appease his injured servant, without inflicting on innocence pains that are only due to guilt, and in the persons of those whom the first and greatest of all laws, the law of nature, particularly obliged him to save and protect.

I can never conceive veneration compatible with horror. I venerate the principle of the elder Brutus, but so far from likewise feeling horror at the deed, I would (I trust) have done the same. But *here* the principle is as false as the act was monstrous. It may be said "But Henry thought it right." Well! but 1. who knows this? 2. and if so, who can say how far bad passions may not have influenced his reason in adopting the principle? an influence always to be suspected in glaring exorbitations of an erring conscience—and lastly, an Inquisitor's conscience prompts first to torture and then burn alive hundreds of women and children for mere words without meaning—by the utmost stretch of charity we may admit his principle as a *palliation* of his crime, but do we *venerate* it? This is not unworthy of notice, for much injury has been done to the morals of men by this rash confounding of actions: 1. by teaching a few Bigots to justify cruelty by the principle, and 2ndly a thousand others to admit no regular guide but that of feeling, liking, and sympathy with the multitude—because, forsooth, we cannot act up to principle, for *principle*, forsooth, leads to such cruel unnatural deeds. In short, either the horror is unjust, and not necessarily arising out of a good and humane disposition, or (which is most often the case), the principle is as erroneous as its consequences are atrocious.

1808

Samuel Daniel, *Poetical Works*, London, 1718.

*Charles Lamb, the whimsical essayist who published under the pen name
"Elia," had been at school with Coleridge, and his essays include several
references to their friendship and shared experiences. Lamb celebrated
Coleridge's annotating habit in "The Two Races of Men" (the "two races"
being those who borrow and those who lend books), saying that Coleridge's notes would triple the value of a book. Lamb was himself an annotator. This edition of Daniel, which belonged to him, contains notes by
both of them. Coleridge wrote a letter to Lamb at the front of each of the
two volumes of the* Works, *pursuing their amicable disagreement about
Daniel's epic poem on the subject of English history up to the accession
of Edward IV,* The Civil Wars between the Two Houses of York and Lancaster, *first published in its complete form in eight books in 1609.*

The Mercury *and* Intelligencer *were periodicals of the late seventeenth
century; variations of these names were used for political journals and
news-sheets in the eighteenth century. "Jacobite" is the name given to
supporters of the Stuarts (James II and his descendants) after the Revolution of 1688.*

[# 26]

Tuesday, Feb. 10. 1808. (*10th or 9th?*)

Dear Charles,

I think more highly, far more, of the "Civil Wars", than you seemed to
do (on Monday night, Feb. 9th 1808)—the Verse does not teize *me*; and
all the while I am reading it, I cannot but fancy a plain England-loving
English Country Gentleman, with only some dozen Books in his whole
Library, and at a time when a "Mercury" or "Intelligencer" was seen by
him once in a month or two, making this his Newspaper & political Bible
at the same time/ & reading it so often as to store his Memory with its
aphorisms. Conceive a good man of that kind, diffident and passive, yet
rather inclined to Jacobitism; seeing the reasons of the Revolutionary
Party, yet by disposition and old principles leaning, in quiet nods and
signs at his own parlour fire, to the hereditary Right—(and of these char-

acters there must have been many)—& then read this poem assuming in your heart his Character—conceive how grave he would look, and what pleasure there would be, what unconscious, harmless, humble self-conceit, self-compliment in his gravity; how *wise* he would feel himself—& yet after all, how forbearing, how much calmed by that most calming reflection (when it is really the mind's own reflection)—aye! it was just so in Henry the 6^{th's} Time/ always the same Passions at work—&c—. Have I injured thy Book—? or wilt thou "like it the better there*fore*?" But I have done as I would gladly be done by—thee, at least.—

                                                                            S. T. Coleridge

John Milton, *A Complete Collection of the Historical, Political, and Miscellaneous Works*, ed. T. Birch, London, 1738.

This long note from the front flyleaves, the only one by Coleridge in this work, is addressed from the office of the daily newspaper, the Courier, *where Coleridge was staying while he lectured on poetry and aesthetics in London. It was written for Daniel Stuart, the editor of the paper, to which Coleridge was an occasional contributor—hence, perhaps, its political and nationalist slant. Advocacy of seventeenth-century writers and patriots (Milton, Taylor, Browne, etc.) as superior to their successors is, however, consistent for Coleridge. Here he praises them at the expense of his and Stuart's contemporaries, the Whig politicians and writers Samuel Whitbread, William Roscoe, and Charles James Fox.*

[# 27] Bought for Mr Stuart, 28 March 1808—price 3 guineas. If G. Britain remain independent (and o! what Extremes of Guilt and Folly must combine in order to the Loss even of her paramounce!) the prose Works of Milton will be more and more in Request. Hooker, Bacon, Harrington, Sidney, Jeremy Taylor, and these Volumes (to which I would add Sir T. Brown, if rich and peculiar Genius could wholly cover quaintness & pedantry of Diction) are the Upper House of genuine English Prose Classics.—This present Century, among many worse things, which cast a gloom over its infancy, will be *notorious* in English Literature for the shameful Incorrectness, with which Booksellers, (too ignorant or too niggardly or both, to employ learned men in the business) have edited the various works of Bacon, Milton, & a number of other Works of great size/ The late Edition in 12 Vol Octavo of Lord Bacon, and Anderson's British Poets in 14 Vol: (thick Octavo, double column (each volume equal to two common Quartos, or even three)) are absolutely *infamous* for their Errata; in the former there exists one error in every second, in the latter from 3 to half a dozen of the *worst** sort of blunders in every, page. This Edition of Milton therefore by the excellent and laborious *Birch*, corrected with a care worthy of the praise of Milton himself, cannot but rise in value: and I dare prophesy, that in less than 20 years it will be sold at not less than ten guineas.—I greatly prefer this Folio to the Quarto Edition of Milton, which some have bought in order to have his prose works uniform with the 4th Edition of his poetical Works, even for the opposite Reason—Admirable to the very height of Praise as Milton's Prose works are, still they are "of a *party*" in country, in religion, in politics, & even in *Morals*— (the Treatise in favor of Divorce)—a party indeed, to which in all respects I cleave with head, heart and body—but yet it is a *Party*. But his Poetry belongs to the whole World/ It is alike the Property of the Churchman and the Dissenter, the Protestant and Catholic, the Monarchist and the Republican—and of every Country on Earth, except the kingdom of Dahomy, in Africa, for the *present* at least, and of France (as long as it shall be inhabited by Frenchmen) *for ever*! A mine of Lead could sooner take wing and mount aloft at the Call of the Sun with the Dews and with the Lark, than the witty discontinuous Intellect, and sensual Sum Total of a Frenchman could soar up to Religion or to Milton & Shakspear. It is impossible. Frenchmen are the *Indigenae*, the *natives* of this Planet—and all the Souls, that are not Wanderers *from* other Worlds, or destined *for* other Worlds, who are not mere Probationers here and Birds of passage— all the *very own* Children of this "*Earth*" enter into the wombs of Frenchwomen, from N. E. S. W. and increase the population & Empire of France. Russia† furnishes such large supplies of French Souls, that they probably will be commanded to abide where they arrive, and form a "New France"—a Nova Gallia—as we have a New England in America, & a Nova Scotia./ And alas! even G. Britain sends large Colonies thither. What are the greater part of the members of the two Houses of Parliament, especially the Whitbreads, & Roscoe-pamphlet Men, but Souls passing thro' the Stomach & Intestines of England, like Misletoe Berries thro' those of the Thrush, or Nutmegs (in the Spice Islands) thro' those of the Eastern Pigeon, in order to be matured for germinating in France & becoming Frenchmen? some in the next—some in the following generation,—And few (Mr Fox for instance) may even take three or four generations, sinking in each into a nearer proximity, before the Soul is compleatly *unsouled* into a proper Gaul—This Process is now so common, that every Englishman has cause for alarm, lest instead of singing with

Angels, or beating off imp-flies with his Tail among the Infernals, his Spirit should some 50 or a 100 years hence be dancing, crouching, and *libidinizing*, beneath the Sceptre of one of Napoleon's Successors.—I know no better way, by which he can assure himself of the contrary, and prove his *Election* either to be a happy angel hereafter, or at worst an honest English Devil, than by his being sincerely conscious, that he reads with delight, feels, understands, and honors the *following Works* of *Milton*. This being, it necessarily follows that he loves Sidney, Harrington, Shakspere, & the *Poet* Milton.

S. T. Coleridge. *348, Strand.*

* "worst sort of blunders": i.e. those which substitute a *stupid sense* for an exquisite beauty. Of the self-conceit of ignorant Compositors instances enough might be collected, from literary men, to make a volume—and a very entertaining one it would be.—

† I write this not from the accident of a war with Russia, but from an intimate knowlege of the Russian Character, gained from two years Intercourse with Russians, of all ages, & rank, and of both sexes. The Russian is a thorough Frenchman, without the Frenchman's Wit.

Jakob Boehme, *Works*, London, 1764–81.

The German mystical writer Jakob Boehme (also spelled Böhme or Behmen), a shoemaker for most of his working life, had an influence long after his death as a theosopher, in the broad sense of someone with intuitive knowledge of God. Coleridge was probably acquainted with his ideas even before acquiring this handsome translation of his works, the gift of Thomas De Quincey. He made good use of it and appears to have written notes on many occasions between 1808 and 1826. The first note here addresses the reader who may be prejudiced against uneducated writers.

The phrase magnis tamen excidit ausis *is from Ovid,* Metamorphoses *2.328; "the vision and the faculty divine" from Wordsworth's* Excursion *1.79;* ast tenet umbra Deum *is adapted from Statius,* Thebaid *4.425. The Greek at the end of the second note is from Pindar,* Olympian Odes *2.85; the motto in the third is one traditionally believed to have been inscribed over the entrance to Plato's Academy. "Waterland and Sherlock" represent Church of England orthodoxy on the subject of the Trinity; Humphry*

Davy (Coleridge often spelled the name differently), later a very eminent scientist and president of the Royal Society, had been a friend in Coleridge's Bristol days. "H.C. and D. C." are Coleridge's sons, Hartley and Derwent, to whom he addresses the note in which he regrets his inattention to mathematics. John Locke, William Paley, and Dugald Stewart are introduced as respected philosophers of a commonsense kind, as opposed to Boehme's unfashionable mysticism. The quotation about Homer nodding (i.e., dozing) is from Horace, Ars Poetica 359. Emanuel Swedenborg (1688–1772) was a Swedish scientist and visionary whose followers founded the New Jerusalem Church in London in 1787.

[# 28]   To the contemptuous and therefore unreasonable:
for what reason for continuing to read what you despise?

Reader

Plato and Aristotle both reprehend this point in Anaxagoras, that having, to his immortal honor in the history of Philosophy, first established the position of a supermundane ΝΟΥΕ, ως το πρωτον, μεσον και ύστατον [MIND, as the first, middle, and last] he yet never makes any regular or determinate Use of this supreme Agent in the course of his System, but does as the Poets do who introduce a God only when their invention fails them, or their Plot has been unskillfully laid—that is, he never introduces the NOUS (= Pure Intelligence) but as a Deus ex machinâ [a god descending from a machine, i.e., a clumsy contrivance] to cut a knot, he is not able to untie.

The fault of the great German Theosopher lies in the opposite extreme. But this ought not to excite thy scorn. For the *Attempt* is dictated by Reason, nay even by Consistency; and if he have failed by soaring too high, magnis tamen excidit ausis [yet he failed in a daring attempt]—and in no spirit of pride did he soar—but being a poor unlearned Man he contemplated Truth and the forms of Nature thro' a luminous Mist, the vaporous darkness rising from his Ignorance and accidental peculiarities of fancy and sensation, but the Light streaming into it from his inmost Soul. What wonder then, if in some places the Mist condenses into a thick smoke with a few wandering rays darting across it & sometimes overpowers the eye with a confused Dazzle? The true wonder is, that in so many places it thins away almost into a transparent Medium, and Jacob Behmen, *the Philosopher*, surprizes us in proportion as Behmen, the Visionary, had astounded or perplexed us. For Behmen was indeed a Visionary in two very different senses of that word. Frequently does he mistake the dreams of his own overexcited Nerves, the phantoms and witcheries from the cauldron of his own seething Fancy, for parts or symbols of a universal Process; but frequently likewise does he give incontestible proofs, that he possessed in very truth

"The Vision and Faculty divine!"

And even when he wanders in the shades, ast tenet umbra Deum [yet the shadow contains a God].

Read then in meekness—lest to read him at all, which might be thy folly, should prove thy Sin.

[# 29] Böem's (or as we say, Behmen's) account of the Trinity is masterly and orthodox. Waterland and Sherlock might each have condescended to have been instructed by the humble Shoe-maker of Gorlitz, with great advantage to themselves, and to the avoidal of the perilous Errors, of which they were at least in jeopardy. Let me add to this Note, that there are three analogous Acts in the human Consciousness, or rather three dim imperfect Similitudes; and if ever we have a truly scientific Psychology, it will consist of the distinct Enunciation, and Developement of the three primary Energies of Consciousness, and be a History of their Application and Results. Humphrey Davy in his Laboratory is probably doing more for the Science of Mind, than all the Metaphysicians have done from Aristotle to Hartley, inclusive. Φωνῶ Συνετοισι [I declare this to the enlightened].

[# 30]

8. Before this Looking-Glass I will now *invite* all Lovers of the holy and highly to be esteemed Arts of *Philosophy*, *Astrology*, and *Theology*, wherein I will lay open the Root and *Ground* of them.

9. And though I have not studied nor learned *their* Arts, neither do I know how to go about to measure Circles, and *use* their Mathematical Instruments and Compasses, I take no great Care about that. However, they will have *so much* to learn from hence, that many will not comprehend the Ground thereof *all* the Days of their Lives.

10. For I use not their Tables, Formulas, or Schemes, Rules and Ways, for I have *not learned* from them, but I have another Teacher, or School-master, which is the whole or total NATURE.

11. From that *whole Nature*, together with its innate, instant Birth or Geniture, have I studied and learned my *Philosophy, Astrology,* and *Theology*, and not from Men, or by Men.

12. But seeing Men *are Gods*, and have the Knowledge of God . . . there-

fore I *despise not* the Canons, Rules, and Formulas of *their* Philosophy, Astrology, and Theology. For I find, that for the most part they stand upon a *right Ground*, and I will diligently *endeavour* to go according to their Rules and Formulas.

13. For . . . their Formula or Scheme is *my* Master, and I have my Beginning and *first* Knowledge from their Formula or Positions: Neither is it my Purpose to go about to amend or cry down theirs, for I cannot do it, neither have I *learned* them, but leave them standing in their own Place and Worth.

To H. C. and D. C.

I shall be obliged to take as my motto ¶s 8, 9, 10, 11, 12, 13—p. 219 of the Aurora, but o! with what bitter regret, and in the conscience of such glorious opportunities, both at School under the famous Mathematician, WALES, the companion of Cook in his circumnavigation, and at Jesus College, Cambridge, under an excellent Mathematical Tutor, Newton, all *neglected* with still greater *remorse*! O be assured, my dear Sons! that Pythagoras, Plato, Speusippus, had abundant reason for excluding from all philosophy and theology not merely practical those who were ignorant of Mathematics. Μηδεις αγεομετρητος εισιτω [Let no one ignorant of geometry enter]—the common inscription over all the Portals of all true Knowlege. I cannot say—for I know the contrary, and the ¶s above referred to express the conviction—that it *cannot* be *acquired* without the *technical* knowlege of Geometry and Algebra—but never can it without them be adequately *communicated* to others—and o! with what toil must the essential knowlege be *anguished-out* without the assistance of the technical!—

S. T. Coleridge—

[# 31]

73. But the holy God is *hidden* in the *Center* of all these Things in his Heaven, and thou canst neither see nor comprehend him; but the *Soul* comprehends him, and the astral Birth but half, for the Heaven is the Partition between Love and Wrath. That Heaven is every where, even in thyself.

74. And now when thou worshippest or prayest to the *holy God* in his Heaven, then thou worshippest or prayest to *him* in *that* Heaven which is *in* thee, and that same God with his Light; and therein the Holy Ghost *breaks* through in *thy* Heart, and generates thy *Soul* to be a new Body of God, which rules and reigns with God in *his* Heaven.

75. For the earthly Body, which thou bearest, is one Body with the whole

kindled Body of this World, and thy Body qualifies, mixes, or unites with the whole Body of this World; and there is no Difference between the Stars and the Deep, as also the Earth and thy Body; it is all one Body. This is the only Difference, thy Body is a *Son* of the Whole, and is in itself as the whole Being itself is.

What practically vital Christian, experienced in the communion with God, and the struggles of and with the Spirit, in prayer whether passive or fervent, can read ¶phs 73, 74—what Philosopher, who is indeed such, can meditate on ¶. 75—without a profound admiration of the Writer, increased into Wonder by the reflection on his Circumstances; his want of Learning; poverty of words; lack of skill and mastery in both the Rhematic and Logical composition and sequency of Words; exclusion from the society of the Learned and Ingenious; and lastly, his scanty Means and manual labor, as a humble Shoe-maker! Verily, it is worse than hardness, it is badness of Heart, to scoff at the wreaths & columns of Smoke from this Altar or Hearthstone of Behmen's Genius—with such heavy damps dripping continually thereon, and with such wet Logs for the Fuel, the marvel is that the smoke did not utterly choke and strangle the flames!— or rather that there was any Smoke even, and that the Spark was not quenched as soon as kindled! The very Delusions of such a mind are more venerable to me than the heartless Sobrieties of a Locke, a Paley, or a Dugald Stewart! Let it be, if you will have it so, that poor Jacob is sometimes *out of his Wits,* and often *out of* his Senses—Yet it is better so, than with the Fascinati [bewitched], to have *lost his Reason.*

[# 32]

For we find that the Woman was taken and formed in the *Fiat* out of *Adam's* Essence, both in Body and Soul. But the Rib betokens *Adam's* Dissolution or Breaking, *viz.* that this Body should and would be *dissolved*; for in the Place of this Rib *Longinus's* Spear must afterwards, when Christ was crucified, enter into the same, and tincture and *heal* the Breach in the Wrath of God with heavenly Blood.

Here B. seems engaged in a fruitless, probably, an impracticable undertaking—the discovering a spiritual (i.e. universal) truth in the mythus of the Rib. But such passages as these are the *Snores* of the sleeping Genius—aliquando bonus dormitat Homerus [sometimes worthy Homer nods].—I have sometimes conjectured that the Chapter was translated into *words* from stone Carvings, or proper Hieroglyphs—and that in the latter there had been some such paronomasia as in our Children's picture-for-word Books: in which an eye stands for I, a Yew for you &c—which translated back into a different dialect would make a most mysterious Mythus, like this of Eve's manufacture—tho' perhaps the picture may have meant nothing more by the rib, than a bone of the Trunk generally, and by this again nothing more than that God made the Woman in the same mould as he had made the Man, only subtracting the greater Hardness, Stiffness, and self-supporting Character of the latter—In the infancy of the World the Mythos was written, & for it—the simpler therefore and more childlike an interpretation is, the more probable ought it to be considered.

[# 33]

> [Boehme considers the Fall and ponders such questions as "Why did Satan choose to speak through the serpent? How was the serpent able to talk?"]

It is painful to observe, how this mighty but undisciplined Spirit perplexes his own intuitions by confusion of the Letter with the Life, and of the Symbolic Life with the Letter! The II Chapter of Genesis appears to be little more than a translation of Sculptured Figures into Words—the serpent being the Egyptian Symbol of intellective Invention, idolized by the Descendants of Ham, but the same, taken separately, as the φρονημα σαρκος [*phronema sarkos*], the wisdom of the Flesh, in Sᵗ Paul. Distinctive & discursive Knowlege was & by the fitness of the symbol remains, represented in the ramifications of a Tree, full of fruit but with the Serpent (which has here a double meaning, as being significant of poison or evil secretly working) wreathing the Boughs—Thus, the Mythos speaks to the Catechumen & to the Adept.—To the Catechumen it states the simple Fact, viz. that Man fell & falls thro' the separation and insubordination of the Fancy, the Appetence, & the discursive Intellect from the Faith or practical Reason—To the Adept it conveys the great mystery, that the origin of moral Evil is in the *Timeless*, εν τω αχρονω—in a spirit, not comprehended within the consciousness,—tho' revealed in the conscience of Man.

[# 34]

> 10. For the Heathens *worshipped* the Stars and four Elements, seeing they knew that they governed the *outward* Life of all Things; their understanding of the compacted sensual Tongue . . . did also enter into the *formed* compacted

. . . *Word of Nature* in them; and one Understanding moved the other, *viz.* the Human Understanding, in their Desire, moved the Understanding in the Soul of the outward World, *viz.* of the *expressed* and formed Word out of the inward dark and Fire-world, and out of the astral and elemental World; in which Soul the *Meaning* of the Sphere of Time is in the Understanding. . . .

12. From *this* Soul, *viz.* from the Horologium of the Understanding of Nature, the Heathens were *answered* by their Images and Idols, *viz.* through the Sense of the *Astrum*, which *their Faith* . . . did move and stir up.

When I consider the age and country in which these and so many other ¶s of equal or greater worth were written; when I recollect the notions held and doctrines enforced by the contemporary Divines, Civilians and Philosophers; and then reflect on the rank and means of *this* Man, only less contrasted with *their* circumstances, opportunities, and *bookish* acquirements than *these* principles with *their* Tenets—it seems to me, that many assertions, that have been favorably received by the Learned of the present day, have met a more decisive oppugnancy on the part of my Reason and Feelings, than the Belief avowed by the Gichtelians*, that Jacob Behmen was favored with a portion of the same spiritual Gift, the outbreathings of which in John and Paul we pronounce θεοδοτα [God-given], and designate by the name of Inspiration.

* a small but most estimable and blameless Church still existing at Amsterdam, who hold Behmen & Behmen's works in the same regard as the Church of the New Jerusalem hold Em. Swedenborg & *his* Writings.

1809

Sir Thomas Browne, *Religio Medici [A Doctor's Faith]*, London, 1669.

These related notes about love were almost certainly written in 1809–10 when Coleridge was living with the Wordsworths and producing a periodical, The Friend. *Their private significance stems from the fact that Coleridge intended to give the book to Sara Hutchinson, Wordsworth's sister-in-law, to whom* The Friend *was being dictated, and with whom he had been in love (chastely and distressingly) for about a decade.*

[# 35]

> I never yet cast a true affection on a woman, but I have loved my friend as I do vertue, my soul, my God. From hence me thinks I do conceive how God loves man, what happiness there is in the love of God.

I have loved—& still do love—*truly* i.e. not in a fanciful attributing of certain ideal perfections to an existing Being, who possesses perhaps no one of them; but in a true & palpable sympathy of manners, sentiments, & affections. So have I loved *one* Woman; & believe that such a love of such a Woman is the highest Friendship—for we cannot love a Friend as a Woman, but we can love a Woman as a Friend.

[# 36] Friendship satisfies the *highest* parts of our nature; but a wife, who is capable of friendship, satisfies *all*. The great business of real unostentatious Virtue is—not to eradicate any genuine instinct or appetite of human nature; but—to establish a concord and unity betwixt all parts of our nature, to give a Feeling & a Passion to our purer Intellect, and to intellectualize our feelings & passions. This a happy marriage, blessed with children, effectuates, in the highest degree, of which our nature is capable, & is therefore chosen by St Paul, as the symbol of the Union of the Church with Christ; that is, of the Souls of all good Men with God, the soul of the Universe—"I scarcely distinguish," said once a good old man, "the wife of my old age from the wife of my youth; for when we were both young, & she was beautiful, for *once* that I caressed her with a

34

meaner passion I caressed her a thousand times with *Love*—& *these* caresses still remain to us!"

Besides, there is another Reason why Friendship is of somewhat less Value, than Love which includes Friendship—it is this—we may love many persons, all *very* dearly; but we cannot love many persons, all *equally* dearly. There will be *differences*, there will be *gradations*—our nature imperiously asks a *summit*, a *resting-place*—it is with the affections in Love, as with the Reason in Religion—we cannot *diffuse* & equalize—we must have a SUPREME—a *One the highest*. All languages express this sentiment. What is more common than to say of a man in love—"he idolizes her," "he makes *a god* of her."—Now, in order that a person should *continue* to love another, better than all others, it seems necessary, that this feeling should be reciprocal. For if it be not so, Sympathy is broken off in the very highest point. A. (we will say, by way of illustration) loves B. above all others, in the best & fullest sense of the word, love: but B. loves C. above all others. Either therefore A. does not sympathize with B. in this most important feeling; & then his Love must necessarily be incomplete, & accompanied with a *craving* after something that *is not*, & yet *might be*; or he does sympathize with B. in loving C. above all others—& then, of course, he loves C. better than B. Now it is selfishness, at least it seems so to me, to desire that your *Friend* should love you better than all others—but not to wish that a *Wife* should.

[# 37]

> I could be content that we might procreate like trees without conjunction, or that there were any way to perpetuate the world without this trivial and vulgar way of coition; it is the foolishest act a wise man commits in all his life, nor is there any thing that will more deject his cool'd imagination, when he shall consider what an odd and unworthy piece of folly he hath committed.

He says, he is a Batchelor, but he talks as if he had been a married man, & married to a Woman who did not love him, & whom he did not love. Taken by itself, no doubt, the act is both foolish, & debasing. But what a misery is contained in those words, "taken by itself"? Are there not thoughts, & affections, & Hopes, & a *Religion* of the Heart,—that lift & sanctify all our bodily Actions where the union of the Bodies is but a language & *conversation* of united Souls?—

John Barclay, *Argenis*, Amsterdam, 1659.

Barclay's Latin romance and political allegory was published in 1621 and is of a kind, as Coleridge observes, with Spenser's Faerie Queene *(1590–96) and Fénelon's* Aventures de Télémaque [Adventures of Telemachus] *(1699). "Roscoe" and "Boswell" stand for two recent best-selling biographies, of Pope Leo X and Dr. Johnson, respectively.*

[# 38] It absolutely *distresses* me when I reflect that this Work, admired as it has been by great men of all ages, and lately, I hear, by the Poet Cowper, should be only not *unknown* to general Readers. It has been translated into English two or three times—how, I know not—wretchedly, I doubt not. It affords matter for Thought, that the last Translation—(or rather in all probability, miserable & faithless Abridgement, of some former) was given under another name. What a mournful proof of the In-celebrity of this great, and amazing Work, among both the *Public* and the *People*!/ for as Wordsworth, the greater of the two *great* men of this Age—(at least, except Davy & him I have *known, read of, heard of,* no others) for as W. did me the honor of once observing to me, the *People* and the *Public* are two distinct Classes, and (as things go) the former is likely to retain a better Taste, the less it is acted on by the Latter. Yet *Telemachus* is in every mouth, in every school-boys & school-girl's Hand.—

It is aweful to say of a work, like the Argenis, the style and latinity of which judged not according to classical pedantry, which pronounces every sentence right which can be found in any book prior to Boetius, however vicious the Age or affected the Author; and every sentence, wrong, however natural & beautiful, which has been of the Author's own combination/ but according to the universal Logic of Thought as modified by feeling, is equal to Tacitus in energy and genuine conciseness, is perspicuous as Livy, and is free from the affectations, obscurities, and lust to *surprize*, of the former, and forms a sort of antithesis to the slowness and prolixity of the Latter. This remark does not however impeach even the *classicality* of the Language, which, considering the freedom & originality, the easy motion and perfect Command of the Thoughts, is truly wonderful—of such a work it is aweful to say, that it would have been well if it had been written in English or Italian Verse/ Yet the Event seems to justify the Notion.—Alas! it is now too late. What modern work even of the size of Paradise Lost, much less of the Faery Queen—(N.B. are even *these* read?) would be *read* in the present Day; or even *bought* or likely to be *bought*, unless it be an INSTRUCTIVE Work, like Roscoe's 5 quartos of Leo X—or Boswell's 3 of Dr Johnson's pilfered brutalities of Wit?—It may be fairly objected, what work of surpassing merit has given the proof?—Certainly, none. Yet still there are ominous facts sufficient, I fear, to afford a certain prophecy of its reception, if such were produced.

Jonathan Swift, *Works*, Vol. 5, Edinburgh, 1768.

This copy belonged to William Wordsworth and may have been annotated in 1809–10, when Coleridge was living with the Wordsworth family. Coleridge comments on the famous Fourth Book of Gulliver's Travels, *containing Gulliver's account of his voyage to the country of the Houyhnhnms—rational talking horses who keep humanoid creatures, the Yahoos, as domestic animals. Lilliput, Brobdingnag, and Laputa are the main sites of Gulliver's adventures in Books 1, 2, and 3.*

[# 39] The great defect of the Houyhnhnms is not its misanthropy, and those who apply this word to it must really believe that the essence of human nature, that the anthrópos misoumenos [hated man], consists in the shape of the Body. Now to shew the falsity of this was Swift's great Object—he would prove to our feelings & imaginations and thereby teach *practically*, that it is Reason and Conscience which give all the loveliness and dignity not only to Man, but to the shape of Man—that deprived of these and yet retaining his Understanding he would be the most loathsome & hateful of all animals—that his understanding would manifest itself only as malignant Cunning, his free will as obstinacy and unteachableness—And how true a picture this is, every madhouse may convince any man/ a Brothel where Highwaymen meet, will convince every philosopher.—But the defect of the work is its inconsistency—the Houyhnhnms are not rational creatures, i.e. creatures of perfect reason—they are not progressive—they have servants without any reason for their natural inferiority or any explanation how the difference acted—and above all, they—i.e. Swift himself—has a perpetual affectation of being wiser* than his Maker, and of eradicating what God gave to be subordinated & used—ex. gr. the maternal & parental affection (στοργὴ [storge])—there is likewise a true Yahooism in the constant denial of the existence of Love, as not identical with Friendship, & yet distinct always & very often divided from Lust—. The best defence is that it is a Satyr—still it would have been felt a thousand times more deeply, if Reason had been truly pourtrayed—and a finer Imagination would have been evinced, if the Author had shewn the effects of the possession of Reason & the moral sense in the outward form & gestures of the Horse/ In short, Critics in general complain of the Yahoos—I complain of the Houyhnnms—

As to the *Wisdom* of adopting this mode of proving the great Truths here exemplified, that is another question—which no feeling mind will find a difficulty in answering, who has read & understood the Paradise Scenes in Paradise Lost, & compared the moral effect on his heart: and his virtuous aspirations of Milton's Adam with Swift's Horses—but different men have different Turns of Genius—Swift's may be good, tho' very inferior to Milton's—they do not stand in each other's way.

* A case in point, and besides utterly inconsistent with the boasted Reason of the Houyhnhnm, may be seen p. 194, 195—where the Horse discourses on the human frame with the grossest prejudices that could possibly be inspired by vanity & self-opinion. That Reason which commands man to admire the fitness of the Horse & Stag for superior speed, of the Bird for Flight, &c &c—must it not have necessitated the rational Horse to have seen and acknowleged the admirable aptitude of the human Hand compared with his own fetlocks—of the human Limbs for climbing, for the management of Tools &c?—In short, compare the *effect* of the Satire, when it is founded in truth & good sense (Chapt. V. for instance) with the wittiest of those passages which have their only support in spleen & want of reverence for the original frame of Man—& the feelings of the Reader will be his faithful guides in the reperusal of the work—which I still think the highest effort of Swift's genius, unless we should except the Tale of the Tub—/ then I would put Lilliput—next Brogdignag—& Laputa I would expunge altogether/ It is a wretched abortion, the product of Spleen & Ignorance & Self-conceit—

1810

James Sedgwick, *Hints to the Public and the Legislature,
on the Nature and Effect of Evangelical Preaching,*
London, 1808–10.

*Hints to the Public, published anonymously as by "A Barrister," was sent
to Coleridge's brother-in-law, Robert Southey, for review. Coleridge's
notes were written to assist Southey in that task.*

*The story of the woman with an issue of blood, healed by Christ, is in
Matt. 9.20–22. The names in the first note are representative, the imagined duchess and Moll Crispin representing the two ends of the social
spectrum; Raphael and Uriel, archangels who might be supposed to be
responsible for souls; Numa and Lycurgus, ancient lawgivers; and Chrysostom and Athanasius, theologians and saints. The reference to the* Quarterly Review *in the second note reminds Southey about a passage he had
quoted in an earlier review, in which a missionary in India wins a convert with the "easier law" of Christianity.*

[# 40]

... in the Evangelical Magazine for the last month, is the following article:—
"... At ———, in Yorkshire, after a handsome collection [for the Missionary
Society] on the preceding evening, a poor man, whose wages are about 28*s.*
per week, brought the next morning, at breakfast-time, a donation of twenty
guineas. Our friends hesitated to receive it, doubting whether it was consistent
with his duty to his family and the world to contribute such a sum; when he
answered to the following effect:—'Before I knew the grace of our Lord I was
a poor drunkard: I never could save a shilling. My family were in beggary and
rags; but, since it has pleased God to renew me by his grace, we have been in-
dustrious and frugal; we have not spent many idle shillings; and we have been
enabled to put something into the Bank; and this I freely offer to the blessed
cause of our Lord and Saviour.'—This is the SECOND donation of this same
poor man, to the SAME AMOUNT!!!"

Whatever these Evangelists may think of such conduct, they ought to be
ashamed of thus basely taking the advantage of this poor ignorant enthusiast. ...

Is it possible to read this affecting Story without finding in it a compleat answer to the charge of demoralizing the lower Classes? Does the Barrister really think, that this generous & grateful Enthusiast is as likely to be unprovided & poverty-stricken in his old age, as he *was* prior to his conversion? Except indeed that at that time his old age was as improbable as his distresses were certain if he did live so long. This is singing Io Paean! [Hail, Apollo!] for the Enemy with a vengeance.—

[# 41]

> A washerwoman has *all her sins blotted out*, in the twinkling of an eye, and while reeking with suds, is received in the family "of the Redeemer's kingdom!!!"
>
> Surely this is a most abominable profanation of all that is serious!—a most monstrous burlesque of all that is sacred! Yet such, according to the evangelists of methodism, is the new birth!!!

And where pray is the absurdity of this? Has Christ declared any antipathy to Washerwomen, or the H.G. [Holy Ghost] to warm Suds? Why does not the B. [Barrister] try his hand at abom. prof. [abominable profanation] in the story of the Woman with the issue of Blood who was made free by touching the Hem of a Garment without the previous knowlege of the Wearer? If a man were at once wicked & hard-hearted enough to repeat the same process, would not something more repulsive to decorous Ears come out than *reeking suds*? This is far, far too childish!

[# 42]

> What is *faith*? Is it not a conviction produced in the mind by adequate testimony?

No! that is not the meaning of Faith in the Gospel! Nor indeed any where else. Were it so, the stronger the testimony, the more adequate—Yet who says, I have *Faith* in the existence of George the Second, as his present Majesty's Antecessor & Grandfather?—If Testimony, then Evidence too—and who has Faith, that the two sides of all Triangles are greater than the Third? In truth, Faith even in common language always implies some effort, something of evidence that is not universally adequate or communicable at will to others—. Well! to be sure, he has behaved badly hitherto; but I have *Faith* in him.—If it were otherwise, how could it be imputed as Righteousness—Can morality exist without choice? nay, strengthen in proportion as it becomes more independent of the Will?—

A very meritorious man! he has *faith* in every proposition of Euclid, which he understands!

[# 43]

> The nostrum of the Mountebank will be preferred to the prescription of the regular Practitioner. Why is this? Because there is something in the authoritative arrogance of the pretender by which ignorance is over-awed.

This is something: and true as far as it goes. That is however but a very little way. The great Power of both spiritual and physical mountebanks rests on that irremoveable property of human Nature, in force of which *indefinite* Instincts and Sufferings find no echo, no resting place in the Definite and Comprehensible. Ignorance unnecessarily enlarges the sphere of these; but a sphere there is, *facts* of mind and Cravings of the Soul there are, in which the wisest Man seeks help from the Indefinite, because it is nearer and more like the Infinite, of which he is made the Image—for even we are infinite, even in our finiteness infinite, as the Father in his Infinity. In many caterpillars there is a large empty space in the head, the destined room for the pushing forth of the antennae of its next state of Being.—

[# 44]

> [Sedgwick quotes Rowland Hill's *Village Dialogues* to the effect that it would be worthwhile for all men to become tinkers if by so doing they became preachers of the caliber of the tinker John Bunyan, author of *Pilgrim's Progress*.] So with the Tinker; I would give him the care of kettles, but I would not give him *the cure of souls*. So long as he attended to the management and mending of his pots and pans, I would wish success to his industry; but when he came to declare *himself* a "chosen vessel," and demand permission to take the souls of the people into his holy keeping, I should think that, instead of *a license*, it would be more humane and more prudent to give him a passport to Saint Luke's.—Depend upon it such men were never sent by Providence to rule or to regulate mankind.

Whoo!!! Bounteous Providence, that always looks at the Baby Clothes & the Parents' Equipage before it picks out the proper Soul for the Baby. Ho! the Dutchess of Manchester is in labor—quick, Raphael or Uriel! bring a Soul out of the *Numa Bin*/ a young Lycurgus—or the Archbishop's Lady—Ho! a Soul from the Chrysostom or Athanasius Locker!—But poor Moll Crispin is in the Throes with Twins—/ Well! there are plenty of Cobler & Tinker Souls in the Hold—*John* Bunyan!—

Why, thou miserable Barrister, it would take an Angel an eternity a post to tinker thee into a Skull of half his Capacity!

[# 45]

> . . . these *anti-moral* editors [of *Pilgrim's Progress*, with notes by J. Newton, Dr. Hawker, and others] assure us, in a note, that "A *truly* awakened conscience can never find relief from the law." (*i.e.* THE MORAL LAW.) "The more he looks for peace *this way, his guilt,* like a heavy burden, becomes more intolerable; when he becomes *dead* to the *law*,—as to *any dependence upon it for salvation*,—by the body of Christ, and married to him, who was raised from the dead, then, and not till then, his heart is set at liberty to run the way of God's Commandments." . . . But here we are taught that the *conscience* can never find relief from *obedience to the law* of the Gospel, and are told, directly in the teeth of it, that the more a man looks for peace *this way,* the more *intolerable* becomes the burden of *his guilt!!*

False! We are told by Bunyan, that the Conscience can never find relief for its *disobedience* to the Law in the Law itself—and this is as true of the Moral as of the Mosaic Law. I am not defending Calvinism or Bunyan's Theology; but if victory, not truth, were my object, I could desire no easier task than to defend it against our doughty Barrister.—Well, but I *repent*—i.e. regret it.—Yes! and so you doubtless regret the loss of an Eye or Arm—will that make it grow again?—Think you this nonsense as applied to morality? Be it so! But yet nonsense most tremendously suited to human Nature is it, as the Barrister may find in the Arguments of the Pagan Philosophers against Christianity, who attributed a large portion of its success to its holding out an expiation, which no other Religion did.— Read but that most affecting & instructive anecdote selected from the Indostan Missionary Account by the Quart. Review! Again let me say, I am not giving my own opinion on this very difficult point; but of one thing I am convinced, that the *I am sorry for it—that's enough* men mean nothing but *regret* when they talk of repentance, and have consciences either so pure or so callous, as not to know what a direful and strange thing *Remorse* is! and how absolutely a fact sui generis [of its own kind]! I have often remarked, & it cannot be too often remarked (vain as this may sound) that this essential *Heterogeneity* of Regret and Remorse is of itself a sufficient and the best, *proof* of Free *Will*, and *Reason*: the coexistence of which in man we call *Conscience*, and on this rests the whole Superstructure of human Religion—God, Immortality, Guilt, Judgment, Redemption. Whether another & different Superstructure may be raised on the same foundation, or whether the same Edifice is susceptible of important alteration, is another question—But such is the Edifice at present—and this its foundation: and the Barrister might as rationally expect to blow up Windsor Castle by breaking wind in one of its Cellars, as hope to demolish Calvinism by such arguments as his.

[# 46]

> On this subject I will quote the just and striking observations of an excellent modern writer [Robert Fellowes, whose *Religion without Cant* is cited in a footnote]:—"In whatever village," says he, "the fanatics get a footing, drunkenness and swearing—sins which, being more exposed to the eye of the world, would be ruinous to their great pretensions to superior sanctity—will, perhaps, be found to decline; but I am convinced, from personal observation, that lying and dishonesty, that every species of fraud and falsehood—sins which are not so readily detected, but which seem more closely connected with worldly advantage—will be found invariably to increase."

In answer this let me make a very just observation, by some other man of my opinion to be hereafter quoted "from an excellent Modern Writer"—and this, that from the Birth of Christ to the present Hour no Sect or Body of Men were zealous in the reformation of manners in society, without having been charged with the same vices in the same words. When I hate a man, & *see* nothing bad in him—what remains possible, but to accuse him of crimes which I cannot see—& which cannot be disproved, because they cannot be proved.—Surely, if Xtn Charity did not preclude *these* charges, the Shame of convicted Parrotry ought to prevent a man from repeating & publishing them.—The very same thoughts, almost the words, are to be found in Lucian of the early Christians—of the poor Quakers, in a hundred Books—of the republicans—of the first Reformers. Why need I say this? Does not every one know, that a jovial Pot-companion can never believe a water-drinker not to be a sneaking cheating Knave that is afraid of his thoughts—that every Whoremonger swears that those who pretend to be chaste, either have their girl in a corner, or far worse—&c—&c— —

Immanuel Kant, *Vermischte Schriften* [*Miscellaneous Writings*], Halle, 1799.

This collection includes Kant's Latin thesis, the "Inaugural Dissertation" of 1770, De Mundi sensibilis atque intelligibilis forma et principiis [On the Form and Principles of the Sensory and Intelligible World].

[# 47] It is an interesting fact in philosophical History, i.e. the History of speculative Philosophy, that the "De Mundi Sensib. et intell. Form. et Prin." that Masterwork of profundity and precision, that model of steady investigation, clear Conception, and (as the Cambridge Mathematicians say) *elegant* Demonstration, was published 15 years before the Critique der reinen Vernunft [*Critique of Pure Reason*]—and produced no sensible effect on the philosophic Public. The former work contains all the main principles of the Latter, and often more perspicuously expressed— yet all remained silent. The Critique der r. V. appeared—& the Universities of Germany *exploded*! What was the cause of this difference? Is it, that the same Thoughts appeared less strange, less paradoxical, in Latin than in the vernacular Tongue? Or that the ordinary proofs of the higher psychology are exposed more openly & expressly in the Crit. d. r. V. than in the former work?—Or lastly, that one's mother tongue however philosophized and technical still produces on us a liveliness of impression which a dead Language cannot produce?—However this be, the former work should always be studied & mastered previously to the study of the Critique d. r. V. & the works that followed it.—The student will find it a better auxiliary than 50 Vol. of Comments, from Reinhold, Schmidt, Schulz, Beck, Tieftrunk, &c &c &c.—

1811

**Richard Baxter, *Reliquiae Baxterianae: or, Mr. Richard
Baxter's Narrative of the Most Memorable Passages of His Life
and Times,* ed. Matthew Sylvester, London, 1696.**

*Coleridge loved memoirs of the seventeenth century partly for the history
and partly for the prose. Two annotated copies of Baxter's autobiography
survive, this one containing notes of 1811 and later. "Ray" is John Ray,
author of* The Wisdom of God Manifested in the Works of Creation.
"Mumpsimus" is a name for someone who adheres obstinately to old errors.

[# 48]

[An account of an old woman who, after the massacre at Bolton, found an infant lying in the street by its dead mother and father, and] put it to her Breast for warmth, (having not had a Child her self of about 30 Years) the Child drew Milk, and so much, that the Woman nursed it up with her Breast Milk a good while. . . .

The great naturalist, Ray, adduces, in treating of the male teat (vide [see] his "Wisdom of God"), a yet stronger instance, that of a father whose breast furnished milk sufficient to preserve the life of the babe, whose mother had perished as they were travelling through the waste plains (then so at least), in the North of Italy, and on seeming good authority. I think that I have myself known a man who could have done it, under a conceived intense stimulus of pity and parental fondness.

[# 49]

In the Presbyterian way I disliked 1. Their Order of *Lay-Elders* who had *no Ordination*, nor *Power to Preach*, nor to *administer Sacraments*: For though I grant that Lay-Elders, or the Chief of the People, were oft imployed to express the Peoples Consent, and preserve their Liberties, yet these were no *Church-Officers* at all, nor had any Charge of private Oversight of the Flocks. . . .

Now this is almost the only thing which I approve of and admire in the Presbyterian form, as constituting a medium and conducting link between the priest and the congregation, so that all may be one well-organised body spiritual without discontinuity; whereas our churches resemble insects, in which the head is connected with the body only by a *thread*, a conjunction disjunctive.

[# 50]

4. When we have craved help for *God's Prayers*, before we come to them, we abruptly put in the Petition for speedy Deliverance "*O God make speed to save us: O Lord make haste to help us.*" without any Intimation of the Danger that we desire deliverance from, and without any other Petition conjoined.

5. It is disorderly in the *Manner*, to sing the Scripture in a plain Tune after the manner of reading.

6. "*The Lord be with you. And with thy Spirit*" being Petitions for Divine Assistance, come in abruptly, in the midst or near the end of Morning Prayer: And "*Let us Pray*" is adjoined when we were before in Prayer.

Oh! these seem to me very captious and unthinking objections. Had good Baxter considered the Liturgy *psychologically*, or as a grand composition of devotional *music*, gradually attuning, preparing, animating, and *working up*, the feelings of men to *public* and *common* prayer, and thanks, and glory-giving, he would have seen the excellence of much which he here condemns. Above all, he should have borne in mind that public prayer and private prayer, nay, I may add an intermediate, viz., domestic prayer, are quite distinct—much in each incongruous with the others—and that *common* prayer neither can, nor was ever intended to, supersede individual prayer. The direful lethargy of the *mumpsimus* Church hirelings then distorted, and alas *still* too often distorts, the judgments of warm and earnest Gospel preachers.

Jeremy Taylor, *A Collection of Polemicall Discourses*, London, 1674.

The most heavily annotated of all the books that passed through Coleridge's hands, containing over 250 notes written between 1811 and 1826, this volume of Taylor belonged to Charles Lamb.

The crux that Coleridge refers to as resting on a Greek "and" appears to be 2 Tim. 3.16: "All scripture is given by God, and is profitable for doctrine, for reproof, for correction, for instruction in righteousness." In Greek mythology "Hippocrene," a name that means "the horse's foun-

tain," was the fountain of the Muses; it was believed to have been opened up by an accidental blow from the hoof of the winged horse Pegasus. In using the phrase "Swedenborg's Hells," Coleridge evokes the environments of nightmare: the Swedish mystical writer described visions of heaven and hell (see # 144–47). The "Star-Chamber Inquisitors" refers to a period in the reign of Charles I when the archbishop of Canterbury, William Laud, used the special jurisdiction of the Star Chamber to persecute the Puritans.

[# 51]

> Lastly. Did not the Pen-men of the Scripture, write the Epistles and Gospels respectively all by the Spirit? Most certainly, *holy Men of God spoke as they were moved by the Holy Ghost*, saith *Saint Peter*. . . . because the Holy Ghost renewed their memory, improved their understanding, supplied to some their want of humane learning, and so assisted them that they should not commit an error in fact or opinion, neither in the narrative nor dogmatical parts, therefore they writ *by the Spirit*.

And where is the proof? And to what purpose, unless a distinct and plain Diagnostic were given of the *divinitùs* [that given from heaven] & the *humanitùs* [that which comes from human motives]? And even then, what would it avail unless the Interpreters & Translators, not to speak of the Copyists in the first & second Centuries, were likewise assisted by inspiration? As to the larger part of the prophetic Books, and the whole of the Apocalypse, we must receive them as inspired Truths, or reject them as inventions or enthusiastic delusions. But in what other Book of Scripture does the Writer assign his own work to a miraculous dictation or infusion? Surely, the contrary is implied in Luke's Preface. Does the hypothesis rest on one possible construction of a single passage in St Paul's? And that construction too resting on a καὶ [and] not found in the oldest mss?—when the context would rather lead us to understand the words as parallel with the other assertion of the apostle, that all good works are given from God? Finally, will not the certainty of the competence & single-mindedness of the writers suffice? And this too confirmed by the high probability, bordering on certainty, that God's *especial* Grace worked in them? and that an especial Providence watched over the preservation of Writings, which, we know, both are and have been of such pre-eminent importance to Christianity—& yet by natural means? We receive the Books ascribed to Matthew & John as their Books on the Judgement of men for whom no miraculous inspiration is pretended, nay, who both in their admission and rejection of other Books we believe to have erred—and we do not complain of the evidence as unsatisfactory. And shall we give less credence to Matthew & John themselves? The miracles and the main doctrines of faith must be believed in order to *ground* the argument for miraculous inspiration—Surely, the heart & soul of every Christian gives him sufficient assurance, that in all things that concern him as a man & a responsible Agent, the words, that he reads, are Spirit and are Truth, & could proceed only from the Great Being who made his heart & soul—without puzzling his mind about a term, the meaning of which it is hard to determine in any application but that one, which Taylor has shewn to be contradictory to the express declaration of the Scripture itself. Alas! any thing will be pretended rather than admit the necessity of internal evidence, or than acknowlege among the external proofs the convictions and spiritual experiences of Believers, tho' they should be common to all the Faithful in all ages of the Church. But in all superstition there is a heart of Unbelief: and vice versâ, where an Individual's Belief is but a superficial acquiescence, credulity is the natural result & accompaniment, if only he be not presumed to sink into the depths of his being, where the sensual man can no longer draw breath. It is not the profession of Socinian tenets, but the *Spirit* of Socinianism in the Church itself that alarms me. This, this, is the Dry Rot—in the beams and timbers of the Temple!—

[# 52]

[A digression in which Taylor discusses "Psalms made by common persons".] And this was not unhandsomely intimated by the word sometimes used by the Ἐυχολόγιον [prayer book] of the Greek Church, calling the publick Liturgie κοντάκιον, which signifies Prayers, made for the use of the *Idiotae*, or private persons, as the word is contradistinguished from the Rulers of the Church. κόντος signifies *contum*, and κόντῳ τλεῖν is as much as προσηκόντως ζῆν, to live in the condition of a private person, and in the vulgar Greek (says *Arcudius*) κόντος & κοντακῆνος ἄνθρωπος signifie a little man, of low stature, from which two significations κοντάκιον may well enough design a short form of Prayer, made for the use of private persons. . . . But this by the way.

Now here dear Jer. Taylor begins to be *himself*: for with all his astonishing complexity yet versatile agility of Powers he was too good & of too catholic a spirit to be a good Polemic! Hence he so continually is now breaking, now varying, the thread of the argument: and hence he is so again and again forgetting that he is reasoning against an antagonist and falls into Conversation with him as a friend—I might almost say, into the literary Chit-chat of a rich Genius and an unwithholding Frankness, whose *sands* are seed-pearl. Of his Controversies those against Popery are the most powerful because there he had subtleties & obscure Reading to contend against, & his Wit, Acuteness, and omnifarious Learning found stuff to work on: those on Original Sin the most eloquent. But in all alike it is the Digressions, Overgrowths, parenthetic *obiter et in transitu* [by the way and in passing] sentences, and above all, his anthropological Reflections and experiences (ex. gr. the inimitable account of a religious Dispute, from the first collision to the spark, and from the spark to the "World in flames," in his Dissuasive from Popery)—these are the costly gems which glitter, loosely set, on the Chain Armour of his polemic Pegasus, that expands his wings chiefly to fly off from the field of Battle—the stroke of whose Hoof the very Rock cannot resist, but beneath the stroke of which the opening Rock sends forth an Hippocrene! The Work in which all his powers are confluent, in which deep yet gentle the full stream of his Genius winds onward, still forming peninsulas in its winding course (distinct parts that are only not each, a perfect Whole)— or in less figurative style—(yet what Language that does not partake of poetic eloquence can convey the characteristics of a Poet & an Orator?) the work, which I read with most admiration but likewise with most apprehension and regret, is the Liberty of Prophesying. If indeed, like some Thessalian Drug or the

> Strong Herb of Anticyre, that helps & harms,
> Which Life and Death have seal'd with counter-charms;

it could be administered by special Prescription; it might do good service as a narcotic for Zealotry or a solvent for Bigotry.

[# 53]

> If these words be understood of Sacramental manducation, then no man can be saved but he that receives the holy Sacrament. For *unless ye eat the flesh of the son of Man and drink his blood, ye have no life in you.* . . .

The error on both sides, Roman & Protestant, originates in the confusion of Sign or Figure, and *Symbol*—which latter is always an essential *Part* of that, of the Whole of which it is the representative. Not seeing this, and therefore seeing no medium between the whole Thing and the mere Metaphor of the Thing, the Romanists took the former or positive Pole of the Error, the Protestants the latter or negative Pole. The Eucharist is a

symbolic, i.e. solemnizing and *totum in parte* [all in a part] Acting of an
Act that in a true Member of Christ's Body is supposed to be perpetual.
Thus the Husband & Wife exercise the duties of their Marriage Contract
of Love, Protection, Obedience &c all year long: and yet solemnize it by
a more deliberate and reflecting Act of the same Love on the Anniversary
of their marriage.—

[# 54]

> Saint *Justin Martyr* affirms, *That when the soul is departed from the body,*
> ἐυθυς γίνεται, *presently there is a separation made of the just and unjust: The*
> unjust are by Angels born into places which they have deserv'd; but the souls
> of the just into Paradise. . . . St. *Ambrose* saith, That *Death is a Haven of rest,*
> *and makes not our condition worse.* . . .

The strange and oftentimes aweful Dreams accompanying the presence
of irritating matters in the lower abdomen—& the seeming appropriation
of sorts of Dream Images & Incidents to affections of particular Organs,
& viscera—Do the material Causes act *positively*—so that with the removal of the Body by Death the total cause is removed & of course the
Effects? Or only *negatively* and *indirectly* by lessening & suspending that
continuous texture of Organic Sensation, which by drawing outward the
attention of the [?soul] *sheaths* her from her own state & its corresponding activities?—A fearful Question, which I too often agitate, and which
agitates me, even in my Dreams—when most commonly I am in one of
Swedenborg's Hells, doubtful whether I am once more to be *awaked*—&
thinking our Dreams to be the true state of the Soul disembodied when
not united with Christ—. On awaking from such dreams I never fail to
find some local *pain*, circa- or infra-umbilical.—Kidney affections, & at
the base of the Bladder with vast water-scenery./.

[# 55]

> The Churches have troubled themselves with infinite variety of questions, and
> divided their precious unity, and destroyed charity, and instead of contending
> against the Devil and all his crafty methods, they have contended against one
> another, and excommunicated one another, and anathematiz'd and damn'd one
> another; and no man is the better after all, but most men are very much the
> worse; and the Churches are in the world still divided about questions that
> commenc'd twelve or thirteen ages since; and they are like to be so for ever
> till *Elias* come. . . .

I remember no passages of the Fathers nearer to inspired Scripture, than this & similar ones of J. Taylor, in which quitting the acute Logician he combines his Heart with his Head, & utters general & inclusive & reconciling Truths of Charity & of Common Sense. All amounts but to this. What is binding on all, must be possible to all. But conformity of intellectual conclusions is not possible: Faith therefore cannot reside fontally in the Understanding. But to do what we believe we ought to do, is possible to all—therefore binding on all—therefore the unum necessarium [one necessary thing] of Christian Faith. Talk not of a bad Conscience— it is like bad Sense—i.e. no sense—and we all know that we may wilfully lie till we involuntarily believe the Lie as Truth—but causa causae est causa vera causati [the cause of a cause is the true cause of the effect].

[# 56]

> That the Scriptures do not contain in them all things necessary to salvation, is the fountain of many great and Capital errors; I instance in the whole doctrine of the Libertines, Familists, Quakers, and Other Enthusiasts, which issue from this corrupted fountain.

as I cannot think that it detracts from a Dial that in order to tell the time the Sun must shine upon it, so neither does it detract from the Scriptures, that tho' the best and holiest, they are yet *Scripture*—& require a pure heart & the consequent assistances of God's enlightening Grace in order to understand them to edification. And what more does the Quaker say? He will not call the written *words* of God the Divine WORD: & he does rightly.

[# 57]

> Against all the authorities almost which are or might be brought to prove the Unlawfulness of Picturing God the Father, or the Holy Trinity, the *Roman* Doctors generally give this one answer; That the Fathers intended by their sayings, to condemn the picturing of the Divine Essence; but condemn not the picturing of those symbolical shapes or forms in which God the Father, or the Holy Ghost, or the Blessed Trinity are supposed to have appeared. To this I reply, 1. That no man ever intended to paint the essence of any thing in the world. A man cannot well understand an Essence, and hath no *Idea* of it in his mind, much less can a Painters Pencil do it.

Noticeable, that this is the only instance I have met in any English Classic before the Revolution of the word "Idea" used as synonimous with a mental *Image*. Taylor himself has repeatedly placed the two in opposition; but even here I doubt that he has done otherwise. I rather think, he meant by the word "Idea" a notion under an indefinite & confused Form, such as Kant calls a Schema, or vague outline—an imperfect embryo of a concrete, to the individuation of which the mind gives no conscious attention, just as when I say—*any thing*—I may imagine a poker or a plate; but I pay no *attention* to its being this rather than that—& the very image itself is so wandering & unstable that at this moment it may be a dim shadow of the one, & in the next of some other thing. In this sense Idea is ✶ [opposed to] Image in opposition of *degree* instead of Kind; yet still contra-distinguished, as is evident by the Sequel—Much less can a Painter's Pencil do it—For were it an Image, individui et concreti [of an individual and concrete thing], then the Painter's Pencil could do it as well as his fancy, or better.

[# 58]

> Now because the great Question is concerning Religion, and in that also my scene lies, I resolved here to fix my considerations; especially when I observed the ways of promoting the several Opinions which now are busie to be such, as besides that they were most troublesome to me, and such as I could by no means be friends withall, they were also such as to my understanding did the most apparently disserve their ends whose design in advancing their own Opinions was pretended for Religion. For as contrary as cruelty is to mercy, as tyranny to charity, so is war and bloudshed to the meekness and gentleness of Christian Religion.

O! had this work been published when the Lie-martyr, Charles, Archbp Laud whose Chaplain Taylor was, and the other Star-chamber Inquisitors were sentencing Prynne, Bastwick, Leighton to punishments that have left a brand-mark on the Church of England, the Sophistry might have been forgiven for the sake of the Motive—which would *then* have been unquestionable!—Or if Jer. Taylor had not retracted, after the Restoration; if he had not as soon as the Episcopal Church had regained the power and resumed the practice of the foulest Persecution, most basely disclaimed and disavowed the principle of toleration, and apologized for the Publication by declaring it to have been a *ruse de guerre* [war stratagem], currying pardon for his past Liberalism by charging—& most probably *slandering*—himself with the guilt of falsehood, treachery, & hypocrisy; his *character* as a man would at least have been stainless! Alas! alas! most dearly do I love Jer. Taylor! most religiously do I venerate his Memory!

But this was too foul a Blotch of the Episcopal Leprosy to be forgiven. He who pardons such an Act in such a man, partakes of its guilt.

John Donne, *Poems*, London, 1669.

Another of Charles Lamb's books.

[# 59] ["The Triple Fool":] One of my favorite Poems. As late as 10 years ago, I used to seek and find out grand lines and fine stanzas: but my delight has been far greater, since it has consisted more in tracing the leading Thought thro'out the whole. The former is too much like coveting your neighbour's Goods: in the latter you merge yourself in the Author— you *become He.*—

[# 60] ["Satire III" ("Kind pity chokes my spleen"):] If you would teach a Scholar in the highest form, how to *read*, take Donne, and of Donne this Satire. When he has learnt to read Donne, with all the force & meaning which are involved in the Words—then send him to Milton—& he will stalk on, like a Master, *enjoying* his Walk.

1812

Baruch Spinoza, *Opera [Works]*, ed. H.E.G. Paulus, Jena, 1802–3.

Coleridge was already an admirer and defender of Spinoza (# 11) when he borrowed this edition from a fellow student of German literature, Henry Crabb Robinson, who had been a foreign correspondent for the Times *and would go on to become a lawyer and one of the founders of University College London, though he is now best known for his diaries. Here Coleridge expresses the suspicion that national prejudice played a part in the misrepresentation of Spinoza among English readers, since their own Francis Bacon, whose philosophical system seems to him to be similar, does not suffer in the same way. "Whose service is perfect freedom" is from the* Book of Common Prayer.

[# 61]

{Every singular thing, or any thing which is finite and has a determinate existence, can neither exist nor be determined to produce an effect unless it is determined to exist and produce an effect by another cause, which is also finite and has a determinate existence; and again, this cause also can neither exist nor be determined to produce an effect unless it is determined to exist and produce an effect by another, which is also finite and has a determinate existence, and so on, to infinity.}

This is the Proposition, on the full Insight into which depends at once the correction and the confirmation of Spinosism. If these finite Causes can be said to act at all, then that on which they act has an equal power of action—: and even as tho' all in God *essentially*, we are yet each *existentially* individual, so must we have freedom in God in exact proportion to our Individuality. It is most necessary to distinguish Spinosism from Spinosa—i.e. the consequences of the immanence in God as the one only necessary Being whose essence involves existence, with the deductions from Spinosa's own mechanic *realistic* view of the World. Even in the latter, I can not accord with Jacobi's assertion, that Spinosism as taught by Spinosa, is Atheism/ for tho' he will not consent to call things essentially disparate by the same name, and therefore denies human intelligence to Deity, yet he adores his *Wisdom*, and expressly declares the identity of Love, i.e. perfect Virtue, or concentric Will, in the human Being, and that with which the Supreme loves himself, as all in all. It is true, he contends for Necessity; but then he makes two disparate Classes of Necessity, the one identical with Liberty (even as the Christian Doctrine, "whose Service is perfect Freedom") the other Compulsion = Slavery. If Necessity and Freedom are not different Points of View of the same Thing, the one the *Form*, the other the Substance, farewell to all Philosophy and to all Ethics. It is easy to see, that Freedom without necessity would preclude all Science, and as easy to see, that Necessity without Freedom would subvert all Morals; but tho' not so obvious, it is yet equally true, that the Latter would deprive Science of its main Spring, its last ground and impulse; and that the Former would bewilder and *atheize* all Morality. But never has a great Man been so hardly and inequitably treated by Posterity, as Spinosa—No allowances made for the prevalence, nay, universality of Dogmatism & the mechanic System in his age—no trial, except in Germany, to adopt the glorious Truths into the family of Life & Power.— What if we treated Bacon with the same Harshness?

Johann Gottfried Eichhorn, *Einleitung in das Neue Testament [Introduction to the New Testament]*, Leipzig, 1804–14.

Coleridge annotated at least seven works (including two copies of this one) by Eichhorn, whose lectures on the Old and New Testaments he had attended in Germany in 1799. Eichhorn added to the "lower criticism" or close study of the text of the Bible what he and his followers called the "higher criticism" of historical and cultural awareness, which led to new theories and interpretations.

[# 62]

{One only sighs over the miraculous in the biographical accounts that they [the Gospels] set forth! It does not exist in the events themselves, but merely in the telling, in the point of view from which they were written, in the folk beliefs that have flowed in upon them in the recounting. . . . Indeed it is difficult for us in an age of completely different orientation to comprehend the events and to separate them from popular interpretations: but could the Evangelists have reckoned with us? Did they intend their treatises for us? Did they even dream, since they were anything but regular and academic writers, that their works, addressed to particular persons, would be read thousands of years later in a large part of the inhabited world?}

This dishonesty absolutely provokes an English Reader.—Death!—Did the Apostles believe that they were commissioned to found a Religion? If so, could they be such Oafs, with the example of the Jewish Sacred Books before them, as not to foresee that written Documents must exist & would be preserved, if the Gospel was received?—Matthew, an eye-witness, revised at least, arranged and augmented the supposed Original Gospel!— And *could* he as a man of common honesty give his sanction to the assertion, that Jesus fed 4000 men with 7 Loaves & a few small Fishes, & with a surplus of *seven* Baskets full of Fragments—when all this was merely what the Mob thought who did not know that Jesus had previously layed up Provender for that number/ and St Matthew, forsooth, meant only to record Christ's humane Fore-thought? And Jesus himself—he cures diseases at once, by word of mouth—or a little sand.—Were ever Diseases in such numbers epilepsy, mania, &c cured without Medicine—or Leprosy? If given, either Christ concealed it & was an impostor—or his Apostles—& then they were Liars—And what in the name of common sense does Eichhorn believe? What remains after he has taken away the Divinity, Incarnation, mysterious Redemption, and all the miraculous coloring of the Facts?—A Quack doctor, who interspersed his Cures with teaching, the moral part of the old Testament separated from the legal— that which belonged to Individuals as men, from that which belonged to the Jews nationally, as Subjects of a particular Statute-Book!—This seems to me the most puerile and at the same time the most sneeking Form of Deism. For the evidence of Historical Christianity is wholly *moral*/ the men report, nay, the thousand-fold attestation of marvellous Cures, proves nothing but what it proves daily, even at this day—viz. Quackery and Credulity. If a Difference, an essential Difference, is not made by the Doctrine and the Character of the Recorders, there is none at all.

William Shakespeare, *Works*, ed. L. Theobald, London, 1773.

Coleridge is believed to have annotated at least six sets of Shakespeare, this being the earliest known, with notes perhaps as early as 1810 but certainly 1812–13, when Coleridge was lecturing on Shakespeare and liv-

*ing with John James Morgan, his wife Mary, and her sister Charlotte
Brent. This copy belonged to Morgan.
"B. & F."—Francis Beaumont and John Fletcher—were collaborat-
ing playwrights, contemporaries of Shakespeare, whose plays Coleridge
often invokes as a point of comparison for judging Shakespeare's; The
Mad Lover is one of theirs. The prolific German dramatist August von
Kotzebue (1761–1819) was sensationally popular in England in Coleridge's day; his Lovers' Vows is familiar yet as the play chosen for private theatricals in Austen's* Mansfield Park.

[# 63] [On *King Lear.*] It is well worthy notice, that Lear is the only serious performance of Shakespear, the interest & situation of which are derived from the assumption of a gross Improbability; whereas Beaumont
& Fletcher's Tragedies are, almost all, founded on some out-of-the-way
Accident or Exception to the general Experience of Mankind.—But observe the matchless Judgement of Shakespear!—First, improbable as the
Conduct of Lear is, in the first Scene, yet it was an old Story, rooted in
the popular Faith—a thing taken for granted already, & consequently,
without any of the *effects* of Improbability. 2^{ndly}—It is merely the can-
vass to the Characters & Passions, a mere *occasion*—not (as in B. & F.)
perpetually recurring, as the cause & sine quâ non of the Incidents &
Emotions.—Let the first Scene of Lear have been lost, & let it be only
understood that a fond Father had been duped by hypocritical professions
of Love & Duty on the part of two Daughters to disinherit a third, previously, & deservedly, more dear to him/ & all the rest of the Tragedy would
retain its interest, undiminished, & be perfectly intelligible. The *Accidental* is no where the ground-work of the Passions; but the καθολον
[universal], that which in all Ages has been & ever will be close & native
to the heart of Man—Parental Anguish from filial Ingratitude, the gen-
uineness of worth, tho' coffered in bluntness, the vileness of smooth In-
iquity—Perhaps, I ought to have added the Merchant of Venice; but here
too the same remarks apply. It was an old Tale: & substitute any other danger, than that of the Pound of Flesh, (the circumstance in which the improbability lies) yet all the situations & the emotions appertaining to them
remain equally excellent & appropriate.—Whereas take away from "the
Mad Lover" the fantastic hypothesis of his engagement to cut out his own
Heart, & have it presented to his Mistress, & all the main Scenes must go
with it.
    Kotzebue is the German B. & F., without their poetic powers & with-
out their vis comica [comic power]. But like them he always deduces his

situations & passions from marvellous Accidents, & the trick of bringing one part of our moral nature to counteract another—as our pity for misfortune & admiration of generosity & Courage to combat our Condemnation of Guilt, as in Adultery, Robbery &c: & like them too, he excels in his mode of telling a story clearly, & interestingly, in a series of dramatic Dialogues. Only the trick of making Tragedy-Heroes & Heroines out of Shopkeepers & Barmaids was too low for the age, & too unpoetic for the genius, of Beaumont & Fletcher, inferior in every respect as they are to their great Predecessor & Contemporary! *How* inferior would they have appeared, had not Shakespear existed for them to *imitate?*—which in every play, more or less, they do—& in their Tragedies most glaringly—and yet (o Shame! Shame!) miss no opportunity of sneering at the divine Man & subdetracting from his Merits!!—

[# 64]

[From *Antony and Cleopatra:*]

ANTONY. . . . Much is breeding:
    Which, like the Courser's hair, hath yet but life,
    And not a serpent's poison.

[Theobald's note:] This alludes to an old opinion, which obtain'd among the vulgar . . . that the hair of a horse in corrupted water would take life, and become an animal.

This is however so far true, that a Horse-hair thus treated will become the supporter of apparently one, worm, tho' probably of an immense number, of small slimy water-lice. The Hair will twirl round a finger, and sensibly compress it. It is a common experiment with the School-boys in Cumberland and Westmoreland.—

1813

Moses Mendelssohn, *Morgenstunden [Morning Hours]*, Frankfurt and Leipzig, 1790.

[# 65]

{All possibilities thus have their ideal existence in the thinking subject, which ascribes them to the object as conceivable. A possibility that is not conceived [by a subject] is an utter absurdity. . . . Therefore all real things must not only be *conceivable* but also must be *conceived* by some being. Each real existence has a corresponding ideal existence in some subject; each thing has a corresponding conception. Without being perceived nothing is perceptible; without being observed there can really be no mark, and without a concept no object.}

Mend. evidently grounds his Position on the inherence of the Thing in the Thought: for supposing them separate, & simply correspondent, as my face to the Image in the Looking-glass, it is absurd to say that my face would not exist or be if there were no Looking-glass. Instead of being an argument therefore from Realities, it is in fact only an argument against them, in any other sense than as modes of mind. For the whole amounts to no more than the impossibility of conceiving a thing per se unconceived—i.e. conceived and not conceived. It would have been far better therefore to have begun with the thesis—We can attach no meaning to the term, *Thing*, *separated* from Thought—or that all *possibility* (by the bye, the German seems to have led M. into an Equivoque, for I should have said, *Potentiality*) is the mere application of Time and Space to Objects—I know Iron, I know Caloric [heat]—They are now together/ & there is a Fluid. I withdraw the latter—there is a solid. I apply to the Objects before me future Time—& imagine the same space to both—and say, Fusion is a potentiality of this Iron.—But Time & Space are forms of Perception—ergo, &c.—But a plain man would answer: Tho' we cannot know any thing but by knowing it, yet having thus known its existence we at the same time learn that it would have been tho' we had not known it.

Friedrich Wilhelm Joseph von Schelling,
System des transcendentalen Idealismus
[System of Transcendental Idealism], Tübingen, 1800.

The surviving annotated books show Schelling to have been the most important influence on Coleridge's thought among the post-Kantian German Idealists, but they also show a process of disillusionment that culminated in Coleridge's rejection of Schelling's system as ultimately pantheistic. The notes in this volume date from 1813 to 1825.

[# 66]

{But with these two problems we find ourselves involved in a contradiction.— *B* calls for a dominance of thought (the ideal) over the world of sense; but how is this conceivable if (by *A*) the presentation is in origin already the mere slave of the objective?—Conversely, if the real world is a thing wholly independent of us, to which (as *A* tells us) our presentation must conform (as to its archetype), it is inconceivable how the real world, on the contrary, could (as *B* says) conform itself to presentations in us.—In a word, for certainty in theory we lose it in practice, and for the certainty in practice we lose it in theory; it is impossible both that our knowledge should contain truth and our volition reality.

If there is to be any philosophy at all, this contradiction must be resolved— and the solution of this problem, or answer to the question: *how can we think both of presentations as conforming to objects, and objects as conforming to presentations?* is, not the first, but the *highest* task of transcendental philosophy.}

Ye Gods! annihilate both Space and Time—and then this ¶ph. may become cogent Logic. But as it is, one might with equal plausibility from the fact of one man's lying on his back deduce the incompossibility of another Man's standing on his feet; or from the incompossibility of both positions in the same Man at the same time infer the impossibility of the two positions successively.—

Besides, the antitheta [things opposed] are not adequate Opposites, much less Contraries. A Wheel presented to me generates without apparent materials the image of the Wheel in my mind. Now if the preconception of a Wheel in the Artist's mind generated in like manner a corporeal wheel in outward Space—or even in a mass of timber—then indeed (tho even so I can see no contradiction in the two hypotheses) a problem would arise, of which the equality or sameness of kind in the two Generators might be the most natural Solution—. Yet even here there is a Flaw in the Antithesis: for to make it perfectly correspondent, the Mass of Wood ought to generate the Image, Wheel/—Where is the inconsistency between the reality (i.e. actual realizing power) of the Will in respect of the relative *position* of Objects and the reality of Objects themselves independent of the *Position*? Is the Marble of a *Statue* less really Marble, than the Marble in the Quarry?—What after all does the problem amount to more than the Fact, that the Will is a vis motrix [motive power], and the Mind a *directive* power at one moment & in relation to the Will, and a Re- or Per-cipient in relation to objects moving, or at rest? Schelling seems at once to deny and yet suppose the Objectivity—on no other ground than that he commences by giving objectivity to Abstractions—A *acting* he calls Will: the same A acted on he calls *Truth* and then, because acting, and being acted on, are Antitheses or *opposite States*, he first turns them into *contrary things*, and then transfers this contrariety to the Subject A/ —That A acts on B, and is itself acted on by C, is a fact, to the *How*? respecting which I may have no other answer than Nescio [I do not know]/ but that my ignorance as to the How makes any contradiction in the Fact, I can by no means admit—any more than that a Mail Coach moving 10 miles an hour on the Road contradicts the fact of the same standing in a Coach House the night following. The whole difficulty lies in the co-existence of Agere et Pati [Active and Passive] as Predicates of the same Subject.

[# 67]

{The self has sensation, in that it intuits itself as originally limited. This intuition is an activity, but the self cannot at once both intuit, and intuit itself as intuiting.*}

I more and more see the arbitrariness and inconveniences of using the same term, Anschauen [intuit], for the productive and the contemplative Acts of the Intelligential Will, which Schelling calls das Ich [the I, or the self]. If * were true, the I could never become conscious: for the same impossibility for the same reason would recur in the second act—& so in fact it is. We can no more pass without a saltus [leap] from mere Sensation to Perception, than from Marble to Sensations.

Whether it is better to assume Sensation as a minimum of Perception, or to take them as originally diverse, and to contend that in all Sensation a minor grade of Perception is comprised deserves consideration.

Gotthold Ephraim Lessing, *Sämmtliche Schriften* [Collected Writings], Berlin, 1784–98.

Coleridge probably acquired his fifteen-volume set of Lessing's works in Germany in 1799—he was thinking of writing a biography of Lessing at the time—but his notes date from 1813 to 1823.

By "David's Poems, or the Gnomonics attributed to Solomon," Coleridge means the Old Testament books of Psalms and Proverbs; Denis Diderot, as a contributor to the French Encyclopédie, *and Tom Paine as the author of the deistic* Age of Reason *(1794) were leading rationalists; Lycurgus and Solon were lawgivers of ancient Greece.*

[# 68]

{It is strange . . . that the same person [Augustine] maintains that the Creed may not be written down. "Sermon 213 . . . To master the exact words of the Creed you must on no account write them down but learn them thoroughly by hearing them said: nor must you write them when you have learned them, but retain them and keep going over them in your memory."}

Lessing has violently perverted the plain meaning of this Passage, which does not imply a prohibition to write what himself & others not only wrote but published—but not to write it down, as a substitute for actually recollecting it. By writing any thing, as in a Mem: [Memorandum] Book so far from impressing it on the memory we rather disburthen the memory of it.

[# 69]

[A passage from Lessing's play *Nathan the Wise*:]

{SALADIN.   If this man gets his wealth from graves, they were certainly not the graves of Solomon and David. Fools lay buried there.

SITTAH.   Or knaves!}

I cannot understand this Speech—Fools (rather *Crackpates*—) or *Villains*? Lessing's Creed, whether it were that of Deism at this time, or of Spinosism, to which in some sense or other he afterwards professed himself a Convert, does not disturb either my Love or Admiration, neither injures him *with* ME as a Man or as a Philosopher—. But that any man could read David's Poems, or the Gnomonics attributed to Solomon, & yet deem the men crazed or scoundrels—that, *that* would exceed my charity—it would imply such a vulgar Bigotry of low unthinking Anti-christianism, as would level Lessing with a Diderot, or Tom Payne. But I trust, I misinterpret the words.—I know one who from a Socinian became a Deist, or rather a Pantheist—and then from his increased & enthusiastic admiration of the character of Moses, considered merely as a Lycurgus or Solon, with rejection of all inspiration & miracle, was gradually led back to a Belief in Revelation, & after intense study declared, he could conscientiously subscribe all the *doctrinal* Articles of the Church of England.

Robert Robinson, *Miscellaneous Works*, Harlow, 1807.

This collection of sermons and political and religious pamphlets belonged to Coleridge's friend Josiah Wade and was probably annotated while Coleridge was staying with Wade in Bristol in 1813–14.

"Principia" is the familiar short version of the title of Isaac Newton's great work, Philosophiae Naturalis Principia Mathematica—*i.e.,* Mathematical Principles of Natural Philosophy—*published in 1687. The phrase "all the means and appliances to boot" comes from Shakespeare's* 1 Henry IV *3.1.29.*

[# 70]

As I may avoid fire without feeling its effects, so I may avoid the truths of christianity; but I cannot admit them without admitting at the same time the effects, which the belief of these truths never fails to produce. On these principles the apostle . . . connects salvation with faith alone, because faith is not alone, but is inseparably connected with repentance, and love, and zeal, and good works, and every other christian excellence: and on these principles we praise the understandings of those, who give sailors bibles *only*, because the gift implies several just and honourable principles; principles, I mean, which do honour to the understandings and hearts of those, who admit them.

First: this donation implies, that in the opinion of the donors, the bible is a *plain*, easy book; either that all the truths of revelation are simple, plain, and clear, or that such truths as are essential to salvation are so. This is a very just notion of revelation. . . .

!! What if I were to call Newton's "Principia" a *plain*, easy Book, because certain detached passages were axiomatic, & because the results were evident to common-sense?—What? The Pentateuch? the Solomon's Song? The Prophets in general, & Ezekiel in particular? What? the Ecclesiastes?

The praise of Jael? of Ehud? of David?—What? Sᵗ John's Gospel, & his Revelations? the *apparent* Discordances of the Evangelists in the most important narration, that of the Resurrection? What? Sᵗ Paul's Epistles, declared by a contemporary Apostle, dark & hard?—are these parts of a plain & easy Book?

The Writer of the preceding Note reverences the Bible, he trusts, as much, & believes its contents with a far stricter Consistency with Protestant Orthodoxy (in the common received meaning of the word, Orthodoxy) than the amiable Author of this Discourse as appears by his own Letters—but never, never, can he believe that the many & various Writings of so many, various, and distant ages, as brought together form "the Book"; that this Book, or Collectaneum, the interpretation of which *has* occupied, & will occupy all the highest powers of the noblest & best Intellects even to the Consummation of all things; can be called in toto [as a whole], or even on the average, "a plain & easy Book!"—That what is necessary for each man's Salvation, (in *his* particular state, he making the best use of the means in his Power, & walking humbly with his God) is sufficiently plain for that *his* purpose, the Writer of the note cheerfully acknowleges, & with thanks to the Author of all Inspiration & of all good Gifts!

[# 71]

> Secondly: the donation of a bible only, implies, that each reader hath *a right of private judgment*. This is another just notion, truly scriptural, and entirely protestant. To give a man a book to read, and to deny him the right of judging of its meaning, seems the summit of absurdity.

Doubtless!—but may there not be folly in giving a Child (and an ignorant man is a Child in Knowlege) a Book, he cannot understand, without any assistances to enable him so to do? To an ignorant Man I would not give Newton at all: for not only he can not understand it, but he may do very well without it. To the same man I *would* give the Bible, tho' a very large part would be worse than unintelligible, for it would be misintelligible—yet as it does concern him, I would give it, only with "all the means & appliances to boot", that would preclude dangerous misinterpretation.

1814

Robert Leighton, *The Expository Works and Other Remains*, Edinburgh, 1748.

This is one of three known copies of Leighton's works annotated by Coleridge. (Leighton had been professor of divinity at Edinburgh and a reluctant archbishop of Glasgow in the reign of Charles II.) His notes record his reaction on being introduced to Leighton at a particularly low time in his own life, when he was struggling to overcome his addiction to opium by simply stopping taking it. He was lent the book by a Bristol acquaintance, William Brame Elwyn. "The trembling Devils" alludes to James 2.19: "Thou believest that there is one God; thou dost well: the devils also believe, and tremble."

[# 72] Surely if ever Work not in the sacred Canon might suggest a belief of Inspiration, of something more than human, this it is. When Mr. E. made this assertion, I took it as an hyperbole of affection, but now I subscribe to it seriously, & bless the Hour that introduced me to the knowledge of the evangelical apostolical Archbishop Leighton.

S. T. Coleridge April 1814

[# 73]

> There is a Truth in it, that all Sin arises from some kind of Ignorance, or, at least, from present Inadvertence and Inconsideration, turning away the Mind from the Light; which therefore, for the time, is as if it were not, and is all one with Ignorance in the Effect; and therefore the Works of Sin are all called *Works of Darkness*. For were the true Visage of Sin seen at a full Light, undress'd and unpainted, it were impossible, while it so appear'd, that any one Soul could be in Love with it, but would rather fly it, as hideous and abominable.

This is the only (defect shall I say 'no' but the only) omission I have *felt* in this divine Writer—for him we understand by feeling—*experimentally*, namely, that he doth not notice the horrible Tyranny of *Habit*—the trembling Devils *believe*. What the Archbishop says is most true of be-

65

ginners in Sin: but this is the Fore-taste of Hell, to see and loathe the deformity of the wedded vice, & yet still to embrace it & nourish.

Robert Southey, *Joan of Arc, an Epic Poem*, Bristol, 1796.

Joan of Arc, published as Southey's but actually a product of close collaboration between Southey and Coleridge in their hotter-headed democratic days, had become something of an embarrassment to both of them by 1814 when Coleridge annotated this copy, not least because of deteriorating personal relations. Coleridge at that time was at a very low ebb, and Southey, who had the day-to-day responsibility for Coleridge's family as well as his own, had run out of patience with him. Coleridge used red pencil for his notes, whence the pun in # 76.

[# 74]

> [From Southey's preface:] The lawless magic of Ariosto, and the singular theme as well as the singular excellence of Milton, render all rules of epic poetry inapplicable to these authors. . . .

N.B.—It is an original Discovery of Southey's that the *excellence* of an Epic Poem should render the rules of Epic Poetry inapplicable to it. Ex. gr.: The Yorkshire pudding been made with consummate culinary art; the art culinary is therefore inapplicable to the making thereof. There is just the same difference between a *Poet*, the most thinking of human Beings, & a mock Poet, as between an egg and an egg shell.

[# 75] *N.B.*—

S.E. means *Southey's English,* i.e. no English at all.
N. means Nonsense.
J. means discordant *Jingle* of sound—one word rhyming or half-rhyming to another proving either utter want of ears, or else very long ones.
L.M. = ludicrous metaphor. I.M. = incongruous metaphor.
S. = pseudo-poetic Slang, generally, too, not English.

[# 76] Mercy on us, if I go on thus, I shall make the Book what, I suppose, it never was before, *red all thro'*. N.B.—Puns are for the *Ear*. Punning & Spelling are natural enemies.

[# 77]

". . . Then might be heard,
"(That dreadful emblem of destruction seen,)
"The mother's <u>anguish'd</u> shriek, the old man's groan
"Of deep despondence. . . ."

Not English. a Participle presupposes a verb—now there is no such verb as "to anguish", ergo, there can be no such participle, as "anguished". To guard with jealous Care the purity of his native Tongue the sublime Dante declares to be the first Duty of a Poet. It is this conviction more than any other which actuates my severity toward Southey, W. Scott &c—all miserable Offenders!—

[# 78]

"Maid beloved of Heaven!"
(To her the tutelary Power exclaimed)
"Of CHAOS the adventurous progeny
"Thou seest; foul missionaries of foul sire,
"Fierce to regain the losses of that hour
"When LOVE rose glittering, and his gorgeous wings
"Over the abyss flutter'd with such glad noise,
"As what time after long and pestful Calms
"With slimy shapes and miscreated life
"Pois'ning the vast Pacific, the fresh breeze
"Wakens the merchant sail, uprising. NIGHT
"An heavy unimaginable moan
"Sent forth, when she the PROTOPLAST beheld
"Stand beauteous on Confusion's charmed wave.
"Moaning she fled, and entered the Profound
"That leads with downward windings to the Cave
"Of darkness palpable, desart of Death. . . ."

These are very fine Lines, tho' I say it that should not: but hang me, if I know or ever did know the meaning of them, tho' my own composition.

[# 79]

He said; and straightway from the opposite Isle
A Vapor rose, pierc'd by the MAIDEN'S eye.
Guiding its course OPPRESSION sate within,

> With terror pale and rage, yet laugh'd at times
> Musing on Vengeance. . . .

These images imageless, these *small-capitals* constituting Personifica-
tions, I despised even at that time; but was forced to introduce them, to
preserve the connection with the machinery of the Poem, previously
adopted by Southey.

The Quarterly Review, Vol. 10, Oct. 1813–Jan. 1814.

*All the notes included here are Coleridge's comments on an anonymous
review of a book on the history of the Puritans; he knew it to be by
Southey. Leibniz's significant modification of a traditional position—that
there is nothing in the mind that was not previously in the senses, "except
mind itself"—was central to Coleridge's philosophy of mind, as to
Kant's.*

[# 80]

> By whatever name the puritans might have been denominated, their history
> would have been the same; their rise was one of the inevitable consequences
> of a religious revolution, and the civil war was as inevitable an effect of their
> progress.

This is an unthinking way of thinking. It is easy to talk of past events as
having been inevitable, because we are forced by the forms of the Understanding* to review them by the logical functions of Cause and Effect.
The writer did not consider that in the very same way we are obliged to
reflect on our own past actions, and that the very same principle, if admitted other than as logical, would do away free-agency. Endless are the
errors and not a few of them most pernicious, from not distinguishing
Principia Logica [logical principles] from the *Principia Entitiva* [princi-
ples of being].

* The *"ipse Intellectus" (per intellectionem, sibi ipsi revelatus)* [mind
itself (itself revealed to itself by intellection)] of Leibnitz in his admirable
reply to the Lockian assertion of the old Peripatetic *"Nihil in Intellectu
quod non prius in sensu"* [There is nothing in the mind that was not previously in the senses]: an adage which my old Master at Christ's Hospital, Bowyer, used to quote when we were under the rod. You must make
a lad *feel* before he will *understand*. All true knowledge is derived *a pos-*

teriori—& therefore properly entitled too we say, Such a man has been well *bottomed*. Fundamental.

[# 81]

It is easy to talk of toleration, and say that the church should have tolerated these schismatics; they would not tolerate the church. . . . "We intended not," says Baxter, "to dig down the banks, or to pull up the hedge and lay all waste and common, when we desired the prelates' tyranny might cease. We must either tolerate all men to do what they will which they will make a matter of conscience or religion . . . or else you must tolerate no error or fault in religion, and then you must advise what measure of penalty you will inflict. My judgment I have always freely made known; I abhor unlimited liberty, or toleration of all."

Southey did not advert to Baxter's use of the word "Religion", which meant with him the *Regula Fidei* [Rule of Faith], or Apostles' Creed; and this too limited to an open opposition to the words of the Creed. Whoever could conscientiously use the words was not to be further questioned.

This is a most unfair quotation from Baxter, who was the nearest to absolute toleration of all Theologians. He proposed that all persons admitted as Church members should be ready to declare, that they desired what was prayed for in the Lord's Prayer, believed what was declared in the Apostles' Creed, and held themselves bound to obey what was enjoined by the Ten Commandments, and that all beyond should be free to each.

[# 82]

We are not the apologists of Laud: in some things he was erroneous, in some imprudent, in others culpable. . . . The bloody sentences of the Star Chamber brought down upon him a more tragic catastrophe than he attempted to avert by them; a milder primate could not have saved the church from her enemies, but he would not have perished by their hands. And in return, it cannot be doubted that when the clergy regained their ascendancy, the severity with which they treated the Dissenters was in no slight degree exasperated by the remembrance of his execution.

God knows my heart, how bitterly I abhor *all* Intolerance—how deeply I pity the actors, when there is reason to suppose them deluded. But is it not clear that this theatrical scene of Laud's death, who was the victim of almost national indignation, is not to be compared with "bloody sentences" in the coolness of secure power? As well might you palliate the horrible atrocities of the Inquisition, every one of which might be justified on the same grounds that Southey has here defended Laud, by detailing the vengeance taken on some one Inquisitor.

Samuel Parr, *A Spital Sermon*, London, 1801.

Parr's well-known sermon was in part a churchman's response to William Godwin's rationalist Enquiry concerning Political Justice *(1793). In this note, Coleridge characteristically considers the root of the ills of his age to be not atheism itself, as a philosophical position, but the materialist attitudes of contemporary science and education.*

The "pious men" to whom he refers—John Locke, Joseph Priestley, David Hartley, and William King—were all believers and influential moral philosophers, but Coleridge had come to the conclusion in each case that their philosophical principles were at odds with their religious convictions. The examples of the Anabaptists at Munster and of the Spanish Inquisition in South America demonstrate that Christian faith is not incompatible with barbaric violence.

[# 83]

[Parr glosses the phrase "Knight Errant of Atheism":] . . . Upon the various effects of Superstition, where it has spread widely, and thriven long, we can reason from *facts*. But in the original frame of the human mind, and in the operations of all those moral causes which regulate our conduct, or affect our happiness, there seems to be a most active, constant, and invincible principle of *resistance* to the encroachments of Atheism. "All nature cries aloud" against them, "through all her works," not in speculation only, but in practice.

I never had even a doubt in *my being* concerning the supreme Mind; but understand too sufficiently the difficulty of any intellectual demonstration of his existence, and see too plainly how inevitably the principles of many pious men (Locke, Priestley, Hartley, even Archbishop King) would lead to atheism by fair production of consequences, not to feel in perfect charity with all good men, atheist or theist; and, let me add, though I now seem to feel firm ground of *reason* under my belief in God, not gratefully to attribute my uniform past *theism* more to general feeling than to depth of understanding. Within this purpose I hope that, without offence, I may declare my conviction, that in the French Revolution atheism was an effect, not a cause; that the same wicked men, under other circumstances and fashions, would have done the same things as Anabaptists within Munster, or as Inquisitors among the South American Indians; and that atheism from conviction, and as a ruling motive and impulse (in which case only can it be fairly compared with superstition) is a quiescent state, and *per se* harmless to all but the atheist himself. Rather is it that overwhelming preference of experimental philosophy, which, by smothering over more delicate perceptions, and debilitating often to impotence the faculty of going into ourselves, leads to atheism as a conscious creed, and in its extreme is atheism in its essence. This rather is, I should deem, the more perilous, and a plainer and better object for philosophical attack. O! bring back *Jack the Giant Killer* and the *Arabian Nights* to our children, and Plato and his followers to new men, and let us have chemistry as we have watchmakers or surgeons (I select purposely honourable and useful callings), as a *division* of human labour, as a worthy profession for a few, not as a glittering master-feature of the education of men, women, and children.—

Richard Field, *Of the Church*, Oxford, 1635.

Coleridge acquired this book in 1814, and his notes date from then to 1824. In 1819, he made a set of notes especially with a view to presenting the work to his son Derwent, who was eventually ordained as a clergyman in 1827.

The political, cultural, and philosophical significance of the roots of words was keenly debated in the period, one of the major works on the subject being the book that Coleridge cites by its Greek title ("Winged Words"; the subtitle was The Diversions of Purley*). The author, John Horne Tooke, maintained that nouns came first, and so all language can be traced back to names for objects; Coleridge and others argued that a verb came first, the point being that agency is thus shown to be in some sense prior to matter. Coleridge often invoked a device that he called "desynonymization," i.e., discriminating among different meanings by redefining supposed synonyms. Two of the examples he gives here—reason and understanding, and imagination and fancy—proved particularly influential. The Latin* ratio *means both "ratio" and "reason." For "Milton's Limbo" see* Paradise Lost *3.486–97. "Cursed Eutyches" is a phrase used earlier by Field.*

[# 84]

{The etymology of a word is one thing, the meaning another. The etymology is considered according to what the word meaningfully derives from: the meaning of a word, however, is considered according to what the word is applied to. (Aquinas)}

An apt motto for a Critique on Horne Tooke's επεα πτεροεντα [Winged Words].

The best service of Etymology is when the sense of a word is still unsettled, and especially when two words have each two meanings, A = a b, and B = a b, instead of A = a and B = b. Thus Reason and Understanding, as at present popularly confounded—Here the etyma, Ratio, the relative proportion of Thoughts and Things, and Understanding, as the power which substantiates phaenomena (*substat* iis [*under-stands* them]) determines the proper sense. But most often, the etyma being equivalent, we must proceed ex arbitrio [according to our best judgment]—as Law *compels*, Religion *obliges*: or take up what had been begun in some one derivative. Thus fanciful and imaginative *are* discriminated—& thus supplies the ground of choice for giving to Fancy and Imagination, to each its own sense. Cowley a *fanciful* Writer; Milton an *imaginative* Poet.— *Then* I proceed with the distinction—How ill *Fancy* assorts with *Imagination*, is instanced in Milton's Limbo.

[# 85]

Nicetas saith, the *Armenians* are *Monophysits*, and that *Immanuel* the Emperour, in the yeare 1170 sent *Theorianus* to conferre with their Catholick or chiefe Bishop, & to reclaime them if it might bee, from that heresie.

It puzzles me to understand what sense Field gave to the word, Heresy. Surely, every slight error even tho' unpersevered in is not to be held a Heresy, or its Assertors accursed. The Error ought at least to respect some point of Faith essential to the great ends of the Gospel. Thus the phrase "*Cursed* Eutyches" is to me *shockingly* unchristian. I could not dare call even the opinion *cursed* till I saw how it injured the faith in Christ, weakened our confidence in him or lessened our love & gratitude.

1815

Encyclopaedia Londinensis, Vol. 12, London, 1814.

This encyclopedia belonged to the Morgans. "The glorious uncertainty of the law" was a famous toast made in 1756. "Jacobinism" refers to the beliefs espoused by the supporters of the French Revolution, or ultradem-ocratic views; it has always been used pejoratively in Britain and borders on being merely a term of abuse.

[# 86]

> [On the entry "Liberty":] It were endless to enumerate all the *affirmative* acts of parliament, wherein justice is directed to be done according to the law of the land; and what that law is, every subject knows, or may know if he pleases; for it depends not upon the arbitrary will of any judge; but is permanent, fixed, and unchangeable, unless by authority of parliament.

Mere declamation! In a rich & populous, a commercial and manufac-turing people, the practical Law exists in Precedents, far more than in Statutes—and every new Judge furnishes new Precedents. Hence the "glorious uncertainty of the Law".—How can it be truly affirmed, that every *man* may know, when it requires the study and practice of a Life to be qualified even to give an opinion; & when nothing is more common than for two men equally qualified to give opposite opinions. Not to men-tion the ruinous expences of a Law suit to all but rich men: so that the power of appeal from lower to higher Court instead of protecting the poor man enables a rich Tyrant, such as the late Lord Lonsdale to ruin whom he chooses. I write this not in complaint for the evil is inevitable, & re-sults from the very nature of Property in the present state of human Na-ture; but because the strongest arguments of Jacobinism are drawn from these rash assertions, & the actual state of things so opposite to them. These positions should be treated as the declared *Ideal* and ultimate *Ob-ject* of Legislation, which every man is bound to hold in view in his ad-ministration of Law, not as the actual Result of Law: and men should be taught, that the Evils here stated are great indeed yet cannot be removed without far greater Evils, & that there are advantages on the other hand, resulting from those very evils, & in some measure counterbalancing them/such as the existence of a large & learned Profession; a Check on Litigiousness; and not least a general sense of the insufficiency of Law, & the consequent praise & value attached to Honor & Morality as contradistinguished from *Legality.*

Ben Jonson, *Dramatic Works*, ed. Peter Whalley, London, 1811.

Coleridge acquired this work in 1815 and turned to it when preparing lectures on the drama in 1818–19. In the last note, "F. C. Fathom and Zelucco" refer to two familiar novels in which the central character is villainous—Smollett's Ferdinand Count Fathom *(1753) and Moore's* Zelucco *(1786).*

[# 87] It would be amusing to collect from our Dramatists from Eliz. to Charles I. proofs of the manners of the Times. One striking symptom of general Coarseness (i.e. of *manners,* which may co-exist with great refinement of morals, as alas! vice versa) is to be seen in the very frequent allusions to the Olfactories and their most disgusting Stimulants—and these too in the Conversation of virtuous Ladies. This would not appear so strange to one who had been on terms of familiarity with Sicilian and Italian Women of Rank: and bad as they may, too many of them, *actually be,* yet I doubt not, thus the extreme grossness of their Language has imprest many an Englishman of the present Aera with far darker notions, than the same language would have produced in one of Eliz.[s] or James 1[sts] Courtiers. Those who have read *Shakespear only,* complain of occasional grossness in *his* plays—Compare him with his Contemporaries, & the inevitable conviction is that of the exquisite purity of his imagination—

[# 88] The Observation, I have prefixed to the Volpone, is the Key to the faint Interest, that these noble efforts of the intellectual power excite—with the exception of the Sad Shepherd—because in that fragment only is there any character, in whom you are morally interested.—On the other hand, the Measure for Measure is the only play of Shakespear's in which there are not some one or more characters, generally many, whom you follow with an affectionate feeling. For I confess, that Isabella of all Shakespear's female Characters interests me the least: and the M. for Meas. is the only one of his genuine Works, which is painful to me.—

Let me not conclude this Remark, however, without the thankful acknowlegement to the Manes [spirit] of Jonson, that the more I study his writings, the more I admire them—and the more the study resembles that of an ancient Classic, in the minutiae of his rhythm, metre, choice of words, forms of connection, &c, the more numerous have the points of Admiration become.—I may add too, that both the Study and the Admiration cannot but be disinterested—for to expect any advantage to the present Drama were ignorance. The latter is utterly heterogeneous from the Drama of the Shakespearian Age—with a diverse Object and a contrary *principle*. The one was to present a model by *imitation* of real Life, to take from real life all that is what it ought to be, and to supply the rest— the other to *copy* what *is* and as it *is*—the best a tolerable, the most a blundering, *Copy*. In the former the Difference was an essential Element—in the latter an involuntary Defect.—We should think it strange, if a Tale *in Dance* were announced, and the Actors did not *dance* at all! Yet such is modern comedy.

[# 89] This admirable indeed, but yet still more wonderful than admirable Play [*Volpone*], is from the fertility and vigor of Invention, Character, Language and Sentiment the strongest proof, how impossible it is to keep up any pleasurable Interest in a Tale in which there is no goodness of heart in any of the prominent characters—After the 3rd Act, this Play becomes not a dead but a painful weight on the Feelings.—F. C. Fathom, and Zelucco are instances of the same truth.—. Bonario and Celia should have been made in some way or other *principals* in the Plot—which they might be, and the objects of Interest, without being made characters—in Novels the Person, in whose fate you are most interested, is often the least marked character of the whole.

If it were practicable to lessen the *paramouncy* of Volpone, a most delightful Comedy might be produced, Celia being the Ward or Niece instead of the Wife of Corvino, & Bonario her Lover—

Johann Gottlieb Fichte, *Die Bestimmung des Menschen [The Vocation of Mankind]*, Berlin, 1800.

[# 90] I propose to myself to consider the philosophizing mind as gradually ascending not a Jacob's Ladder, but a sort of geometrical Stair-case with several Rests or Landing-Places—each invisible to those below it, but commanding them and their Points of View—and on leaving any one to make it clear & lively why the mind in question could not but attempt to climb higher, and why so many remained there & believed nothing above but Clouds and the Sky. Now Fichte has not given us the pourtraiture either of the natural state of the mind previous to reflection ("It is there: for I *see* it") or of the second state, or that of *reflexion* and hypothesis—Anima modificata suarum mutationum Conscia [the soul modified, conscious of its own changes]—Locke, the Newtonian Opticians &c but hurries at once into the third state, Idealismus autoplasticus Defluence ab intra, ✳ Influence ab extra [self-shaping Idealism is a flowing-down from inside, as contradistinguished from a flowing-in from outside].—And then [. . .] both.

1816

Johann Gottfried Herder, *Von der Auferstehung [On the Resurrection]*, Frankfurt and Leipzig, 1794.

The quotation about faith is an adaptation of a line from Milton, Paradise Lost *2.667.*

[# 91] It is hard under one name to designate Herder's Faith—*"if Faith it may be call'd, which Faith is none"*. It is, or seems to be, composed of contrary Elements in the act of balancing each other, but not yet balanced, & thence substantial; but still glowing in restless vibrations.—A *sensibility*, a certain refined Epicurism of moral Sense, a desire to possess the sympathies of the Mass of Christians & to govern them thereby—and yet an equal desire to be respected by the Philosophers, *the Intellectuals*./ He will linger in and about the Camp of the *Religious*, but then he will have, or will forge for himself, a Ticket, a Certificat from the Philosophists, authorizing him so to do!—Alas! but is not this very like *a Spy?*—The most amusing thing in all Herder's Theological Tracts is the cool (*vornehm*) *"quality*-like" looking down upon all the Founders of Christianity—!! Poor simple Creatures!—excuse them, Gentlemen!—they had very good hearts—& tho' they were somewhat silly, yet really put ourselves in their place, suppose that instead of our rank, education, & various immeasurable Superiority, we had been vulgar ignorant Jew-blackguards, like Peter, John, &c, we should have thought & acted much the same!—And this is a Defence of Christianity!!!—

Henry Fielding, *Tom Jones*, London, 1773.

The rivalry between Fielding and Richardson (Fielding parodied Pamela, *and* Tom Jones *was in part a response to* Clarissa Harlowe*) led generations of readers to feel that they had to declare a preference, as Coleridge does in this note written in a friend's copy of* Tom Jones.

[# 92] Manners change from generation to generation, and with manners morals appear to change,—actually change with some, but appear to change with all but the abandoned. A young man of the present day who should act as Tom Jones is supposed to act at Upton, with Lady Bellaston, &c. would not be a Tom Jones; and a Tom Jones of the present day, without perhaps being in the ground a better man, would have perished rather than submit to be kept by a harridan of fortune. Therefore this novel is, and, indeed, pretends to be, no exemplar of conduct. But, notwithstanding all this, I do loathe the cant which can recommend Pamela and Clarissa Harlowe as strictly moral, though they poison the imagination of the young with continued doses of *tinct. lyttae* [Spanish Fly, an aphrodisiac], while Tom Jones is prohibited as loose. I do not speak of young women;—but a young man whose heart or feelings can be injured, or even his passions excited, by aught in this novel, is already thoroughly corrupt. There is a cheerful, sun-shiny, breezy spirit that prevails everywhere, strongly contrasted with the close, hot, day-dreamy continuity of Richardson. Every indiscretion, every immoral act, of Tom Jones, (and it must be remembered that he is in every one taken by surprise—his inward principles remaining firm—) is so instantly punished by embarrassment and unanticipated evil consequences of his folly, that the reader's mind is not left for a moment to dwell or run riot on the criminal indulgence itself. In short, let the requisite allowance be made for the increased refinement of our manners—and then I dare believe, that no young man who consulted his heart & Conscience only, without adverting to *what the World* would say—could rise from the perusal of Fielding's Tom Jones, Joseph Andrews, and Amelia, without feeling himself a better man—at least, without an intense conviction that he *could* not be guilty of a *base* Act.—

If I want a servant or mechanic, I wish to know what *he does*—but of a Friend, I must know what he *is*. And in no Writer is this momentous distinction so finely brought forward as by Fielding. We do not care what Blifil *does*—the *deed*, as separate from the agent, may be good or ill—but Blifil *is* a villain—and we feel him to be so, from the very moment he, the Boy Blifil, restored Sophia's poor captive Bird to its native & rightful Liberty!

[# 93]

[Tom Jones's letter to Lady Bellaston:] "... O lady *Bellaston*, what a Terror have I been in, for fear your Reputation should be exposed by these perverse Accidents. There is one only Way to secure it. I need not name what that is. Only permit me to say, that as your Honour is as dear to me as my own; so my sole Ambition is to have the Glory of laying my Liberty at your Feet; and believe me when I assure you, I can never be made completely happy, without you generously bestow on me a legal Right of calling you mine for ever."

Even in the most questionable part of Tom Jones, I cannot but think after frequent reflection on it, that an additional paragraph, more fully & forcibly unfolding Tom Jones's sense of self-degradation on the discovery of the true character of the relation, in which he had stood to Lady Bellaston—& his awakened feeling of the dignity & manliness of Chastity— would have removed in great measure any just objection/ at all events, relatively to Fielding himself, & taking in the state of manners in *his* time.

John Reynolds, *The Triumphes of Gods Revenge agaynst the Cryinge, & Execrable Sinne, of (Willfull, & Premeditated) Murther expressed in thirtye severall, tragicall Historyes*, London, 1657.

This gathering of true-crime stories belonging to Charles Lamb appears to have been annotated between 1816 and 1820. All Coleridge's notes are included here.

The phrase "brevities epistolary" is an allusion to 2 Henry IV 2.2.135. "Lockians" are followers of John Locke, whose generally accepted philosophy of mind Coleridge vehemently rejected. Sir Philip Sidney (1554–86), author of the prose romance Arcadia, *is mentioned as a more famous near contemporary of Reynolds. The* Newgate Calendar *was an eighteenth-century counterpart to Reynolds, a collection of the life stories of prominent criminals. Coleridge's acquaintance Thomas Clarkson, known for his leadership in the campaign against the slave trade, was actively involved in the period 1812–20 in prison reform and in opposition to the death penalty.*

[# 94] It is exceedingly entertaining to observe, how absolutely & integrally J. Reynold's heart & soul are swallowed up in the notion "Murder", & in all other crimes only as far as they lead to Murder. The most execrable Wretch about to be murdered, becomes "poor innocent man"— "worthy harmless Gentleman", &c—and the most heroic Character, as that of chaste Perina, "execrable bloody Lady", as soon as she forms the thought of punishing the horrible crimes to herself and her poisoned Lord

& Husband, & his Mother, on the old Monster who had perpetrated them.—And then his never for a moment, not for half a sentence, relaxing or elanguescing, from the height & top gallant of Sensibility & impassioned Moralizing upon all & every act, however often repeated, from p. 1. to p. 486—so flatly delicious, so deliciously flat!—I LIKE JOHN REYNOLDS.

P.S. Almost every tale in this Folio is maimed, as a Tale, thro' its being catastrophied by Torture—& yet, so totus in illis [wholly absorbed in these things] is J. R., that it seems never once to have suggested itself to his mind, tho' he was an Englishman, that the same horrible agonies which overpowered the guilty, spite of all their Interests & strongest predeterminations, would equally overpower the Innocent, nay, more so for the Innocent & Guilty would be the same in preferring Death to such Tortures (or else the Guilty would not have confessed) and the former would have hopes in another world which the latter could not have.—But no such notion occurred to honest Murthero-maniacal John Reynolds—& then the Judges—they are such glorious Abstracts, one & all, of omnisciency, incorruptibility, & firmness. They are not Judges; but Justice & Judgement.—But the Beauties of this Work are endless. There is something half-celestial in that infantine Combination of intense feeling with the vulgarest Truisms, the merest mouldy Scraps, of generalizing Morality. "It is an excellent felicity to grow from Vertue to Vertue, & a fatall misery to run from Vice to Vice. Love & Charity are always the true marks of a Christian, & Malice & Revenge &c &c"—but the nicest feeling is that concerning Duels, which verbally he always condemns as Loss both of Body & Soul/ of course, as leading to the same Hell as Murder—but yet this is all matter of course. In the Author's *feelings* as shewn in the event of his Stories, these Duels are always innocent or virtuous. O what a beautiful Concordia Discordantium [harmony of discordant things] is an unthinking good-hearted Man's Soul!—

[# 95]

[One character sends a challenge to another in a letter:] You have given the first breach to our friendship: for sith you have treacherously bereaved me of my Mistris, you must now both in honour and justice, either take my life, or yeeld me yours in requitall. If you consider your own ingratitude, you cannot tax, much lesse condemn this my resolution: the Place, the West end of the Park; the hour, four or five after Dinner; the manner, on foot, with Seconds; the

Weapon, if you please, two single Rapiers, whereof bring you one, and I the other, and I will be content to take the refusal, to give you the choyce. If your courage answer your infidelity, you will not refuse to meet me.

Reminds one of Shakespere, who in his affected *brevities epistolary* probably had his eye on similar Stories. The style was not imaginary. This Letter might have occurred in Shakespere, & no one have found the least Dissonance with his manner.

[# 96] The chief pain, I feel, in reading these stories is that of a true Theorist. I cannot but perceive, what apparent strength they lend to the Lockians & Materialists, who hold Conscience to be nothing more than the Prejudice of Education—to the same being the most atrocious action will make no pang in the Conscience, if it be but according to the custom of the Age—& the most innocent the cruellest pangs of Remorse, if against the Custom. This *may* be sufficiently answered; but then the answer requires powers of reflection extraordinary, & the statement seems to be of undeniable facts, which every man understands at once.

[# 97] Notice thro' all these tales, & in the writings of Sir P. Sidney & many others, that the natural antipathy (as has been since supposed) of English to French Men, had not commenced. E contra [on the contrary], our Writers in general speak of the French with a manifest predilection, and of all the nations we find the feeling of the great Commonwealth of Christendom predominant. A King is a King, sacred tho' an enemy—a Nobleman always a Nobleman/ the ranks common to all as yet outweighed the differences, by which country was distinguished from Country. With them the Emphasis was layed on the last word, as with us on the first, in the phrase—French Nobleman.

[# 98]

> But as it is the nature of Adultery to be accompanied and waited on by other sins, so *Victorina* is not only content to love *Sypontus*, but she makes a farther progression in impiety, and will needs hate her Husband *Souranza*; who <u>poor honest Gentleman</u>, sick with the Gout, and a Cough of the Lungs, is now distastfull, and which is worse, odious to her. . . .

damn'd old Scoundrel.

[# 99]

. . . *Sypontus*, not to fail of his promise to *Victorina*, in the execution of his bloody and damnable attempt, takes his *Gondola*, and hovers in the direct passage betwixt *Lucifizina* and *Venice*, for *Souranza* his arrivall, who, <u>poor harmlesse Gentleman,</u> loved his young wife so tenderly and dearly, as he thought this short time long that he had wandred from her. . . .

filthy old Dotard!

[# 100]

She very secretly provides her self of a Friers compleat weed, as a sad russet Gown and coule . . . and in one of the pockets of this Frock, she puts a small begging box . . . as also a new breviary . . . but in the other pocket thereof she puts a couple of small short Pistols which she had secretly purloined out of her Father *Placedo*'s Armory, and had charged each of them with a brace of Bullets, fast rammed down, with priming powder in the pans, and all these fatall trinckets, she . . . packs and tyes up close in the Gown, expecting the time and hour to work this her cruell and lamentable feat on <u>innocent</u> *Sanctifiore*, who little thinks or dreams what a bloody Banquet his old love, and now his new enemy *Ursina* is preparing for him.

there is something very amusing in this Writer's sudden change of Feeling as soon as a Villain, a Monster, or even a Murderer himself, is about to be murdered. And the levis macula [light stain] on the conscience when these murders are effected by Duels, how ever unfair & savage, is curious, as a proof how much of what Superstition *calls* Conscience, is mere Love of Reputation, Character, Admission into accustomed Society, &c. Hence the utility of penal Laws, Death not so much as deterring from the crime when tempted to it, but as by prior blind horror precluding the temptation & the very thought. O Mr Clarkson & Co little think how much of the *guilt* of Murder &c in men's Consciences originate in the Gallows & the Newgate Calendar.

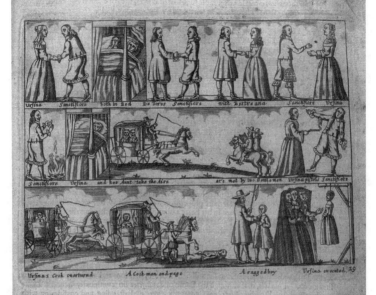

Gods revenge againſt the Crying and Exécrable Sinne of Murther.

HISTORY XXIX.

Sanctiſiore (upon promiſe of marriage) gets Urſina with child, and then afterwards very ingratefully and treacherouſly rejecteth her, and marrieth Bertranna. Vrſina being ſenſible of this her diſgrace, diſguiſeth her ſelf in a Friers habit, and with a caſe of Piſtols kils Sanctiſiore as he is walking in the fields, for the which ſhe is hanged.

IT is a poor profit, a wretched pleaſure, for the ſatisfaction of choller and revenge, to imbrue our hands in the innocent blood of our neer kindred, ſith in ſeeking to wound him, we more properly kill our ſelves in ſoule and body; ſtriking him (who is the figurative Image of God) we preſumptuouſly ſtab at the Majeſty of God himſelf, by whom our ſouls muſt, without whom they can never be ſaved. Therefore if we will not know as we are men, yet we ought firmely both to know and believe as we are Chriſtians, that Revenge and Murther are the two prodigious twins of Sathan, the laſt being engendred and propagated of the firſt; and both from Hell: For Revenge is not half ſo ſweet in the beginning as bitter in the end; nor murther by many degrees ſo pleaſing as it proves pernicious to her Authors, as this enſuing Hiſtory will verifie, and make apparant unto us.

Q q   Le

A page from John Reynolds's *Triumphes of Gods Revenge* (1657), reproduced by permission of the Thomas Fisher Rare Book Library, University of Toronto

1817

Hans Christian Oersted, *Ansicht der chemischen Naturgesetze* *[Survey of the Chemical Laws of Nature],* **Berlin, 1812.**

[# 101]

{In recent times Davy, as is known, has asserted that the so-called oxidized hydrochloric acid is a simple body [an element] to which he gave the name chlorine, and which with hydrogen produces hydrochloric acid. . . . However, what contradicts this is the great analogy of chlorine to sulphuric and nitric acid. . . . It is therefore clear that one cannot, without getting entangled in serious difficulties, regard oxidized hydrochloric acid, or Davy's chlorine, as a simple substance; but continued experimental research must show whether these difficulties might be overcome.}

It is of highest importance in all departments of Knowlege to keep the Speculative distinct from the Empirical. As long as they run parallel, they are of the greatest service to each other: they never meet but to cut and cross. This is Oersted's fault—the rock of offence on which this Work strikes. Davy is necessarily right: for he follows the established Regula recta [right rule] of empirical Chemistry, viz. that all Bodies shall be considered as simple, till they shall have been *shewn* to be compound. On this Rule Chlorine, and Iodine claim the title of simple Bodies (Stoffen) with the same right as Oxygen or the Metals: while the Speculative Chemist sees a priori, that all alike must be composite.

William Shakespeare, *Dramatic Works,* **ed. Samuel Ayscough, London, 1807.**

This two-volume Shakespeare with the plays printed in tight double columns was interleaved with blank paper so that Coleridge could use it when he prepared his lectures on Shakespeare, delivered in 1818–19. (These and other records of the lectures are available in his Lectures 1808–1819: On Literature, *ed. R. A. Foakes.)*
The first note (which is continued and completed in Foakes's edition)

84

takes up the much debated "irregularity" of Shakespeare, that is, the ways in which his plays violate the neoclassical doctrine—originating in Aristotle but codified by French critics—of the unities of time, place, and action. Coleridge is aware of addressing a problem not fully resolved by the English predecessors whom he names—Dryden, Farquhar, and Johnson. To the frank artifice of painters such as Jan van Huysum and Benjamin West he contrasts the three-dimensional imitations of a marble peach and a waxworks display. In his compliment to John Flaxman (1755–1826), the sculptor and illustrator, he is probably thinking of Flaxman's well-known outline designs on classical themes. Schiller's Wallenstein offers an ambitious protagonist comparable to Macbeth, and enables Coleridge to promote his own translation of Schiller's play. The "electrical pictures" were showpieces of popular science. Heraclitus and Democritus are traditionally "the laughing philosopher" and "the weeping philosopher," representing opposite responses to human folly. The "Horn of Huon," in the French romance Huon of Bordeaux, *is a magical horn that can make people sing and dance against their will. The defensive tone of the note dated January 7, 1819, arises from newspaper reports of the lectures that said Coleridge should not claim as his own discoveries about Shakespeare that had been published earlier by the German critic A. W. Schlegel: Coleridge calls to witness a reputable friend, Sir George Beaumont, and a hostile reviewer, William Hazlitt, to support his claim to priority.*

[# 102] We commence with the Tempest, as a specimen of the Romantic Drama. But Whatever Play of Shakespere's we had selected, there is one preliminary point to be first settled, as the indispensable Condition not only of just and genial criticism, but of all consistency in our opinions.— This point is contained in the words, probable, natural. We are all in the habit of praising Shakespear, or of hearing him extolled for his fidelity to Nature. Now what are we to understand by these words, in their application to the Drama? Assuredly, not the ordinary meaning of them. Farquhar the most ably and if we except a few sentences in one of Dryden's Prefaces (written for a partic. purp. and in contrad. to the opinions elsewhere supported by him) first exposed the ludicrous absurdities involved in the supposition, and demolished as with the single sweep of a careless hand the whole Edifice of French Criticism respecting the so called Unities of Time and Place.—But a moment's reflection suffices to make every man conscious of what every man must have before felt, that the Drama is an *imitation* of reality not a *Copy*—and that Imitation is contradistinguished from Copy by this, that a certain quantum of Difference is essential to the former, and an indispensable condition and cause of the pleasure, we derive from it; while in a Copy it is a defect, contravening its name and purpose. If illustration were needed, it would be sufficient to ask—why we prefer a Fruit View of Vanhuysen's to a marble Peach on a mantle piece—or why we prefer an historical picture of West's to Mrs Salmon's Wax-figure Gallery. Not only that we ought, but that we actually do, all of us judge of the Drama under this impression, we need no other proof than the impassive Slumber of our Sense of Probability when we hear an Actor announce himself a Greek, Roman, Venetian or Persian in good Mother English. And how little our great Dramatist feared awakening on it, we have a lively instance in proof in Portia's Answer [in *The Merchant of Venice*] to Neaera's question, What say you then to Falconbridge, the young Baron of England?—to which she replies—You know, I say nothing to him: for he understands not me nor I him. He hath neither Latin, French or Italian: and you will come into the Court and swear that I have a poor Penny-worth in the English.

Still, however, there is a sort of Improb.^{y} with which we are shocked in dramatic repres.^{n} no less than in the narration of real Life—Consequently, there must be Rules respecting it, and as Rules are nothing but Means to an end previously ascertained (the inattention to which simple truth has been the occasion of all the pedantry of the French School) we must first ascertain what the immediate End or Object of the Drama is— Here I find two extremes in critical decision—The French, which evidently presupposes that a perfect Delusion is to be aimed at—an Opinion which now needs no fresh confutation—The opposite, supported by Dr Johnson, supposes the auditors throughout as in the full and positive reflective knowlege of the contrary. In evincing the impossibility of Delusion he makes no sufficient Allowance for an intermediate State, which we distinguish by the term, Illusion. In what this consists, I cannot better explain, than by referring you to the highest degree of it, namely, Dreaming. It is laxly said, that during Sleep we take our Dreams for Realities; but this is irreconcilable with the nature of Sleep, which consists in a suspension of the voluntary and therefore of the comparative power. The fact is, that we pass no judgement either way—we simply do *not* judge them to be unreal—in conseq. of which the Images act on our minds, as far as they act at all, by their own force as images. Our state while we are dreaming differs from that in which we are in the perusal of a deeply interesting Novel, in the degree rather than in the Kind, and from three causes—First, from the exclusion of all outward impressions on our senses the images in Sleep become proportionally more vivid, than they can be when the organs of Sense are in their active state. Secondly, in sleep the Sensations, and with these the Emotions & Passions which they counterfeit, are the causes of our Dream-images, while in our waking hours our emotions are the effects of the Images presented to us—(*apparitions so detectible*) Lastly, in sleep we pass at once by a sudden collapse into this suspension of Will and the Comparative power: whereas in an interesting Play, read or represented, we are brought up to this point, as far as it is requisite or desirable gradually, by the Art of the Poet and the Actors, and with the consent and positive Aidance of our own will. We *chuse* to be deceived.— The rule therefore may be easily inferred. What ever tends to prevent the mind from placing it or from being gradually placed, in this state in which the Images have a negative reality,

[# 103] The opening of Macbeth contrasted with that of Hamlet—. In the latter the gradual ascent from the simplest forms of conversation to the language of impassioned Intellect, yet still the Intellect remaining the *seat* of Passion—in the Macbeth the invocation is made at once to the Imagination, and the emotions connected therewith. A Superstition in both; yet in each not merely different but opposite. The Wierd Sisters, as true a *Creation* of Shakspear's as his Ariel and Caliban—the Fates, the Furies, and the *materializing* Witches being the elements.—

The II Scene illustrated by reference to the Play in Hamlet, in which the Epic is substituted for the Tragic in order to make the latter be felt as the *real-Life* Diction.

Scene III. That I have assigned the true reason for the first appearance of the Weird Sisters, as the Key-note of the character of the whole Play is proved by the re-entrance of the Sisters—after such an order of the King's as establishes their supernatural powers of information.*

The wish that in Macbeth the attempt might be made to introduce the flexile character-mask of the Ancient Pantomime—that a Flaxman might contribute his Genius to the embodying of Shakspear's.

King hereafter was still contingent—still in Macbeth's moral will— tho' if he yielded to the temptation & thus forfeited his free-agency, then the link of *cause* and *effect more physico* [in a physical manner] would commence—& thus the prophetic Visions afterwards. I surely need not say, that the *general* Idea is all that can be required from the Poet—not a scholastic logical consistency in all the parts so as to meet metaphysical Objections.

But O how truly Shakspearian is the opening of Macbeth's Character given in the *unpossessedness* of Banquo's mind, wholly present to the present Object—an unsullied un-scarified Mirror—& in strict truth of Nature that he and not Macbeth himself directs our notice to the effect produced on Macbeth's Mind, rendered *temptible* by previous dalliance of the Fancy with ambitious Thoughts. (See Wallenstein's Soliloquy, Part I.)

> Good Sir, why do you start?—and seem to fear
> Things that do sound so fair?

And then again, still unintröitive, addresses the appearances—The questions of Banquo those of natural Curiosity—such as a Girl would make after she had heard a Gypsey tell her School-fellow's Fortune—all perfectly general—or rather *planless*. But Macbeth, lost in thought, rouses himself to Speech only by their being about to depart—Stay, you imperfect Speakers—and all that follows is reasoning on a problem already discussed in his mind—on a hope which he welcomes, and the doubts concerning its attainment he wishes to have cleared up—. His eagerness—the eager eye with which he had pursued their evanition, compared with the easily satisfied mind of the self-uninterested Banquo

> The Earth hath bubbles—
> Whither are they vanished?
> M[ACBETH].   Into the Air—and what seem'd corporal melted
> As Breath into the wind—Would they had stay'd!

Is it too minute to notice the appropriateness of the Simile "As Breath" in a cold Climate?

Still again Banquo's wonder that of any Spectator "Were such things here"—and Macbeth's recurrence to the *self-concerning*—Your Children shall be Kings—. So truly is the guilt in its Germ anterior to the supposed cause & immediate temptation—. Before he can cool, the *confirmation* of the tempting half of the Prophecy—and the *catenating* tendency fostered by the sudden coincidence.

> Glamis and Thane of Cawdor—The greatest is behind— ⚹ [as opposed to] Banquo's what can the Devil speak true—

I doubt whether *enkindle* has not another sense than that of *stimulating*—whether the Kind, & Kin—as in Rabbits *kindle*—However, Macbeth hears no more *ab extra* [from without]. "Two truths &c" And (p. 365) the necessity of recollecting himself—I thank you, Gentlemen!—in the third line of his speech.—30–45, Col. β—confirm. of the remark on the birth-date of guilt.—And then the warning of the Conscience—& the mode of lulling it—If chance will have me King, why &c—and the suspicion that others might see what was passing in his mind, all prospective, by the LIE—wrought with Things *forgotten*—and instantly the *promising Courtesies* of a Usurper in intention.—

And O the affecting beauty of the Death of Cawdor, and the King's presentimental remark, interrupted by the "Worthiest Cousin"! on the entrance of the deeper Traitor to whom Cawdor had made way—and here in contrast with Duncan's "plenteous Joys" Macbeth has nothing but the commonplaces of Loyalty, in which he hides himself in the "our".—and in the same language of *effort* "The REST is Labor &c"—at the moment that a new difficulty suggests a new crime. This, however, seems the first distinct notion, as to the *plan* of realizing his wishes—and here therefore with great propriety Macbeth's Cowardice of his own Conscience discloses itself.

Macbeth described by Lady M. so as at the same time to describe her own character—intellectually considered, he is powerful in all, but has strength in none.—morally, *selfish* i.e. as far as his weakness will permit him. Could he have every thing, he wanted, he would *rather* have it innocently—ignorant, as alas! how many are! that he who wishes a temporal end for itself does in truth will the *means*—hence the danger of indulging fancies—

"Lady Macbeth = with the valor of my Tongue." Day-dreamer's valiance.

* yet still information/

[# 104]

[From *Julius Caesar:*]

> BRUTUS.   It must be by his death; and, for my part,
> I know no personal cause to spurn at him,
> But for the general. He would be crown'd:—
> How that might change his nature, there's the question.
> It is the bright day, that brings forth the adder;
> And that craves wary walking. Crown him? That;—
> And then, I grant, we put a sting in him,
> That at his will he may do danger with.
> The abuse of greatness is, when it disjoins
> Remorse from power: And, to speak truth of Caesar,
> I have not known when his affections sway'd
> More than his reason. . . .

This is singular—at least, I do not at present see into Shakspear's motive, the rationale—or in what point he meant Brutus's character to appear. For surely (this I mean is what I say to myself, in my present quantum of Insight, only modified by my experience in how many instances I have ripened into a perception of Beauties where I had before descried faults)—surely, nothing can seem more discordant with our historical pre-conceptions of Brutus, or more *lowering* to the intellect of this Stoico-platonic Tyrannicide, than the Tenets here attributed to him, to *him*, the stern Roman Republican—viz.—that he would have no Objection to a King, or to Caesar, a Monarch in Rome, would Caesar be as good a Monarch as he now seems disposed to be—. How too could Brutus say, he finds no personal cause/ i.e. none in Caesar's past conduct as a man? Had he not passed the Rubicon? Entered Rome as a Conqueror? Placed his Gauls in the Senate?—Shakespear (it may be said) has not brought these things forward. True! and this is just the Ground of my perplexity. What character does Sh. mean *his* Brutus to be?—

[# 105]

[From *King Lear:*]

KENT. I thought, the king had more affected the duke of Albany, than Cornwall.

GLOUCESTER. It did always seem so to us: but now, in the division of the kingdom, it appears not which of the dukes he values most; for equalities are so weighed, that curiosity in neither can make choice of either's moiety.

It was [not?] without forethought, and it is not without its due significance, that the triple division is stated here as already determin'd, and in all its particulars, previously to the Trial of Professions, as the relative rewards of which the Daughters were to be made to consider their several portions. The strange yet by no means unnatural, mixture of Selfishness, Sensibility, and Habit of Feeling derived from & fostered by the particular rank and usages of the Individual—the intense desire to be intensely beloved, selfish and yet characteristic of the Selfishness of a loving and kindly nature—a feeble Selfishness, self-supportless and Leaning for all pleasure on another's Breast—the selfish Craving after a sympathy with a prodigal Disinterestedness, contradicted by its own Ostentation and the mode and nature of its Claims—the anxiety, the distrust, the jealousy, which more or less accompany all selfish Affections, and are among the surest contradiction of mere fondness from Love, and which originate Lear's eager wish to enjoy his Daughter's violent Professions, while the inveterate habits of Sovereignty convert the wish into claim and positive Right, and the incompliance with it into crime and treason—these facts, these passions, these moral verities, on which the whole Tragedy is founded, are all prepared for, and will to the retrospect be found implied in, these first 4 or 5 lines of the Play.—They let us know that the Trial is but a Trick—and that the grossness of the old King's rage is in part the natural result of a silly Trick suddenly and most unexpectedly baffled, and disappointed. *Here* notice the improbability and nursery-tale character of the tale./ prefixed as the *Porch* of the Edifice, not laid as its foundation— So Shylock's Lb [pound] of Flesh—item, an old popular Ballad—with how great judgment which still remains is combatable. This having been provided in the fewest words, in a natural reply to as natural question, which yet answers a secondary purpose of attracting our attention to the difference or diversity between the characters of Cornwall and Albany, the premises and *Data*, as it were, having been thus afforded for our after-insight into the mind and mood of the Person, whose character, passions and sufferings are the main *subject-matter* of the Play—from Lear, the Persona PATIENS [person who suffers/ is acted on] of his Drama Shaksp. passes without delay to the second in importance, to the Main *Agent*, and prime Mover—introduces Edmund to our acquaintance, and with the same felicity of Judgement in the same easy, natural way prepares us for his character in the seemingly casual communication of its origin and occasion.—From the first drawing up of the Curtain he has stood before us in the united strength and beauty of earliest Manhood. Our eyes have been questioning him. Gifted thus with high advantages of *person*, and further endowed by Nature with a powerful intellect and a strong energetic Will, even without any concurrence of circumstances and accident, Pride will be the Sin that most easily besets him/. But he is the known, and acknowleged Son of the princely Gloster—Edmund therefore has both the germ of Pride and the conditions best fitted to evolve and ripen it into a predominant feeling. Yet hitherto no reason appears why it should be other than the not unusual pride of Person, Talent and Birth, a pride auxiliary if not akin to many Virtues, and the natural ally of honorable [deeds?] But, alas! in his own presence his own father takes shame to himself for the frank avowal—that he is his Father—has blushed so often to acknowlege him that he is now braz'd to it. He hears his Mother and the circumstances of his Birth spoken of with a most degrading and licentious Levity—described as a Wanton by her own Paramour, and the remembrance of the animal sting, the low criminal gratifications connected with her Wantonness and prostituted Beauty assigned as the reason, why "the Whoreson must be acknowleged."—This and the consciousness of its notoriety—the gnawing conviction that every shew of respect is an effort of courtesy which recalls while it represses a contrary feeling—this is the ever-trickling flow of Wormwood and Gall into the wounds of Pride—the corrosive Virus which inoculates Pride with a venom not its own, with Envy, Hatred, a lust of that Power which in its blaze of radiance would hide the dark spots on his disk—pangs of shame, personally undeserved, and therefore felt as wrongs—and a blind ferment of vindictive workings towards the occasions and causes, especially towards a Brother whose stainless Birth and lawful Honors were the constant remembrancers of *his* debasement, and were ever in the way to prevent all chance of its being unknown or overlooked—&—forgotten. Add to this that with excellent Judgement, and provident for the claims of the moral sense, for that which relatively to the Drama is called Poetic Justice; and as the fittest means for reconciling the feelings of the Spectators to the horrors of Gloster's after Sufferings—at least, of rendering them somewhat less unendurable—(for I will not disguise my conviction, that in this one point the Tragic has been urged beyond the outermost Mark and Ne plus Ultra [Go no further] of the Dramatic)—Shakspeare has precluded all excuse and palliation of the guilt incurred by both the Parents of the base-born Edmund by Gloster's confession, that he was at the time a married man and already blest with a lawful Heir of his fortunes. The mournful alienation of brotherly Love occasioned by Primogeniture in noble families, or rather by the unnecessary distinctions engrafted thereon, and this in Children of the same Stock, is still almost proverbial on the Continent— especially as I know from my own observation in the South of Europe, and appears to have been scarcely less common in our own Island, before the Revolution of 1688, if we may judge from the characters and sentiments so frequent in our elder Comedies—the Younger Brother, for instance, in B. and F's [Beaumont and Fletcher's] Scornful Lady, on one side, and the Oliver in Sh's own As you like it, on the other. Need it be said how heavy an aggravation the stain of Bastardy must have been— were it only, that the younger Brother was liable to hear his own dishonor and his Mother's infamy related by his Father with an excusing shrug of the shoulders, and in a tone betwixt waggery and Shame.

By the circumstances here enumerated, as so many predisposing causes, Edmund's Character might well be deem'd already sufficiently explained and prepared for. But in this Tragedy the story or fable constrained Shakespear to introduce wickedness in an outrageous form, in Regan and Gonerill. He had read Nature too heedfully not to know, that Courage, Intellect, and strength of Character were the most impressive Forms of Power: and that to Power in itself, without reference to any moral end, an inevitable Admiration & Complacency appertains, whether it be displayed in the conquests of a Napoleon or Tamurlane, or in the foam and thunder of a Cataract. But in the display of such a character it was of the highest importance to prevent the guilt from passing into utter *monstrosity*—which again depends on the presence or absence of causes and temptations sufficient to *account* for the wickedness, without the necessity of recurring to a thorough fiendishness of nature for its origination—For such are the appointed relations of intellectual Power to Truth, and of Truth to Goodness, that it becomes both morally and poetic unsafe to present what is admirable—what our nature compels to admire—in the mind, and what is most detestable in the Heart, as co-existing in the same individual without any apparent connection, or any modification of the one by the other. That Shakspeare has in one instance, that of Iago, approached to this, and that he has done it successfully, is perhaps the most astonishing proof of his genius, and the opulence of its resources.—But in the present Tragedy, in which he compelled to present a Goneril & Regan, it was most carefully to be avoided—and therefore the one only conceivable addition to the inauspicious influences on the preformation of Edmund's character is given in the information, that all the kindly counteractions to the mischievous feelings of Shame that might have been derived from co-domestication with Edgar & their common father, had been cut off by an absence from home and a foreign education from Boyhood to the present time—and the prospect of its continuance, as if to preclude all risk of his interference with the Father's Views for the elder and legitimate Son. "He hath been out nine years, and away he shall again"—

[# 106]

[On *Lear* III iv, when Lear and his companions encounter Edgar, disguised as a madman, on the heath.]

What a World's *Convention* of Agonies—surely, never was such a scene conceived before or since—Take it but as a picture, for the eye only, it is more terrific than any a Michael Angelo inspired by a Dante could have conceived, and which none but a Michael Angelo could have executed—or let it have been uttered to the Blind, the howlings of convulsed Nature would seem concentered in the voice of conscious Humanity—

[# 107]   Romeo and Juliet

We have had occasion to speak at large on the subject of the three Unities, Time, Place, and Action, as applied to the Drama in abstract, and to the particular stage for which Shakspeare wrote as far as he can be said to have written for any stage but that of the universal Mind. We succeeded in demonstrating that the two former, instead of being Rules were mere inconveniences attached to the local peculiarities of the Athenian Drama; that the last alone deserved the name of a Principle, and that in this Shakspear stood pre-eminent.

Yet instead of Unity of Action I should great prefer the more appropriate tho' scholastic and uncouth words—Homogeneity, proportionateness and totality of Interest.—The distinction or rather the essential difference betwixt the Shaping skill of mechanical Talent, and the creative productive Life-power of inspired Genius. In the former each part separately conceived and then by a succeeding Act put together—not as Watches are made for wholesale—for here each part supposes a preconception of the Whole in *some* mind—but as the Pictures on a motley Screen. (N.b. I must seek for a happier illustration.)

Whence the Harmony that strikes us in the wildest natural landscapes? In the relative shapes of rocks, the harmony of colors in the Heath, Ferns, and Lichens, the Leaves of the Beech, and Oak, the stems and rich chocate-brown Branches of the Birch, and other mountain Trees, varying from varying Autumn to returning Spring—compared with the visual effect from the greater number of artificial Plantations?—The former are effected by a single energy, modified ab intra [from within] in each component part—. Now as this is the particular excellence of the Shakespearian Dramas generally, so is it especially characteristic of the Romeo and Juliet.—First, the groundwork of the Tale is altogether in family Life, and the events of the Play have their first origin in family-feuds—Filmy as are the eyes of Party-spirit, at once dim and truculent, still there is commonly some real or supposed Object in view, or Principle to be maintained—and tho but = the twisted Wires on the Plate of rosin in the preparation for electrical pictures, it is still a guide in some degree, an assimilation to an Outline; but in family quarrels, which have proved scarcely less injurious to States, wilfulness, and precipitancy and passion from the mere habit and custom can alone be expected—With his accustomed Judgement Shak. has begun by placing before us a lively picture of all the impulses of the Play, like a prelude/ and human folly ever presents two sides, one for Heraclitus & one for Democritus, he has first given the laughable absurdity of the Evil in the contagion of the Servants—The domestic Tale begins with Domestics that have so little to do that they are under the necessity of letting the superfluity of sensorial power fly off thro' the escape-valve of Wit-combats and Quarreling with Weapons of sharper edge—all in humble imitation of their Masters—Yet there is a sort of unhired fidelity, an *our*ishness about it that makes it rest pleasant on one's feelings—and all that follows to p. 968, 55, β—is a motley dance of all ranks and ages to one Tune, as if the Horn of Huon had been playing—

[# 108] Scene IV introduces Mercutio to us—O how shall I describe that exquisite ebullience and overflow of youthful Life, wafted on over the laughing Wavelets of Pleasure & Prosperity, Waves of the Sea like a wanton Beauty that distorted a face on which she saw her lover gazing enraptured, had wrinkled her surface in the Triumph of its smoothness—Wit, ever wakeful, Fancy busy & procreative as Insects, Courage, an easy mind that without cares of its own was at once disposed to laugh away those of others & yet be interested in them/ these and all congenial qualities, melting into the common copula of all, the man of quality and the Gentleman, with all its excellencies & all its foibles—/

[# 109] [*Hamlet.*] Hamlet was the Play, or rather Hamlet himself was the Character, in the intuition and exposition of which I first made my turn for philosophical criticism, and especially for insight into the genius of Shakespear, *noticed*, first among my Acquaintances, as Sir G. Beaumont will bear witness, and as M[r] Wordsworth knows, tho' from motives which I do not know or impulses which I *cannot* know, he has thought proper to assert that Schlegel and the German Critics *first* taught Englishmen to admire their own great Countryman intelligently—and secondly, long before Schlegel had given at Vienna the Lectures on Shakespear which he afterwards published, I had given eighteen Lectures on the same subject, *substantially* the same, proceeding from the same, the *very* same, point of view, and deducing the same conclusions, as far as I either then or now agree with him/ I gave them at the Royal Institution, before from six to seven hundred Auditors of rank and eminence, in the spring of the same year in which Sir H. Davy, a fellow-lecturer, made his great revolutionary Discoveries in Chemistry. Even in detail the coincidence of Schlegel with my Lectures was so extra-ordinary, that all at a later period who heard the same *words* (taken from my Royal Instit. Notes) concluded a borrowing on my part from Schlegel.—M[r] Hazlitt, whose hatred of me is in such an inverse ratio to my zealous Kindness toward him as to be defended by his warmest Admirer, C. Lamb who (besides his characteristic obstinacy of adherence to old friends, as long at least as they are at all down in the World,) is linked as by a charm to Hazlitt's conversation, only under the epithet of *"frantic"*—Mr Hazlitt himself replied to an assertion of my plagiarism from Schlegel in these words—"That is a Lie; for I myself heard the very same character of Hamlet from Coleridge before he went to Germany and when he had neither read or could read a page of German." Now Hazlitt was on a visit to my Cottage at Nether Stowey, Somerset, in the summer of the year 1798, in the September of which (see my Literary Life [*Biographia Literaria*, 1817]) I first was out of sight of the Shores of Great Britain.—

Recorded by me, S. T. Coleridge, Jany 7, 1819. Highgate.

[# 110]

HAMLET.	A little more than kin, and less than kind.
KING.	How is it that the clouds still hang on you?
HAMLET.	Not so, my lord; I am too much i' the sun.

[Footnote:] Mr. Farmer questions whether a quibble between *sun* and *son* be not here intended.

A little more than kin yet less than kind—Play on words—either to 1. exuberant activity of mind, as in Shakespear's higher Comedy. 2. Imitation of it as a fashion which has this to say for it—why is not this now better than groaning?—or 3 contemptuous Exultation in minds vulgarized and overset by their success—Milton's Devils—Or 4 as the language of resentment, in order to express Contempt—most common among the lower orders, & origin of Nick-names—or lastly as the language of suppressed passion, especially of hardly smothered dislike.—3 of these combine in the present instance.—and doubtless Farmer is right in supposing the equivocation carried on into too much in the *Son*.

[# 111]

HAMLET.	The king doth wake to-night, and takes his rouse,
	Keeps wassel, and the swaggering up-spring reels:
	And, as he drains his draughts of Rhenish down,
	The kettle-drum, and trumpet, thus bray out
	The triumph of his pledge.

In addition to the other excellencies of Hamlet's Speech concerning the *Wassel* Music, so finely revealing the predominant idealism, the ratiocinative meditativeness, of his character, it has the advantage of giving nature and probability to the impassioned continuity of the Speech instantly directed to the Ghost. The momentum had been given to his mental Activity—the full current of the thoughts & words had set in—and the very forgetfulness, in the fervor of his Argumentation, of the purpose for which he was there, aided in preventing the Appearance from benumming the mind—Consequently, it acted as a new impulse, a sudden Stroke which increased the velocity of the body already in motion while it altered the direction.—The co-presence of Horatio, Marcellus and Bernardo is most judiciously contrived—for it renders the courage of Hamlet and his impetuous eloquence perfectly intelligible/. The knowlege, the *unthought-of* consciousness, the *Sensation*, of human Auditors, of Flesh and Blood Sympathists, acts as a support, a stimulation *a tergo* [from behind], while the *front* of the Mind, the whole Consciousness of the Speaker, is filled by the solemn Apparition. Add too, that the Apparition itself has by its frequent previous appearances been brought nearer to a Thing of this World. This accrescence of Objectivity in a Ghost that yet retains all its ghostly attributes & fearful Subjectivity, is truly wonderful.

[# 112]

> KING.   O, my offence is rank, it smells to heaven;
>   It hath the primal eldest curse upon 't,
>   A brother's murder! . . . What then? what rests?
>   Try what repentance can: What can it not?
>   O wretched state! O bosom, black as death!
>   O limed soul; that, struggling to be free,
>   Art more engag'd! Help, angels, make assay!
>   Bow, stubborn knees! and, heart, with strings of steel,
>   Be soft as sinews of the new-born babe;
>   All may be well!

The King's Speech well marks the difference between Crime and Guilt of Habit. The Conscience is still admitted to Audience. Nay, even as an audible soliloquy, it is far less improbable than is supposed by such as have watched men only in the beaten road of their feelings.—But it deserves to be dwelt on, that final "All may be well"!—a degree of Merit attributed by the self-flattering Soul to its own struggle, tho' baffled—and to the indefinite half-promise, half-command, to persevere in religious Duties. The divine Medium of the Christian Doctrine of Expiation—in the—Not what you have done, but what you *are*, must determine—Metanoia [repentance]

1818

Francis Beaumont and John Fletcher, *Dramatic Works*, ed. George Colman, London, 1811.

This copy of Beaumont and Fletcher contains a few notes dating from about 1815, but most belong to 1817–19 when Coleridge was giving lectures on literature. They display his concern with practical and technical aspects of playwriting, particularly meter. Richard Bentley (d. 1742) and Richard Porson (d. 1808) were eminent classical scholars.

[# 113] We can never expect an authentic Edition of our elder *dramatic Poets* (for in their times a Drama was a Poem) until some man undertakes the work, who has studied the philosophy of metre. This has been found the main Torch of sound Restoration in the Greek Dramatists by Bentley, Porson, and their followers: how much more then in our own Tongue!— It is true, that *Quantity*, an almost iron Law with the Greek, is in our language rather a subject for a peculiarly fine ear, than any law or even rule— but then we instead of it have first, Accent, 2^{ndly} emphasis, and lastly, retardation & acceleration of the Times of Syllables according to the meaning of the words, the passion that accompanies them, and even the Character of the Person that uses them.—With due attention to these, above all to that, which requires the most attention & the finest taste, the last; MASSINGER, *ex. gr.* might be reduced to a rich and yet regular metre. But then the REGULAE [rules] must be first known—tho' I will venture to say, that he who does not find a Line (not corrupted) of Massinger's flow to the *Time total* of an Iambic Pentameter Hyperacatalectic, i.e. four Iambics ($\smile$ $-$) and an Amphibrach ($\smile$ $-$ $\smile$) has not read it aright.— By power of this last principle (ret. and accel. of time) we have even Proceleusmatics and Dispondaeuses—proceleusmatics ($\smile$ $\smile$ $\smile$ $\smile$) and Dispondaeuses ($-$ $-$ $-$ $-$) not to mention the Choriambics, the Ionics, the Paeons and the Epitrites.—Since Dryden the metre of our Poets leads to the Sense: in our elder and more genuine Poets the Sense, including the Passion, leads to the metre.—Read even Donne's Satires as he meant them to be read and as the sense & passion demand, and you will find in the lines a manly harmony.

[# 114] In respect of Style and Versification this Play [*The Queen of Corinth*] and the Bonduca may be taken as the best, and yet as *characteristic*, specimens. Particularly, the first Scene of Bonduca—. Take the Richard the second of Shakespear, and having selected some one scene of about the same number of Lines, and consisting mostly of long Speeches, compare it with the first scene of Bonduca/ not for the idle purpose of finding out which is the better, but in order to see and understand the difference. The latter (B. and F.) you will find a well arranged bed of Flowers, each having its separate root, and its position determined aforehand by the *Will* of the Gardener—a fresh plant a fresh Volition. In the former an Indian Fig-tree, as described by Milton—all is growth, evolution, γενεσις [genesis]—each Line, each word almost, begets the following—and the Will of the Writer is an interfusion, a continuous agency, no series of separate Acts.—Sh. is the height, breadth, and depth of Genius: B. and F. the excellent mechanism, in juxta-position and succession, of Talent.

Jean Paul Richter, *Museum von Jean Paul*
[Jean Paul's Museum], Stuttgart, 1814.

This book belonged to a German merchant, Carl Aders, who was introduced to Coleridge in 1812 after attending his 1811 lectures.

[# 115]

> {. . . seemingly drowned persons (according to Unzer) heard in the water the distant tinkling of bells, swaying in a blissful state of being, as though they were lying at the half-open gate of death and paradise, and breathing in an intoxicating fragrance of the earth.}

I can attest from *my own experience* that this is the Case with outward insensibility in consequence of Frost. For I was recovered from such a state, with a distinct recollection of my feelings during the earlier part—what they were, if any, during the *interval*, I cannot say.

[# 116]

> {A person's first thought when he cannot find something is that it has been stolen from him; and no matter how much more frequent losing and misplacing are than the occasional theft, nevertheless he will believe in a thief again the next time.}

This is, I am sure, a mere *subjective* peculiarity. *I* never think of any thing having been stolen that I had mislaid; but always that the *Women* had swept it or put it away in their rage of neatness. The cause is obvious— the act of mislaying or overlaying presents no *image* round which one's pet and vexation may climb up and support itself. And yet the image must be uncertain, and wavering—for a distinct individualized Image rather puts a sudden stop to the Pet—for all Passions can neither do without Images or *with* clear and definite ones. The Reason alone is self-sufficing— The Passions are all Parasite Plants, the strangling Joy; Tempers the Tree, Mosses affections the Grape-vines & Woodbines

Karl Wilhelm Ferdinand Solger, *Philosophische Gespräche [Philosophical Dialogues]*, Berlin, 1817.

Coleridge was beginning to develop a following among men of a younger generation. The most important to him in the end was the owner of this book, Joseph Henry Green, a well-connected surgeon. On the first occasion of their meeting in June 1817, both Green and Coleridge were excited by accounts of the aesthetic philosophy of Solger, and Green left shortly after to study under Solger in Berlin. On his return he began an informal program of reading German philosophy with Coleridge. Eventually, Green became president of the Royal College of Surgeons; acted as one of Coleridge's executors; and wrote Spiritual Philosophy, *based on Coleridge's teaching.*

The German poet Hans Sachs, a Meistersinger of Nuremberg, was a shoemaker by trade.

[# 117]

{It clearly cannot be denied that Kant's ideas about the state, about freedom and equality, about the division of governmental powers, and about many other things of this kind, would probably have taken another form if they had not been devised at the time of the French Revolution. How much Fichte served the interests of his time, which he believed himself to be so vehemently and vigorously attacking, Friedrich Schlegel has strikingly enough demonstrated. . . .}

I cannot admit this without serious limitations even of Fichte, still less of Kant: who thought and wrote *for* his Age, not *with* it—or *with* it only as far as the *form* and *method* extend. Kant had 1st to overthrow, 2.nd to build the best possible temporary Shed and Tool-house, both for those ejected from the old Edifice, & for the Laborers &c. Lastly, in this Shed to give the Hints & great Ideas for the erection of a new Edifice. What since Kant is not in Kant as a Germ at least?

[# 118]

{And it is therefore doubtless preferable to recognize the eternal truth in the great developments of history and in our own profession and to apply the recognized truth vigorously. Thus science and practical life will be most intimately fused so that we have only one practical science and one scientific practice.}

Of all wearisome Cant this Cant of Action, practical Truth, diese in unserem eigenen Berufe [these in our own profession], & the like, is the most sickening. What, the Devil! does it mean? We must get our bread and therefore for our own sakes and as honorable men, try to do what we do as well as possible. Who does not know this?—And what has it to do with a man's meditations in his leisure Hours? or, if he should be a Shoemaker, &c, even while he is working? Hans Sachs composed 20 folios of Verses, and never made a Shoe the less.—

[# 119]

{. . . what has been submissively revered by mankind as the actual force determining their wishes and achievements . . . what has been revealed to the artist with strict truth as vital existence . . . what is called public spirit in the state, driving every individual to his particular advantage and yet with wonderfully operating predestination guiding the totality of men to the harmony of virtue as members of one single community devoted to the good—this and nothing else is the subject of philosophy.}

In short, Philosophy is the spiritual Light in and by which we behold and affirm the Human in Man, the Natural in Nature; the Godlike in All, and God every where and over all! Add the Consciousness of dependency, the conscience of imperfection add Love, as the Indiffe[re]ncing of Individuality and Community: add Prayer, as the unity of Thought and Act, of Insight and Life: and P. becomes RELIGION.

Wilhelm Gottlieb Tennemann, *Geschichte der Philosophie [History of Philosophy]*, Leipzig, 1798–1817.

Coleridge's many notes in this learned history of ancient and medieval philosophy, borrowed from Green, include datings from 1818 to 1827. The first note below takes up one of his favorite subjects, the nature of dreams

and related visionary, mystical, and parapsychological experiences.
"Magnetic Clear-seeing"—a translation of the French clairvoyance—
refers to a phenomenon associated with a form of mesmerism or animal
magnetism (or "zoo-magnetism," as Coleridge sometimes calls it) in
which the patient, in a trance, is apparently able to see the interior of
the body and to describe, for example, the condition of internal organs.
Oneiromancy and oneiroscopy, from the Greek oneiros, *"dream," mean,*
respectively, divination or prophecy based on dreams and the examina-
tion or interpretation of dreams. "Mrs. Ibbetson"—Agnes Ibbetson, a
botanist who published her results in scientific periodicals—produced
striking illustrations of her observations by using a device called a solar
microscope that projected an enlarged image onto a wall or screen.

[# 120]

> {Does the soul not show its divine nature far more plainly in sleep, which has
> so much resemblance with death because then it works with more freedom,
> and even has some presentiments of the future?} [Tennemann goes on to quote
> a long passage from Xenophon's *Cyropaedia* or *Boyhood of Cyrus* to illustrate
> this proposition. Xenophon was a follower of Socrates and author of bio-
> graphical memoirs about him.]

The deeply interesting extract from the Cyropaedia (beyond doubt *So-
cratica* verba [Socrates' words]) must refer to magnetic *Clear-seeing*—
for it is too glaringly false of ordinary Sleep, or of *Dreams* properly so
called—i.e. a shifting Current in the shoreless Chaos of the Fancy in
which the streamy *Continuum* of passive Association is broken into *zig-
zag* by Sensations, from within or from without—ex. gr. distension from
wind in the Stomach, or a knot in the bed-cloathes: the judgment being
suspended, alike in both its functions, that of affirming and that of denying the reality of the Images presented to the Mind. Granting even, that a
science or an empirical art, of Oneiromancy, or Oneiroscopy (i.e. the Interpretation of Dreams pro- or retro-spectively) were real or possible; still
the power of thus inferring the Future or the Past would belong to the
Waking Intellect. How indeed can the Soul *be made free* (μαλιστα
ελευθεροῦται [it is most untrammeled]) during Sleep when the Suspension of the Free-will is a main Constituent of Sleep? How said to be free'd
from the Body when the passiveness of the Soul to the Body is the principal Character of Sleep?—Supposing (as Socrates and Plato did suppose
& believe) the *fact*, the actual existence, of inward Vision answering to
the *Clair-voyance* of the Zoo-magnetists, not ὕπνος (= Sleep) but

ἄνθυπνος (= the opposite to Sleep, or Counter-sleep) would be the more appropriate designation of such a State.

[# 121]

{But it was even more difficult to link the Church's dogmatic definitions of the Trinity to these rational concepts, to derive these definitions from those concepts. To assume the unity of the divine being and three different persons in it without assuming a plurality of gods, without abrogating the unity and oneness of the divine being; to assume the difference of persons without accepting attributes and a difference of being—this was a problem which was bound to be beyond the greatest skill and cleverness of the human understanding. Nevertheless Anselm, borne on the wings of faith, dared to attempt this venture, and he succeeded in kindling a light, for believers at least, which a cooler and more calmly testing reason cannot find.}

Divide Mankind into two very disproportionate parts, the Few who have and who have cultivated, the faculty of thinking *speculatively*, i.e. by reduction to Principles, and the Many who either from original defect or deficience, or from want of cultivation, do not, in this sense, think at all: and you may then, according to my belief, subdivide the former Class, the illustrious Minority, into two Species, scarcely less disproportionate in the comparative number of Individuals contained in each, viz. the *born* Conceptionists, the spiritual Children of Aristotle, and the born Ideists or Ideatae, the spiritual Children of Plato. The former System is comprehended in the latter, and therefore of admitted Truth in all, it affirms, and false, if false, by denial only of the distinctive Tenets of the latter.—The Aristotelean therefore is completely intelligible to the Platonist, while the Platonist is mere *Sound*, vox et praeterea nihil [a sound and nothing more], to the Aristotelean. The Ideatae are but somniloquent Ideotae [common folk talking in their sleep]. The difference being innate, all controversy is hopeless, and, could it be ascertained in any particular instance, useless.—Supposing, however, that the Platonist is in the right, he alone is the Philosopher—and the Men of Thought might be divided into Philosophers and Philologists—/ Now this Tenet of the Trinity is an excellent Test. As a Conception it can never be defended, because it can never be rendered intelligible—the words have no meaning, vix ῥήματα, μὴ οτι γε λογοι [scarcely utterances, let alone meaningful words]. If, nevertheless, it be a truth for Man, and the object of a rational Faith, being true neither in Sense or in Conception, it must be true in the Idea—and consequently Ideas *are*.—

No wonder, therefore, that Tenneman saw Anselm's Undertaking as impracticable, and this Ascent of the Soul as a mere Flying in Sleep. For he examines the doctrine by the laws of Conception—asks for analogies; for instances of the same in the world of sensible experience; for generic Characters, &c. But this is unfair. For the Doctrine is affirmed as *inconceivable,* i.e. as an *Idea.* Consequently, the utmost that Tenneman was entitled to say, is "For me, who am conscious of no *Ideas* (i.e. Inconceivable Truths known intuitively, and yet not by intuitions of Sense) and who suspect their existence in other Men, the Doctrine of the Trinity appears a wilful Affirmation of express Contradictions."—But as a *moral* Man he ought to have added—"I dare not however attach that fullness of conviction, that untroubled Confidence of Certainty to this my Judgement, which I should have done, had I been ignorant of the Fact, that some of the most powerful and profound Intellects that have ever given dignity to Human Kind, have thought otherwise—have maintained the verity of Intuitions not sensuous, and have declared that in the Idea of the Tri-une God they beheld the Source and intelligible Principle of all true Unity in all that is called One, and of all true distinction in all that is seen distinctly. I do not, I confess understand these great men; but neither do I clearly understand how the supposition of their words having *no* meaning is to be reconciled with my experience of their superior insight in all points, that I do understand, or with their intimate acquaintance with all the arguments and grounds of argument against their belief. I rest therefore in subjective *Un*belief, without advancing to a *Dis*belief dogmatical & objective.—Or as Bauer said of Mrs Ibbetson's Beholdings. "Well! well! either she has better eyes than mine or a more creative Solar Microscope."— Such, I say, is the Language which Morality & Modesty should have dictated to Tenneman and all other *born* Aristoteleans. But it is not, I fear, without cause objected to Tenneman, that he turns the Critical Philosophy into Dogmatism.

[# 122]

{. . . Gerson then proceeds to a closer treatment of contemplation. But in this he offers less that is distinctly his, and he chiefly repeats the thoughts of Richard of St. Victor, though occasionally explaining them with good psychological observations. Contemplation can be achieved neither by imagination nor even by reason alone, for it is elevated by pure intelligence to knowledge of the eternal and immaterial, which are susceptible of no images of the imagination.}

Gerson's & St Victore's Contemplation is in my System = *Positive* Reason, or R. in her own Sphere as distinguished from the merely *formal* Negative Reason, R. in the lower sphere of the Understanding. The + R = Lux: − R = Lumen a Luce [Positive Reason is the Light: Negative Reason is a Light from the Light]. By the one the Mind contemplates Ideas: by the other it meditates on Conceptions. Hence the distinction might be expressed by the names, Ideal Reason)([as distinguished from] Conceptual Reason.

The simplest yet practically sufficient Order of the Mental Powers is, beginning from the

lowest	highest
Sense	Reason
Fancy	Imagination
Understanding.	Understanding.
Understanding	Understanding
Imagination	Fancy
Reason.	Sense.

Fancy and Imagination are Oscillations, *this* connecting R. and U; *that* connecting Sense and Understanding.

[# 123]

{Then one must assume that God himself limits his infinite existence, and in so far as limitations are nothing other than negations, that God contains in himself the basis not only of all *existence* but also of all *non-existence* and is subject to a blind fate, not indeed external but internal.}

Since Spinoza is chargeable with the same confusion, I cannot perhaps call this Objection to *his* Scheme *unfair*. But as an argument subversive of the System itself, it is necessary to expose the fallacy and falsehood of the Position, that all Circumscription is Negation. What can be more distinct than the Outline of a Leaf, or of one of Rafael's female Figures, and a Line formed by my Arm while I am trying to stretch it as far as I can from above my head to my knee? Distinct, did I say? Is it not as diverse as Position and Negation themselves? Imagine the birth of a living Circle. The Circumference may be formed by the Radii all stopping there because they could go no farther = Negation; but it may likewise be formed because the Radii had pre-determined to go back again, both in order to form the circumference and in order to be conscious of its having so done = Position.

N.B. I can confidently acquit myself of Vanity *when*, and tho', I say that the above is a *most important* Remark.

Gotthilf Heinrich von Schubert, *Ansichten von der Nachtseite der Naturwissenschaft [Views from the Dark Side of Natural History]*, Dresden, 1808.

Several of the notes in this volume are addressed to another reader, probably Joseph Henry Green.

[# 124]

{Is it not possible that the size of the comets, if I may use this image, is proportionate to their orbits (by which we mean only the position and inclination of the comet), just as the size of the blood-current which flows through this or that part of the body depends on the larger or smaller size of the vessels? Even the periodicity of the return of the comets (the periodic revolution) would be connected with this, and perhaps it would be possible to measure the period by other means than by way of elliptic or parabolic computation of the orbit; in fact, it may well be that the doctor who recently composed a humorous weather forecast was near the truth when he said that the periodic return of the comets resembled that of the Northern Lights.}

Alas! but this does not "hang together" with the preceding ¶: which seems to require a continuous action. Perhaps if Pulsation were better understood, some analogy might be supported—at present, it seems obscurum per obscurius [explaining what is obscure by reference to what is more obscure]. Yet I myself have often had wild notions, yea shapings of worlds, while gazing at the Waves and counting their intervals—or in hanging over a torrent stream as from Greta Bridge—

[# 125]

{That momentary individual life is already contained, through the mediation of a higher whole, in the cosmic moments of inorganic nature. In magnetism it is through the mediation of the two physical poles of the earth, or the two most excitable points of the planet, that the magnet, whose dominant pole always turns towards the nearer of these points, receives the higher influence of life; and in electricity too it is through mediate or immediate communion with the earth that bodies receive a first glimmer of independent life.}

Alas! that the Author had but told us, what he means by *Life!* The Foci of
Glasses; the concentric Circles on a Pond, are beautiful WORDS for its
phaenomena, could we but first learn what *it* is. If I say, I *know* it—yet
how can I then apply *that* "it" to a magnet?

[# 126]

> {Especially in humid or hot years we find some certain regions full of vege-
> tation of which there was not a trace in other years.}

This is a Longing Desire to make a Mystery out of a plain matter. Schu-
bart does not dare to say downright, that the germs and seeds of these
plants did not pre-exist in the Soil, either left there since the last Season
favorable to their vegetating or wafted thither: for there are too many
facts/ in proof of the contrary, some of the lowest Fungi alone presenting
any difficulty. But he would forget this and have the Reader forget it: it is
so pleasant to both parties to wander and wonder awhile in gleamy dreamy
Twilight.

[# 127]

> {All juices squeezed out of plants and not entirely deprived of the possibility
> of fermentation tend to undergo a new fermentation at the time when the plants
> from which they are extracted come into bloom, and many can be kept only
> until that time.}

This fact I have often met with in Books—I wish, I could meet with some
individual verification of it. At the reblossoming of *the* Vine from whose
Grapes a Cask of Wine had been expressed, the Wine will ferment anew
if it have not passed beyond the last Fermentation. And this is asserted of
all expressed Plant-juices.—

On mentioning this fact a young Lady assured me on her own repeated
Experience that a spot or stain from Fruit on a Gown may be washed out
while that sort of Fruit continues in season; but becomes indelible if delayed beyond that time.

1819

Martin Luther, *Colloquia Mensalia: or, Dr. Martin Luther's Divine Discourses at his Table,* trans. Henry Bell, London, 1652.

More than twenty of Luther's followers kept records of his conversation, or "table-talk," which were digested into a single volume and then further abridged by Bell, the English translator. This heavily annotated copy, with notes dating from 1819 to 1829, belonged to Charles Lamb.

Erasmus defended the freedom of the human will, whereas Saavedra represented it as very severely limited. The "body of this death" and the "thorn in the flesh" are quotations from Saint Paul, Rom. 7.24 and 2 Cor. 12.7, which Coleridge applies to sinful addiction (such as his own, to opium). Thomas Chalmers, mentioned in conjunction with Jeremy Taylor for his hard line on repentance, visited Coleridge at Highgate in 1827 and 1830. The "Vision of Mirza" was a well known allegory of life from Addison's periodical The Spectator: *Coleridge playfully suggests that Luther was at least as guilty as his contemporary Zwingli of the faults of which he accuses him.*

[# 128]

Bullinger said once in my hearing (said *Luther*) that hee was earnest against the Anabaptists, as contemners of God's Word, and also against those which attributed too much to the literal word, for (said hee) such do sin against God and his Almightie power; as the Jews did in naming the Ark, God. But (said hee) whoso holdeth a mean between both, the same is taught what is the right use of the Word and Sacraments.

Whereupon (said *Luther*) I answered him and said: *Bullinger* you Err, you know neither your self, nor what you hold; I mark well your tricks and fallacies: *Zuinglius* and *Oecolampadius* likewise proceeded too far in this your ungodly meaning: but when *Brentius* withstood them, they then lessened their opinions, alleging, they did not reject the literal Word, but onely condemned certain gross abuses. By this your Error (said *Luther* to *Bullinger*) you cut in sunder and separate the Word and the Spirit. . . .

108

In my present state of mind and with what Light I now enjoy (may God increase it, and cleanse it from the dank mist into the Lumen Siccum [Dry Light] of sincere Knowlege!) I cannot persuade myself, that this vehemence of this dear Man of God against Bullinger, Zuinglius & Oecolampadius on this point could have had other origin, than his misconception of what they intended! But Luther spoke often (I like him & love him all the better *therefore*!) in his moods and according to the Mood.—Was not that a different *mood*, in which he called James's Epistle *a Jack-straw-poppet*—and even in this work selects one verse as the *best* in the whole letter? evidently meaning, the only verse of any great value.—Besides, he accustomed himself to use the term, the Word, in a very wide sense when the narrower would have cramped him. When he was on the point of rejecting the Apocalypse, then *The Word* meant *the Spirit* of the Scriptures collectively.

[# 129]

> [Luther expounds John 20.23, "whose soever sins ye remit, they are remitted unto them; and whose soever sins ye retain, they are retained."] But who hath power to forgive or to detein sins? Answer, The Apostles and all Church-servants, and (in case of necessitie) everie Christian. Christ giveth them not power over monie, wealth, Kingdoms, &c. but over sins and the Consciences of humane creatures, over the power of the Divel, and the throat of Hell.

Few passages in the Sacred Writings have occasioned so much mischief, abject Slavishness, bloated pride, tyrannous Usurpation, bloody persecution with Kings even against their will—the Drudges, false soul-destroying quiet of Conscience, than this Text misinterpreted. It is really a tremendous proof of what the misunderstanding of a few words can do.—That even Luther partook of the delusion, this ¶ph. gives proof. But that a delusion it is—that the Commission was confined to the Seventy whom Christ sent out to proclaim and offer the Kingdom of God, and refers exclusively to the gifts of miraculous Healing which our Lord at that time and for that especial Mission conferred on them—and that, per figuram Causae pro Effecto [according to the figure of cause for effect], Sins here mean Diseases, I have not the smallest doubt—

[# 130]

> Ah Lord God (saith *Luther*)! why should wee anie waie boast of our Free-will, as if it were able to do anie thing in divine and spiritual matters were they never so smal? . . .

> I confess, that mankinde hath a Free-will, but it is to milk Kine, to build houses, &c. and no further: for so long as a man sitteth well and in safetie, and sticketh in no want, so long hee thinketh, hee hath a Free-will which is able to do somthing; but when want and need appeareth, that there is neither to eat nor to drink, neither monie nor provision, Where is then the Free-will? It is utterly lost, and cannot stand when it cometh to the pinch. But Faith onely standeth fast and sure, and seeketh Christ.
>
> Therefore Faith is far another thing then is Free-will, nay, Free-will is nothing at all, but Faith is all in all.

Luther confounds Free Will with efficient *Power*—which neither does nor can exist, save where the finite Will is one with the Absolute Will.

That Luther was practically on the right side in this famous Controversy, and that he was driving at the truth, I see abundant reason to believe—But it is no less evident, that he saw it in a Mist, or rather as a Mist, with dissolving outline—and as he saw the Thing as a Mist, so he ever and anon mistakes a mist for the Thing. But Erasmus & Saavedra were equally indistinct; & shallow & unsubstantial to boot. But in fact, till the appearance of Kant's Kritique der reinen, and die der practischen, Vernunft [*Critique of Pure,* and *of Practical Reason*] the Problem had never been accurately or adequately stated—much less solved.

[# 131]

> When Satan saith in thy heart, God will not pardon thy sins, nor bee gracious unto thee, I pray (said *Luther*) how wilt thou then, as a poor sinner rais up and comfort thy self, especially when other signs of God's wrath besides do beat upon thee, as sickness, povertie, &c. And that thy heart beginneth to preach and say, Behold, here thou lyest in sickness, thou art poor and forsaken of every one, &c. How canst thou as then know, that God is gracious unto thee? then thou must turn thy self to the other side. . . .

Oh! how true, how affectingly true is this! And when too Satan, the Tempter, becomes Satan, the Accuser, saying in my heart—This Sickness is the consequence of Sin or sinful infirmity—& thou hast brought thyself into a fearful dilemma—thou canst not hope for salvation as long as thou continuest in any sinful practice—and yet thou canst not abandon thy daily dose of this or that poison without suicide. For the Sin of thy Soul has become the Necessity of thy Body—daily tormenting thee, without yielding thee any the least pleasurable sensation, but goading thee on by terror without Hope. Under such evidence of God's Wrath how can'st thou expect to be saved?—Well may the Heart cry out—Who shall deliver me from the *Body* of this Death! from this Death that lives and tyrannizes in my body!—But the Gospel answers—There is a Redemption from the Body promised—only cling to Christ. Call on him continually, with all thy heart and all thy Soul, to give thee strength, to be strong in thy weakness—and what Christ doth not see good to relieve thee from, suffer *in hope.*

It may be better for thee to be kept humble and in self-abasement. The thorn in the flesh may remain—& yet the Grace of God thro' Christ prove sufficient for thee. Only *cling* to Christ, and do thy best. In all love, and well-doing gird thyself up to improve & use aright what remains free in thee and if thou doest aught aright, say and thankfully believe, that Christ hath done it for thee. O what a miserable despairing Wretch should I become, if I believed the doctrines of Bishop Jer. Taylor in his Treatise on Repentance—or those I heard preached by Dr Chalmers! If I gave up the faith, that the Life of Christ would *precipitate* the remaining dregs of Sin in the crisis of Death, and that I shall rise a pure *capacity* of Christ, blind to be irradiated by his Light, empty to be possessed by his fullness, naked of merit to be cloathed with his Righteousness!—

[# 132]

> Sir! you saie, *Paul* was justified, that is, was received to everlasting life, onely for mercie's sake. Against which, I saie, if the piece-meal or partial Caus, namely, our obedience followeth not; then wee are not saved, according to these words, *Wo is mee, if I preach not the Gospel*, 1 Cor. 9.
>
> No piecing or partial Caus (said *Luther)* approacheth thereunto; For Faith is powerful continually without ceasing; otherwise, it is no Faith. Therefore what the works are, or of what value, the same they are through the Honor and Power of Faith, which undeniably is the Sun or Sun-beam of this shining.

This is indeed a difficult question: and one, I am disposed to think, which can receive its solution only by the Idea, or the Act and fact of Justification by Faith self-reflected. But humanly considered, this Position of Luther's provokes the mind to ask—Is there no receptivity of Faith, considered as free gift of God, pre-requisite in the Individual? does Faith commence by generating the receptivity of itself? If so, there is no difference either in kind or in degree between the Receivers and the Rejectors of the Word, at the moment preceding this Reception or Rejection: and a Stone is as capable a Subject of Faith as a Man?—How can obedience exist, where disobedience was not possible?—Surely, two or three

Texts from St Paul detached from the total organismus of his Reasoning
ought not to outweigh the plain fact, that the contrary position is implied
in, or an immediate Consequent of, our Lord's own Invitations & Assurances! Every where a something is attributed to the Will.

S.T.C.*

* Mem. I should not have written the above Note in my present state
of Light. Not that I find it false; but that it may have the effect of falsehood by not going deep enough.   July 1829

[# 133]

> God oftentimes (said *Luther*) hath altered His Sacraments and Signs in the
> world; for from *Adam*'s time to *Abraham*'s, the Church for Sacraments had Of-
> ferings and Sacrifices, insomuch that Fire came down from Heaven . . . which
> was a far more glorious sign, then those which wee have. Afterwards, *Noah*
> had for a sign the Rain-bow. *Abraham* thereupon had the Circumcision. The
> Circumcision stood and remained until Christ came. From the time of Christ,
> to this present daie, Baptism hath continued. *Signa sunt subinde facta minora,*
> *Res autem & facta subinde creverunt* [The signs continually became less, but
> the facts and the actions continually grew].

A valuable Remark! As the Substance waxed (i.e. became more evident)
the ceremonial Sign waned—till at length in the Eucharist the Signum
[Sign] united with the Significatum [Thing signified], and became Con-
substantial. The ceremonial Sign, viz. the eating the Bread and drinking
the Wine, became a *Symbol*—i.e. a solemn instance and exemplification
of the *Class* of mysterious Acts, which we are, or as Christians *should* be,
performing daily & hourly in every social duty and recreation.—This is
indeed to re-create the Man in and by Christ. Sublimely did the Fathers
call the Eucharist, the extension of the Incarnation—only I would have
preferred the perpetuation & application of the Incarnation.

[# 134]

> Ambition and Pride (said Luther) are the ranckest poison in the Church when
> they are possessed by Preachers. *Zuinglius* thereby was mis-led, who did what
> pleased himself, as his interpreting of the Prophets sheweth, which is stuffed
> full with presumption, pride, and ambition; hee presumed to contemn every
> man, yea also, the Potentates and Princes, for thus hee wrote, Yee honorable
> and good Princes, must pardon mee, in that I give you not your Titles: for the

Glass-windows are as well illustrious as yee. In like manner *Grickle* and *Jeckle* behaved themselvs in proud and haughtie manner in the Convocation at *Muntzer*. To conclude, Ambition is a consuming fire.

One might fancy in the Vision of Mirza Style that all the angry, contemptuous, haughty Expressions of good and zealous Men, Gallant Staff-officers in the Army of Christ, formed a Rick of Straw and Stubble, which at the last day is to be divided into more or smaller Haycocks, according to the number of kind & unfeignedly humble and charitable Thoughts and Speeches that had intervened/ and that these were placed in a file, Leap-frog fashion, in the narrow road to the Gate of Paradise, and burst into flame as the Soul of the Individual approached—so that he must leap over and thro' them. Now I cannot help thinking, that this dear Man of God, heroic Luther, will find more opportunities of shewing his Agility, and reach the Gate in a greater Sweat, and with more Burn-blisters, than his Brother Hero, Zuinglius! I guess, that the Latter's Comment on the Prophets will be found almost sterile in these Tyger-Lilies and Brimstone Flowers of polemic Rhetoric, compared with the former's controversy with our Henry the 8th—Replies to the Pope's Bulls &c &c!—

[# 135]

> It is the highest grace and gift of God, to have an honest, a God-fearing houswifely consort, with whom a man may live peaceable, in whom hee may put in trust his wealth and whatsoever hee hath, yea his bodie and life, with whom hee getteth children. But God thrusteth many into the state of matrimonie before they bee aware and rightly bethink themselves.

Alas! alas! this is the misery of it that so many wed and so few are christianly married! But even in this the analogy of Matrimony to the Religion of Christ holds good; for even such is the proportion of nominal to actual Christians—all *christened*, how few baptized!—But in true matrimony it is beautiful to consider, how peculiarly the marriage state harmonizes with the doctrine of Justification by free Grace thro' Faith alone. The little quarrels, the imperfections on both sides, the occasional frailties, yield to the one thought—there is Love at the bottom. If Sickness or other sorer Calamity visit me, how would the Love then blaze forth. The faults are there but they are not imputed/—The Prickles, the acrid rind, the bitterness or sourness, are transformed into the ripe Fruit—and, the foreknowlege of this gives the name and virtue of the ripe fruit to the fruit yet green on the Bough.

[# 136]

[Luther considers the case of a man who married the sister of his dead wife.] . . . the same marriage in this degree is not to bee suffered nor endured; therefore accordingly it is acknowledged void, and that those two persons bee separated the one from the other. Also by reason of their exercised leacherie, to terrifie others by their example, they shall bee laid in prison, and there remain certain weeks, and the begotten childe to bee brought up and maintained by the parents on both sides. And whereas the minister (without the advice and instruction of his lawful magistrat and spiritual superattendent) did permit that marriage in a prohibited degree, therefore hee shall also bee punished with eight daies imprisonment.

I look on this as a very doubtful case. Bp Jeremy Taylor justifies, nay, recommends such marriages. There is much & of much weight to be advanced on both sides.—If first Cousins may marry, *then* I should confidently decide, that a man may marry his Wife's Sister. But as I do not approve of the former, neither dare I give a positive opinion for the lawfulness of the latter.—Is it a mere whim?—But somehow or other I contemplate the man's marrying his deceased Wife's Sister with more tolerance than a Widow's marrying her Husband's Brother.

Johann Heinrich Jung, *Theorie der Geister-Kunde [Theory of Pneumatology]*, Nuremberg, 1808–9.

[# 137]

{Soon afterwards the young man died, and now his master waited for his visit, and for news from the other world. About three weeks after the death of the journeyman, when the master . . . had just climbed into bed and was still sitting up in it, he noticed on the opposite wall a bluish glimmer of light that took on the shape of a human figure. He then asked without fear: "Is it you, John?"—The spirit answered audibly: "Yes!"}

There often take place fits of Slumber so brief and momentary as to escape the Slumberer's own consciousness. In these cases the Images and Sounds from the Brain blend with those from the Outward Senses, their distance being determined by their comparative vividness—just as reflected and transmitted Light, where a window fronts the fire-place. We see the Fire among the Bushes in the Garden, for instance—(supposing the window to overlook a Garden) and nearer and nearer as it grows darker & darker. Now the impossibility of proving, that this Johannes [John] was not a Dream or Brain-creature of this kind, amounts to a proof that it *was/*

[# 138]

> {There is no reason to think that through the progress of the Enlightenment the number of ghost stories has decreased; the ignominy of fanaticism and of superstition with which they are charged is the reason why one does not speak of them; and besides, each family prefers to keep such matters secret.}

But if these ghostly Occurrences have not diminished in frequency, and the comparative number of the Experti is still so mighty, how is this *Shame* possible? If I believe Jung, there are not fewer persons in Germany, who have had intercourse with the World of Spirits, than who have travelled into Spain, or seen Naples. Were this true, the one Witness would support the other as instantly and decisively in the former as in the latter case—or if not, it must be because they are themselves inwardly *uncertain* as to the outward reality of their own Experiences: and endeavor to make up for this sense of certainty by sensations and correspondent expressions of *positiveness*, as often as they can talk in a snug corner to such as are willing to listen and already want only an excuse for believing.

Bryan Waller Procter, *Dramatic Scenes and Other Poems*, London, 1819.

Procter's pen name was Barry Cornwall. It seems that Charles Lamb invited Coleridge to comment on the poems by annotating the book, and then passed the book on (perhaps by prearrangement) to the author.

[# 139] Barry Cornwall is a Poet, me saltem judice [in my opinion, at least]: and in that sense of the term in which I apply it to C. LMB and WW [Charles Lamb and William Wordsworth]. There are poems of great merit, the Authors of which I should yet not feel impelled so to designate.—

The faults of these Poems are no less things of Hope than the Beauties—Both are just what they ought to be: i.e. NOW.

If B. C. be faithful to his Genius, it in due time will warn him that as Poetry is the *identity* of all other Knowleges, so a Poet cannot be a *great*

Poet but as being likewise & inclusively an Historian and Naturalist in the Light as well as the Life of Philosophy. All other men's Worlds (κοσμοι) are *his* Chaos.

Hints *obiter* are—Not to permit Delicacy & Exquisiteness to seduce into effeminacy.

Not to permit Beauties by repetition to become Mannerism/

To be jealous of *fragmentary* Composition—as Epicurism of Genius, and Apple Pie made all of Quinces.

Item, that Dramatic Poetry must be Poetry *hid* in Thought and Passion, not T. or P. disguised in the dress of Poetry.

Lastly, to be economic and withholding in similies, figures, &c.— They will all find their place sooner or later, each as the Luminary of a sphere of its own. There can be no *Galaxy* in Poetry; because it is Language, ergo, successive, ergo, every the smallest Star must be seen singly.

There are not five Metrists in the Kingdom, whose works are known to me, to whom I could have held myself allowed to have spoken so plainly. But B. C. is a Man of Genius, and it depends on himself (Competence protecting him from gnawing or distracting Cares) to become a rightful *Poet*—i.e. a great Man.

O! for such a man worldly Prudence is transfigured into the highest spiritual Duty. How generous is Self-interest in *him*, whose true Self is = all that is good and hopeful in all ages, as far as the Language of Spencer, Shakspeare and Milton shall become the Mother Tongue!

A map of the road to Paradise drawn in Purgatory on the Confines of Hell by S. T. C.—July 30, 1819.—

P.S. The pause after the second Syllable in Pentameter Iambic Blank Verse is frequent in the Poems of Mr Southey and of his Imitators. But should it be imitated? Milton uses it, when the weight of the first Iambic, Trochee, or Spondee, of the second Line, requires a *pause* of preparation at the last foot of the preceding.

Thomas Gray, *Works*, London, 1814.

[# 140]

[From the "Ode on a Distant Prospect of Eton College":]

> Wanders the hoary Thames along
> His silver-winding way.

We want, methinks, a little treatise from some man of flexible good sense, and well versed in the Greek poets, especially Homer, the choral, and other lyrics, containing first a history of compound epithets, and then the laws and licenses. I am not so much disposed as I used to be to quarrel with such an epithet as "silver-winding;" ungrammatical as the hyphen is, it is not wholly *illogical*, for the phrase conveys more than silvery and winding. It gives, namely, the unity of the impression, the co-inherence of the brightness, the motion, and the line of motion.

John Webster, *The Displaying of Supposed Witchcraft*, London, 1677.

These notes may have been written for Charles Augustus Tulk, whom Coleridge met when he was on holiday at Littlehampton in 1817. Tulk was a founder of the Swedenborg Society, created to ensure the publication of Swedenborg's works, though not himself a member of the Swedenborgian New Jerusalem Church. For Coleridge's interest in reports of paranormal events—including prophetic trances and visions, oracles, miracles, animal magnetism, and the like—see the Tennemann entry (# 120).

"Behmen [Boehme], Helmont" etc.: Coleridge lists famous figures from ancient times to the present who described their own and others' apparently supernatural experiences. Friedrich Anton Mesmer (1732–1815) developed a method of healing supposedly based on invisible forces. One of Swedenborg's accounts of his experience of angels is quoted below, # 144.

[# 141]

> [Webster tells a story from Johannes Baptista Porta, "a great Naturalist, and a person of competent veracity," of a witch who was observed to anoint herself with an ointment that put her into a deep sleep in which she apparently dreamed of journeys and adventures that she reported, when she woke up, as having really taken place. While insensible she was also severely beaten, but retained afterward no memory of the incident.]

This of Porta's is not the only well attested instance of the use of the Cataleptic properties of narcotic Ointments and Potions in the Pharmacy of the poor Self-bewitched. They are a traditional Derivative from Pagan Antiquity (Pocula Circëia [Circeian draught] &c) and even in the earliest mention of them seem, like most superstitions, to be the cadaver et putrimenta [corpse and decaying parts] of a defunct Natural Philosophy. In many respects the voluntary confessions of Witches would lead one to suppose that an empirical Animal Magnetism was in play; but there is this characteristic difference, that the magnetized Cataleptic retain no memory of what they said or imagined during their Trance.

Q.y Might this difference arise from the Witches remaining unquestioned and unroused, unexcited ab et ad extra [from and towards the outside] during the magnetic torpor? Or by the continuance & sequelae [those things that follow from it, i.e. consequences] of the narcotic Influence, so as not to afford any chasm, or abrupt transition into the waking & natural state? That Self-magnetism is in certain conditions, those indeed of the rarest occurrence, possible, has been rendered highly probable, at least. The cases of Behmen, Helmont, Swedenborg, and the assertions of Philo Judaeus of himself, and Porphyry both of Plotinus and of himself might at all events receive a natural solution from the hypothesis. Indeed, the best service which mesmerism or zoomagnetism has yet done is that it enables us to explain the Oracles & a score other superstitions without recourse either to downright Self-conscious Lying and Imposture on the one side, or to the Devil and his Works on the other—reducing the whole of Daemonology and Diabolography [writing about the Devil] to Neuro-pathology.

[# 142]

> This pretended League [between Devil and witch] must needs be a lye and a figment, because of the effects that are feigned to follow, as to have carnal copulation with the Devil, to raise storms and tempests, to flye in the air, and to kill men and beasts. For if these things be done, they are either performed by the Witches own natural power, or by the Devils. If by the Witches natural power, or the force of her resuscitated imagination and strength of will to work *ad nutum* [at a nod] (as *Van Helmont* seems to hold) then the Devil operateth nothing, but in playing the Imposter, and deceiving the Witch, and that he may easily do by internal and mental delusion, and needs no visible League to bring it to pass.

How very close Van Helmont seems to have been to the full discovery of Mesmerism, or theletic manipulation [manipulation by the will]. That the Will can extend its power, by some immediate vehicle or instrument secreted, accumulated, and directed by its own *intension*, beyond the surface of the visible Body, is evident in the Torpedo, Gymnotus, and other Aquatilia Electrica [the electric eel, and other electric water creatures]/

that there is an appropriate electrical apparatus in these animals does not prove that there need be one in so perfect an Organismus as the human, but on the contrary the multiplication of appropriate instruments the lower we descend in the scale of animal organization & in some proportion to the descent (thus, several of the Insect Tribes and the Crustacea are a perfect *Shop* of Tools) furnishes a strong analogical presumption against such necessity—not to say, that our present ignorance of a galvanöid structure in the human frame is no proof of its non-existence.— This point, I meant to observe, Helmont had in full and clear view; and he had himself accidentally discovered, that the root of the Napellus [Monkshood], & probably other vegetable Narcotics, was capable of specifically exciting the ganglia of the pectoral Region (Plexus Solaris) so as to alter the polarity of the Nervous System. All that remained therefore for him to have ascertained was whether the *Will* (say of A) could act analogously i.e. as a narcotic, on the nervous system of B, the latter being previously disposed by natural or *for-the-purpose-induced*, disease, so as to bring about the same excited state of the pectoral Ganglia. This would have completed the discovery after made by Mesmer. Whether the Will of A act directly on B, or by means of a material tho' imponderable effluence from the body of A; or by a peculiar narcotic secretion from his Skin, as Stieglitz supposes, and applies to cases of *Fanatical* Contagion in crowded *Preachings*, or by an organ of *Temperature* in the cutaneous Nervous Net-work, a Caloric sui generis [heat of its own kind, unique], as Schelling Conjectures; or by a nervous atmosphere as Humbold, Blumenbach, Soemmering & others; are ?s that belong to the Theory not to the *Facts*.

[#143]

> [A case reported by Helmont:] "So (he saith) we have in times past seen at *Lira* the children of *Orphans* to have cast up by vomit an artificial Horse and Cart, drawn forth by the hands of the by-standers; to wit a four footed board accompanied with its ropes, and wheel. And what way soever it were placed, it was easily greater than the double throat."

The *story* may be true, & the more probable from *Fits* being so common in the Foundling Hospitals of the continent: tho' the *Telling* is Self-contradictory: for how could it have been vomited if it had been too large to have been swallowed? A *most* singular instance occurred at Keswick, in my own and Robert Southey's (the Poet Laureate's) own presence— of a Pike sent us as a present from Mr Leathe's of Leathe's Water or

Thirlmere, the lake between Grasmere and Keswick—& which had 3 pounds & a half of Stones in its stomach, the *smallest* of which could not be forced down the throat of the Fish without lacerating it. We made the exactest inquiries, tracing it from the persons who caught and were present at the time in the boat (two of them the young Mr Leatheses) to the moment of its delivery, and received the most solemn assurances that no trick had been played—The throat was entire & in its natural state—

Emanuel Swedenborg, *De coelo et ejus mirabilibus, et de inferno, ex auditis et visis [Concerning Heaven and its Wonders, and Hell, from Things Heard and Seen]*, London, 1758.

Like William Blake, who was also a friend of Tulk's, Coleridge took a serious interest in the visions and doctrine of Swedenborg, without becoming a convert to his system. He annotated at least eight of his works, several of them gifts from Tulk, and considered publishing on Swedenborg. Among the topics proposed were an intellectual biography, a dictionary of "correspondences," and a companion to True Christian Religion.

"Trinitarians and Solifidians" represent different and in some ways conflicting aspects of Protestantism, Solifidians adhering to the belief that faith alone is sufficient for salvation, and Trinitarians emphasizing the role of Christ as Redeemer. "Reigning love" is Coleridge's literal translation of amor regnans *in Swedenborg: Swedenborg suggests that human beings are defined as spiritual beings according to the thing they love most in life.*

[# 144]

{Now let us turn to experience. That angels are human forms or men has been seen by me a thousand times. I have talked with them as man with man, sometimes with one, sometimes with several together, and I have seen nothing whatever in their form different from that of man. . . . Indeed, I have quite often told them that men in the Christian world are in such blind ignorance about angels and spirits as to believe them to be minds without form, even pure thoughts, of which they have no idea except as something ethereal in which there is some vitality.}

I have met (in books at least) with some tho' few, who have doubted like myself whether Scripture teaches us, *as an article of Faith*, the existence of any other rational Creatures but men either such as they are in the present or such as they become in the spiritual World. But I never met with any who, believing in Angels as originally super-human, supposed them to be without Form & personal Characteristics, tho' invisible to our bodily Sense. The Common Man throughout Christendom represents them to himself as sexless Men, beautiful luminous and with Wings.

One of my scruples respecting the *reality* of Swedenborg's Experiences (N.b. *not* respecting *his* veracity, which God forbid!) is grounded on this: that the notions, & doctrines, which he attributes to others, seem always like the opinions which one Man forms of another Man's Belief whom he supposes to differ from himself, and not like what the Man's own statement of his own conceptions would be. This is especially striking in the confessions of Faith put in the mouths of Trinitarians and Solifidians by Swedenborg—which no learned Trinitarian or Calvinist would acknowlege for his own.

[# 145] If these marginal notes should fall under any other eyes but my own, I would wish to premise to the remark below that I am almost persuaded that the errors objected to are mainly in the use of undefined terms—and that the Author actually meant every where the form intelligible, or that spiritual Intuition/ rather, perhaps that Object of spiritual intuition, by which living Truths are distinguished from each other: and not the *shape*, or *image*.

[# 146]

{God cannot be thought of except in human form; and what is incomprehensible does not fall into any idea, so neither into belief. . . .}

This is true or false, according to the sense in which the terms Idea and incomprehensible are used. If Idea be employed as the synonime of Idol, or visual Image, and incomprehensible mean unpicturable, or that which cannot be contained within an Outline,—then it is, doubtless, true, or rather it is a truism. But if Idea be opposed to ειδωλον or image, and if for incomprehensible we substitute inapprehensible, then it is not only false but a very pernicious falsity—as has been ably shewn by Kant in his Tract, De Mundo *Intelligibili* et Sensibili [*Concerning the Form and Principles of the Intelligible and Sensible World*]. Besides, there is, I suspect, another equivocation latent in all these positions de formâ [concerning form] of Swedenborg's (besides the repetition of the former in the confusion of the forma antecedens and the forma consequens sive apparens [the antecedent form and the consequent or visible form]) viz. the subjective necessity of apprehending a Truth *with* some visual image, and the objective necessity of the Image in the Truth and in order to the distinct apprehension of the same.—Ex. gr. Suppose an animalcule to require to be magnified by the microscope 500 times in order to appear the size of the smallest mite—The truth, viz. that it is 500 times less than the appearance, is a perfect distinct cognition—which I accompany with an Image, as its proper representative, that at the same I contradict. In fact, it is doubtful to me whether the *sensation* of Magnitude does not constitute *the Image*, i.e. is not that which renders the perception an Image. Now this connection with magnitude & whatever is merely passive impress, Swedᵍ. expressly forbids. His "Ideas" therefore must be pure Intuitions of *Relations*, co-existing severally or diversely in each several Integer. Thus the *Substance*, the *Being*, is the generic or universal; the Relations are the Specific; and the Copula, i.e. the Intuition of these as *existing*, is the Individual or the Form.

Now if I understand Sw. aright, he means to say that in the spiritual World the Forms or Ideas arise in and out of each Spirit's subjective Insight into or Construction of the *specific Relations*, in and with which every *Each* exists in the absolute Being—in the immediate Act of determining that existence numerically—and again that this Process depends on laws of Similitude and Assimilation, and not as in this World by the operation of *Intermedia* of diverse nature both from the Percipient and the Perceptum [thing perceived], such as material Light, elastic Fluids, &c.— So far this is a system of subjective Idealism = the monads or vires representativae [representing powers] of Leibnitz. But whence the Objectivity?—the proper Perceiving?—In the Will of God, or the absolute Esse [Being] as the Act that causes the universal Reality—id per quod omnia sunt quatenus sunt [that by means of which all things are such as they are]? Is this at once the Light and the percipient Faculty as far as both are common to the Spirits: but modified in each by the essential Relations of each, & by the individual Will? And in proportion as the latter is the same with the former or absolute Will, is the Perception more perfect? All will causative? And thence even the wicked Will so far causative as to assimilate the superficies indifferens [neutral surface] of the Good sufficiently to engender *a form* correspondent to its essence & its contrariety to the Divine Order?—

Nota bene. One great occasion of the perplexity in Metaphysical Reasoning is the different senses confounded in the Mathematical = ["equals" sign] when introduced into Metaphysical use. We sadly want

two or three additional characters for the different sorts of equality.—
Thus B + a = A respectivè ad [respectively to] a; but in genetics A cannot be said to be = B: it is only = a, i.e. to itself, which acts on B but sus-
tains no re-action. But I again repeat my conviction, that Swedenborg's
Meaning is the truth—and the duty of his followers is, to secure this
meaning to the Readers of his Works by collecting from his numerous
Volumes those passages, in which this meaning is conveyed in terms so
plain as not to be misconceived: an introduction of 50 pages would suffice for this purpose.

This modification of = is above all requisite in the formation of an
right Judgement respecting Swedenborg for with a true philosopher the
final question will be—thus—Spirits in Sw. = B, C, D (i.e. such and such
philosophic truths, psycho- or physio-logical Facts.) But are B. C. D =
Spirits?

[# 147]

{I can testify from much experience that it is impossible to implant the life of
heaven in those who in the world have lived a life opposite to the life of heaven.
For there were some who had believed that they would readily receive Divine
truths after death, when they heard them from the angels, and that they would
believe them, and consequently live a different life, and could thus be received
into heaven. But this was tried with very many, although it was confined to
those who held this belief, and was permitted in their case that they might learn
that repentance is not possible after death. Some of those with whom the experiment was made understood truths and seemed to receive them; but as soon
as they turned to the life of their love they rejected them, and even spoke
against them. Others were unwilling to hear them, and at once rejected them.
Others wished to have the life of love that they had contracted from the world
taken away from them, and to have the angelic life, or the life of heaven, in-
fused in its place. This, too, was permitted to be done; but as soon as the life
of their love was taken away they lay as if dead, with their powers gone.}

What Sw. included in his "reigning love" or ruling passion, I do not distinctly understand. But this I *feel* with tremendous depth, that for a man
enthralled in any *habit* condemned by himself, and bitterly bitterly inces-
santly groaned over—exempli gratiâ [for example], the ruinous use of an-
odynes & opiates, which he loathes while he takes, yet still takes, goaded
on by pain, and more than pain, and by the dread of both—that for such
a man, I say, this Chapter is of unspeakable Horror—& the next on the
facilities of acquiring Heaven = 1. negative, and 2. progressive perfec-

tion, calls forth a piteous plaint from the wounded Conscience/ O favored Man! Why mockest thou me?—

There are, however, other Passages in Sw's Works, thro' which a Ray of Promise breaks. May I not represent to myself the Gospel Mean between the extremes of arbitrary Mercy and determined Judgement in some such Parable as this? Claudius and Lelius both sorely sick are under the same compassionate Physician. But Claudius is diseased in the vital principle itself—all that the nature of the case, the inmost order of things, leaves possible to the skill of the kind Physician, is to soothe & alleviate the symptoms. But in Lelius *the organs* are diseased—not however by any outward calamity but by his own fault. Now in this latter case will the inmost sorrow and penitence & abhorrence of the originating Guilt avail nothing? Will earnest unselfish Love & Thankfulness toward the believed Redeemer, the Lord God of Forgiveness, avail nothing—unless the entire victory over all the results & outward or bodily consequences of the Evil has been won even in this Life!—Shall the poor Sinner be forbidden to die with—Mercy! Mercy! Mercy, Lord! on his Lips?

1820

Robert Southey, *The Life of Wesley; and the Rise and Progress of Methodism*, London, 1820.

Southey himself presented this copy of his most successful biographical work to Coleridge upon publication. Coleridge wrote his notes on various occasions, dating some as late as 1832.

Pelagians believe in the possibility of redemption by one's own efforts, as opposed to the Trinitarian Church of England emphasis on divine grace and redemption through Christ. "Leibnitz" is the German philosopher Gottfried Wilhelm Leibniz (1646–1716); Coleridge alludes to his view that truth is not the property of one party but is dispersed in fragments among many different systems of belief. The Moravians, a Protestant sect originating in Germany in the eighteenth century, were an important early influence on Wesley. "Nitrous oxyd" we know as "laughing gas."

[# 148] Memento!—It is my desire and request that this Work should be presented to its Donor & Author, Robert Southey, after my Death. The Substance and character of the marginal annotations will abundantly prove the absence of any such intention in my mind at the time, they were written. But it will not be uninteresting to him to know that the one or the other Volume was the book more often in my hands than any other in my ragged Book-regiment, and that to this work, and to the Life of R. Baxter, I was used to resort whenever Sickness & Languor made me feel the want of an old friend, of whose company I could never be tired. How many and many an hour of Self-oblivion do I owe to this Life of Wesley—how often have I argued with it, questioned, remonstrated, been peevish & asked pardon—then again listened & cried, Right! Excellent!—& in yet heavier hours intreated it, as it were, to continue talking to me—for that I heard & listened & was soothed tho' I could make no reply. Ah! that Robert Southey had fulfilled his intention of writing a history of the Monastic Orders—or would become the Biographer at least of Loyola, Xavier, Dominic, & the other remarkable Founders.

Grove, Highgate.   S. T. Coleridge
                                                                          Aug. 1825

[#149]

[Archbishop Potter's advice to Wesley:] "If you desire to be extensively useful, do not spend your time and strength in contending for or against such things as are of a disputable nature; but in testifying against open, notorious vice, and in promoting real, essential holiness."

If de facto disputata et de jure disputabilia [things actually disputed and things in principle susceptible of dispute] were the same things; and if the words real essential Holiness, had the same meaning for all Parties; Archb? Potter's Advice would be a profitable Rule. As it is, I cannot think highly of a maxim, better calculated to soothe and justify a Socinian in his Pelagian Self-redemption, than to direct a Minister of the Gospel in preaching the whole truth in Christ. But so it is & ever has been! A Church is first collected and established by the fervent preaching of Doctrines and Mysteries, the Interest in which is distinctive of Man either as a rational, or as a responsible, or as a fallen and sinful, Creature—When the Church is firmly established & richly endowed with wealth or influence or both, Indolence & Jealousy of commencing or apprehended Rivalry join in inducing an infrequency and virtual discouragement of doctrinal, (the alone powerful & soul-reaching) Sermons: and the Church is ruined or brought to the verge of Ruin, by preaching *Morality*—i.e. first Platonic, then Stoic, and lastly Epicurean Ethics under the usurped names, first of real substantial *Holiness*, then of Good & exemplary Living, and lastly, of Christian *Charity*, and Good Works—till by little & little the Church is divorced from the affections of the People, the only reliable source of her influence, or like the Romist, retains them in a sense of dependency by multiplying, encouraging and enforcing the most debasing and demoralizing Superstitions. The subtle Poison of the easy Chair had begun to work on Wesley himself toward the end of his Life: and to this far more than to increased experience and riper Judgement may we attribute the change in the tone & spirit, and the relaxation even in the most characteristic principles, of his Preaching & Conversation. And what have the "Great Revivals" of Methodism been but the recurrence of some of its Itinerants to the Tone, Spirit & Doctrines by which it was founded?

[# 150]

It rained heavily, and the woman, when he was three miles off, cried out "Yonder comes Wesley, galloping as fast as he can;" a circumstance which it certainly required no aid from the devil to foresee.

A sufficient Solution: as far as this particular case is concerned. But the co-incidence throughout all of these Methodist Cases with those of the Magnetists' makes one wish a solution that would apply to all—now this sense, or appearance of a sense of the Distant both in Time & Space is common to almost all the Magnetic Patients, in Denmark, Germany, France, & North Italy—to many of which the same or a similar Solution could not apply. Likewise, many have been recorded at the same time in different Countries by Men, who had never heard of each other's names and where the simultaneity of publication proves the independence of the Testimony—and among the Magnetizers & Attesters are to be found names of men, whose competence in respect of integrity & incapability of intentional falsehood is fully equal to Wesley, and their competence in respect of physio- and psycho-logical insight and attainments incomparably greater. Who would dream, indeed, of comparing Wesley with a Cuvier, Hufeland, Blumenbach, Eschenmeyer, Reil, &c?—Were I asked what *I* think—my answer would be—that the Evidence enforces Scepticism & a Non liquet [it is not clear]. Too strong & consentaneous for a candid mind to be satisfied of its falsehood, or its solvibility in the supposition of Imposture or casual Co-incidence—too fugacious and infixible to support any Theory that supposes the always potential & under certain conditions & circumstances occasionally actual existence of a correspondent faculty in the human Soul. And nothing less than such an hypothesis would be adequate to the *satisfactory* explanation of the Facts—tho' that of a metastasis of specific functions of the nervous energy taken in conjunction with extreme nervous excitement, + some delusion, + some illusion, + some imposition + (plus) some chance & accidental coincidence, might determine the direction, in which the Scepticism vibrated. Nine years has the subject of Zoo-magnetism been before me—I have traced it historically—collected a Mass of documents in French, German, Italian, & the Latinists of the 16th Century—have never neglected an opportunity of questioning Eye witnesses (ex. gr. Tieck, Treviranus, De Prati, Meyer, and others of literary or medical celebrity) and I remain where I was, & where the first perusal of Klug's Work had left me, without having advanced an Inch backward or forward. Treviranus the famous Botanist's reply to me, when he was in London, is worth recording. Ich habe gesehen was (ich weiss das) ich nicht wurde geglaubt haben auf ihren erzählung, &c. I have seen what I am certain I would not have believed on *your* telling; and in all reason therefore I can neither expect nor wish that you should believe on mine.

[# 151]

> ... a generation of Clergymen had grown up, not inferior as a body to those
> of any age or country, in learning, in ability, or in worth. Their sincerity was
> put to the proof, and it appears that full <u>two-thirds</u> of them were ejected <u>for fi-
> delity to their king and their holy office.</u>

It is strange that no one of the Dissenters have brought this assertion to
the Test of Documents—& a Symptom of the Decay of Learning among
their Ministers. O ever highly prized and fondly remembered Southey!
Methinks, I could have walked to Keswick bare-foot, with only Bread &
Water to support me, and have knelt to you, if by so doing I could have
snatched these four pages from the Mss Pacquet for the Printer—Pages
alike irreconcilable with faith of History, with philosophic Calmness and
with Christian Charity—in one word, with Robert Southey!—

[# 152]

> Wesley took the volume ["one of the spurious treatises ascribed to Dionysius
> the Areopagite"] to Fetter-lane, and read these words before the jarring soci-
> ety, "The Scriptures are good; prayer is good; communicating is good; reliev-
> ing our neighbours is good: but to one who is not born of God none of these
> are good, but all very evil. For him to read the Scriptures, or to pray, or to com-
> municate, or to do any outward work is deadly poison. First let him be born of
> God. <u>Till then let him not do any of these things. For if he does, he destroys
> himself.</u>"

I strongly suspect either misquotation here, or misinterpretation. What
can be more unfair, than to pinch out a bit of a book this way! Most candid Critic! what if I By way of joke pinch out your eye? then holding up
the gobbet, cry—Ha! Ha! that Men should be DOLTS! Behold this slimy
Dab! & He who own'd it, dreamt that it could *see*! The Idea were mighty
analytic—But should you like it, candid Critic?
    I cannot help thinking that the Biographer has been in several instances
led by his venial partiality for his Hero into the neighborhood of his
Hero's faults.—It was a fault common to Wesley and Swedenborg to limit
the words of their opponents to the worst possible sense, instead of seeking as Leibnitz did, the truest sense—& thus finding the error in the insufficiency & exclusiveness of the position. The Moravian Leaders, being
such as Southey himself has described them, could not be ignorant, methinks! that the act of restraining & withholding is as much a positive energy, if not more, than the act of *doing this or that*: and doubtless, for

many minds the more profitable. Their error consisted in universalizing the position, and instead of "many" putting "all".

[# 153]

> After the breach had been thus formally announced, Count Zinzendorff published an advertisement, declaring that he and his people had no connection with John and Charles Wesley. The Moravians forbore from all controversy upon the subject, but Wesley did not continue the tone of charity and candour in which he had addressed them upon the separation.

R. Southey is an Historian worth his weight in diamonds, & were he (which Heaven forfend!) as fat as myself, and the Diamonds all as big as Birds' eggs, I should still repeat the appraisal. He may err in his own deductions from Facts; but he never deceives, by concealing any known part of the Grounds & Premises, on which he had formed his conclusions— or if there be any exception—and p. 318–321 are the only ground or occasion for this "if"—yet it will be found to respect a complex Mass of Facts to be collected from jarring & motley narratives, all as accessible to his Readers as to himself. So *here.* That I am vexed with him for not employing stronger and more empassioned words of reprobation & moral Recoil in this *black blotch* of Wesley's Heart and Character, is in another point of view the highest honor to Southey as an Historian—since it is wholly and solely from his own statement of the Incidents that my impressions have been received.—The manner in which this most delightful of all Books of Biography has been received by the Wesleyan Methodists, demonstrates the justice of the main fault which judicious men charge against the work, viz. partiality toward the Sect & its Founder—a venial fault indeed, the liability to which is almost a desirable qualification in a Biographer.

[# 154]

> . . . powers like his [Wesley's] produce an inward restlessness, and a perpetual uneasy sense of discontent, till they find or force their way into action: but now when those powers were fully developed, and in full activity, at once excited and exerted to the utmost in the service of that God, whom he surely loved with all his heart, and with all his soul, and with all his strength, the world did not contain a happier man than Wesley, nor, in his own eyes, a more important one.

High, yea, an aweful Eulogy—perilously high as applied to any Mortal; but strangely inconsistent with Southey's own clear and discriminating

character of Wesley's Mind both in its present state and generally—
Rooted Ambition, restless Appetite of Power and Primacy, with the most
vindictive Spirit, breaking out into the foulest Slanders, against those who
interfered with his ruling Passion—and a logical shadow-fight with notions and words, sustained by the fervor of the game, with an entire absence and insusceptibility of Ideas and tranquil Depths of Being—in
short, *my*, *my*, *my* Self in a series of Disguises and Self-delusions—such
is the sum of Southey's Statement, and are these compatible with the same
Wesley at the same time assuredly loving God with *all* his heart, and with
all his Soul and with all his Strength? If it were right and possible for a
Man to love himself in God, yet can he love God in himself, otherwise
than by making his Self his God?

[# 155]

> On the day following the preacher met the Society, "in order to wrestle with
> God in behalf of those who were in distress." Pawson went full of sorrow,
> "panting after the Lord as the hart after the water-brooks." When the prayer
> for those in distress was made, he placed himself upon his knees in the mid-
> dle of the room, if possible, in greater anguish of spirit than ever before.
> Presently a person, whom he knew, "cried for mercy, as if he would rend the
> very heaven."—"Quickly after, in the twinkling of an eye," says Pawson, "all
> my trouble was gone, my guilt and condemnation were removed, and I was
> filled with joy unspeakable. I was brought out of darkness into marvellous
> light. . . ."

What shall I say to these and other instances? Disbelieve the Narrators?
I can not. I dare not. I seem to be assured, that I should quench the Ray,
and paralyze the Factual Nerve, by which I have hitherto been able to dis-
criminate veracity from falsehood, and Deceit from Delusion. Is it then
aught real, tho' subjectively real—as the Law of Conscience! When I find
an instance recorded by a Philosopher of himself, he still continuing to
be a Philosopher—recorded by a man, who can give the distinctive
marks, by which he had satisfied himself that the Experience was not ex-
plicable physiologically, nor psychologically, I shall think it time to ask
myself the question.—Till then, I find no more rational solution than that
afforded by *disorder* of the Nervous Functions, from mental Causes, no
physical or external disturbing forces being present, and no *Disease*. In
such cases we may, I should think, anticipate certain sudden refluxes of
healthful secretions & internal actions of the organs—this & that & a
third perhaps baffled & drawn back, till at length, either strengthened by

accumulated Sensation, as availing itself of a quieter moment or conspir-
ing Circumstances, it makes head again & flows in on the empty Channel in a *Bore*—and this of course would take its shape, and as it were articulate itself, or interpret itself, by the predominant Thoughts, Images, &
Aims of the Individual. Even as Life returns upon the Drowned, and as
moderate Warmth has been known to intoxicate & produce all the thrilling
overwhelming synthesis of impatient appetite & intolerable fruition that
some Constitutions have undergone from inhaling the nitrous Oxyd.

*S. T. C.**

* Add to this the important fact that Christianity in its genuine doctrines contains so much of Spiritual Verities that can only be spiritually
discerned; but which will to such Individuals *seem* akin to their recent ex-
altations, and therefore actually supply a *link*—so that by these Spiritual
Verities they become without any sensible discontinuity connected with
the whole series of the Duties, Humanities, Charities of Religion—but
verbum sat ["a word is enough" to the wise man]. In short, the Man awak-
ens so gradually & opens his eyes by little & little to objects so similar to
his Dream, that the Dream detaches itself, as it were, from Sleep, and becomes the commencing Portion of the new Day-thoughts.

**Richard Baxter, *Reliquiae Baxterianae: or, Mr. Richard
Baxter's Narrative of the Most Memorable Passages
of his Life and Times*, ed. Matthew Sylvester, London, 1696.**

*This second copy of Baxter belonged to George Frere, president of the
Law Society, and the notes date from 1817 onward, with a marked burst
of activity about 1820.*

*Coleridge cites Hammond and Baxter, Milton and Jeremy Taylor, to
show that there could be good people on both sides of a political or religious dispute. In the Civil War period and the aftermath, Hammond and
Taylor were associated with the Royalist party loyal to the Church of England, Baxter and Milton with the Parliamentarian and Puritan party of
Cromwell, Hampden, Ireton, and others. Medio tutissimus ibis is from
Ovid,* Metamorphoses *2.137. The "Revolution" is the bloodless English
Revolution of 1688. Luther's* Table Talk *or* Colloquia mensalia, *like Bax-
ter's autobiography, contains some accounts of supernatural events that
would have been treated more skeptically by Coleridge's time. "Mr.
Kenyon"—John Kenyon, poet and philanthropist—was a mutual friend*

of Coleridge and Southey. Milton wrote An Answer to Eikon Basilike.
"Polar logic" is a crucial feature of the philosophical system that Coleridge struggled to elaborate, and he found traces of it in other philosophies ancient and modern. It is "polar" because it assumes a framework of opposites; it avoids simple dichotomy by positing four poles instead of two. "Hercules Furens . . ." is a bookish pun appropriate to its context, describing the schoolmaster's prowess as a disciplinarian: Hercules Furens (The Madness of Hercules) *is the title of a tragedy by Seneca, and "phlogistic" is used not in its scientific sense but as equivalent to "flogging."*

[# 156] Mem. Among the grounds for recommending the perusal of our elder writers, Hooker, Taylor, Baxter, in short almost any of the Folios composed from Edward VI to Charles II

1. The overcoming the habit of deriving your whole pleasure passively from the Book itself, which can only be effected by excitement of Curiosity or of some Passion. Force yourself to reflect on what you read ¶ph by ¶ph, and in a short time you will derive your pleasure, an ample portion at least, from the activity of your own mind. All else is Picture Sunshine.

2. The conquest of party and sectarian Prejudices, when you have on the same table the works of a Hammond and a Baxter; and reflect how many & how momentous their points of agreement; how few and almost childish the differences, which estranged and irritated these good men! Let us but reflect, what their blessed Spirits now feel at the retrospect of their earthly frailties: and can we do other than strive to feel as they now *feel*, not as they once felt?—So will it be with the Disputes between good men of the present Day: and if you have no other reason to doubt your Opponent's Goodness than the point in Dispute, think of Baxter and Hammond, of Milton and Jer. Taylor, and let it be no reason at all!—

3. It will secure you from the narrow Idolatry of the Present Times and Fashions: and create the noblest kind of Imaginative Power in your Soul, that of living in past ages, wholly devoid of which power a man can neither anticipate the Future, nor even live a truly human life, a life of reason, in the Present.

4. In this particular work we may derive a most instructive Lesson that in certain points, as of Religion in relation to Law, the "Medio tutissimus ibis [You will go most safely by the middle way]" is inapplicable. There is no *Medium* possible; and all the attempts, as those of Baxter, tho' no more were required than, "I believe in God thro' Christ," prove only the

mildness of the Proposer's Temper, but as a rule would be either $= 0$, at least exclude only the two or three in a century that make it a matter of religion to declare themselves Atheists; or just as fruitful a rule for a Persecutor as the most complete set of Articles that could be framed by a Spanish Inquisition. For to "believe" must mean to believe aright, and "God" must mean the true God, and "Christ" the Christ in the sense and with the attributes understood by Christians who are truly Xtians. An established Church with a Liturgy is the sufficient solution of the Problem de Jure Magistratus [Concerning the Legal Authority of the Chief Magistrate (or Sovereign)]. Articles of Faith are superfluous; for is it not too absurd for a man to hesitate at subscribing his name to doctrines which yet in the more aweful duty of Prayer & Profession, he dares affirm before his maker? They are therefore *merely* superfluous—not worth reenacting, had they never been done away with—not worth removing now that they exist.

5. The characteristic Contra-distinction between the Speculative Reasoners of the Age before the Revolution and those since then is this: The former cultivated metaphysics without, or neglecting, empirical Psychology; the latter cultivate a mechanical Psychology to the neglect and contempt of Metaphysics. Both therefore almost equi-distant from true *Philosophy*. Hence the belief in Ghosts, Witches, *sensible* Replies to Prayer &c in Baxter, and a 100 others—See p. 81: and look at Luther's Table Talk, &c &c.

6. The earlier part of this Volume is interesting as materials for medical History. The state of medical Science in the reign of Charles the First almost incredibly low!

[# 157]

> I tried, when I was last with you, to revive your Reason, by proposing to you the Infallibility of the Common Senses of all the World; and I could not prevail though you had nothing to answer that was not against Common Sense. And it is impossible any thing controverted can be brought nearer you, or made plainer than to be brought to your Eyes and Taste and Feeling: and not yours only, but all Mens else. Sense goes before Faith. Faith is not Faith but upon Supposition of Sense and Understanding; if therefore Common Sense be fallible, Faith must needs be so.

This is one of those two-edged Arguments, which (not indeed *began* but) began to be *fashionable*, just before & after the Restoration—I was half converted to Transsubst. [Transubstantiation] by Tillotson's *Common*

Senses against it, seeing clearly that the same grounds totidem verbis et syllabis [in the same number of words and syllables] would serve the Socinian against all the mysteries of Christianity. If the Rom. Cath. had pretended that the *phaenomena* Bread & Wine were changed into the *Phaenomena*, Flesh and Blood, this Objection would have been legitimate & irrestible; but as it is, it is mere sensual Babble.—The whole of Popery lies in the assumption of *a Church*, as a real Agent, a numerical Unit— infallible in the highest degree, inasmuch as both what *is* Scripture and what Scripture teaches is infallible by derivation only from an infallible decision of the Church. Fairly undermine or blow up this; & all the remaining peculiar Tenets of Romanism fall with it—or stand by their own insight, as opinions of individual Doctors.—

An Antagonist of a complex bad System, a *System* however notwithstanding—& such is Popery—should take heed above all things not to *disperse* himself. Keep to the *sticking* place. But the majority of our Protestant Polemists seem to have take for granted, that they could not attack Romanism in too many places or on too many points: forgetting, that in some they will be less strong than in others; and that if in any one or two they are repelled from the assault, the feeling of this will extend itself over the whole—Besides, what use of 13 reasons of a Witness's not appearing in Court, when the first is that the Man had died since his subpoena? It is as if a party employed to root up a tree were to set one or two at that work, while others were hacking the Branches, & others sawing the Trunk at different heights from the ground.

N.B. The point of attack suggested below in disputes with the Romanists is of especial expediency in the present day: because a number of pious & reasonable Catholics are not aware of the dependency of their other tenets on this of the Church—but are themselves shaken & inclined to explain it away. This once fixed, the Scriptures rise uppermost: & the Man is already a Protestant, tho' his opinions should remain near to the Roman than the Reformed Church.

[# 158] Mr Kenyon yesterday, 1 Septr 1825, observed, that R. S. could not *mediate* and that I could not *militate*—that even when it was Southey's own purpose to sit as an Arbiter, he was sure, before he was aware, to stand up as a Partisan, and drop the Scales in order to wield the Sword— while I was so engaged in tracing the diverging Branches to a common Trunk both for Right and Wrong that both Parties took to the Sword against *me*. S. saw all Difference as Diversity; while I was striving to reduce supposed Contraries into compatible Opposites, whose worst error consisted in their reciprocal Exclusion of each other. S. found positive falsehoods where I saw half-truths, and found the falsehood in the partial Eclipse.—S. = a Grey-hound: S. T. C. a Pointer.—I have amplified our common Friend's Observation in my own metaphorical way; but I give the conclusion in his own words—In short, Southey should write Books and you write notes on them.—It may serve to confirm this Judgement, if I mediate here between Baxter & the Bishops. Baxter had taken for granted, that the King had a right to promise a revision of the Liturgy, Canons & Regiment of the Church; and that the Bishops ought to have met him and his Friends as Diplomatists on even ground. The Bishops could not with discretion openly avow all, they meant; and it would be High Church Bigotry to deny that the Spirit of Compromise had no In-dwelling in their Feelings or Intents. But nevertheless it is true, that they thought more in the Spirit of the English Constitution than Baxter & his Friends—This, thought they, is THE LAW of the Land, quem nolumus mu-tari [which we refuse to change]—and it must be the King with and by the advice of his Parliament, that can authorize any part of his Subjects to take the question of its Repeal into Consideration. Under other Cir-cumstances a King might bring Bishops and the Heads of the Romish Party together—to plot against the Law of the Land. No! We would have no other Secret Committees, but of Parliamentary Appointment. We are but so many Individuals. It is in the Legislature that the Congregations, the party most interested in this Cause, meet collectively in their Repre-sentatives.—

Lastly, let it be overlooked, that the root of the Bitterness was common to both Parties—viz. the conviction of the vital importance of Unifor-mity—and this admitted, surely an undoubted majority in favor of what is already Law must decide *whose* Uniformity it is to be.

[# 159]

Since this, Dr. *Peter Moulin* hath in his Answer to *Philanax Anglicus*, declared that he is ready to prove, when Authority will call him to it, that the King's Death and the Change of the Government, was first proposed both to the *Sorbonne,* and to the Pope with his Conclave, and consented to and concluded for by both.

The Pope in his Conclave had about the same influence on Charles's Fate as the Pope's Eye in a Leg of Mutton. The Letter intercepted by Cromwell was Charles's Death-warrant. Charles knew his power; & Cromwell and Ireton knew it likewise—and knew, that it was the Power of Man who was within a yard's Length of a Talisman, only not within an Arm's length, but which in that state of the public mind, could he but have once grasped it, would have enabled him to blow up Presbyterian & Independent. If ever a lawless Act was defensible on the principle of Self-preservation, the Murther of Charles might be defended. I suspect, that the fatal delay in the publication of the Eikon Basilike, is susceptible of no other satisfactory Explanation. In short, it is absurd to burthen this Act on Cromwell or his Party. The guilt, if guilt it was, was consummated at the Gates of Hull—i.e. the first moment, that Charles was treated as an Individual, Man against Man. Whatever right Hampden had to defend his Life against the King in Battle. Cromwell & Ireton had in yet more imminent danger against the King's Plotting, Milton's reasoning on this point is unanswerable—& what a wretched hand does Baxter make of it!

[# 160]

> I had been Twenty Six Years convinced that Dichotomizing will not do it; but that the Divine Trinity in Unity, hath exprest it self in the whole Frame of Nature and Morality. . . .

Among Baxter's philosophical merits we ought not to overlook, that the substitution of Trichotomy for the old & still general plan of Dichotomy in the Method and Disposition of Logic, which forms so prominent & substantial an excellence in Kant's Critique of the Pure Reason, of the Judgement, &c belongs originally to Richard Baxter, a century before Kant—& this not as a Hint but as a fully evolved & systematically applied Principle. Nay, more than this! Baxter *grounded** it on an absolute Idea *pre*supposed in all intelligential acts: whereas Kant takes it only as a *Fact* of Reflection—as a singular & curious Fact, in which he seems to anticipate or suspect some yet deeper Truth latent & hereafter to be discovered.—

* On recollection I am disposed to consider *this* alone as Baxter's *peculiar* claim. I have not indeed any distinct memory of Giordano Bruno's Logica Venatrix Veritatis; but doubtless the principle of Trichotomy is necessary involved in the Polar Logic: which again is the same with the Pythagorean *Tetractys*—i.e. the eternal Fountain or Source of Nature; & this being sacred to contemplation of Identity & prior in order of Thought to *all* division, is so far from interfering with Trichotomy, as the univer-

sal form of Division (more correctly, or distinctive Distribution in Logic) that it implies it.—Prothesis being by the very term anterior to Thesis can be no part of it—Thus in

Prothesis

Thesis   Antithesis

Synthesis

we have the Tetrad indeed in the intellectual & intuitive Contemplation; but a Triad in discursive Arrangement, and a Tri-unity in Result.—

[# 161]

> If you think not only Imposition to be essential, but also that nothing else is essential, or that all are true Ministers that are ordained by a lawful Bishop *per manuum impositionem* [by the imposition of hands], then do you egregiously *tibi ipsi imponere* [impose upon yourself].

Baxter, like most Scholastic Logicians, had a sneaking affection for Puns. The cause is: the necessity of attending to the primary sense of words, i.e. the visual image or general relation exprest, & which remains common to all the after senses, however widely or even incongruously differing from each other in other respects.—For the same reason, School-masters are commonly Punsters.—"I have indorsed your Bill, Sir!" said a Pedagogue to a Merchant—meaning, that he had flogged his Son William. "Nihil in intellectu quod non prius in sensu [There is nothing in the understanding not derived from the senses]", my old Master, R^d [Reverend] J. Boyer, the Hercules Furens of the phlogistic Sect, but else an incomparable Teacher, used to translate—first reciting the Latin words & observing that they were the fundamental article of the Peripatetic School— "You must flog a Boy before you can make him understand"—or "You must lay it in at the Tail before you can get it into the Head."—

Robert Leighton, *Genuine Works*, London, 1819.

In April 1816, Coleridge was accepted as a patient and lodger by James Gillman, a surgeon living in Highgate. They quickly became friends, and Coleridge stayed with the family for the rest of his life. This second copy of Leighton belonged to Gillman.

[# 162]

> . . . *They shall see God.* What this is we cannot tell you, nor can you conceive it: but walk heavenwards in purity, and long to be there, where you shall know what it means; *for you shall see him as he is.*

We say "Now I *see* the full meaning, force and beauty of a passage—we see them *thro'* the words." Is not Christ THE WORD? the substantial, con-substantial Word, ὁ ων εν κολπω πατρος [which is in the bosom of the Father]—not as *our* words, arbitrary: nor even as the words of Nature, phaenomenal merely? If even through the words [of] a powerful and perspicuous Author—(as in the next to inspired Comment[y] of Archb. Leighton—for whom God be praised! I identify myself with the excellent Writer and his thoughts become my thoughts; what must not the Bliss be, to be thus identified first, with the filial WORD, and then with the Father in and thro' him?

[# 163]

> In this elementary world, light being (as we hear) the first visible, all things are seen by it, and it by itself. Thus is Christ, among spiritual things, in the elect world of his church; *all things are made manifest by the light,* says the apostle, Eph. v. 13, speaking of Christ, as the following verse doth evidently testify. It is in his word that he shines, and makes it a directing and convincing light, to discover all things that concern his church and himself, to be known by its own brightness. How impertinent then is that question so much tossed by the Romish church, how know you the scriptures (say they) to be the word of God, without the testimony of the church? I would ask one of them again, how they can know that it is day-light, except some light a candle to let them see it? They are little versed in holy scripture, that know not that it is frequently called light; and they are senseless that know not that light is seen and known by itself. If our gospel be hid, says the apostle, it is hid to them that perish; the god of this world having blinded their minds against the light of the glorious gospel, &c. no wonder if such stand in need of a testimony. A blind man knows not that it is light at noon-day, but by report: but to those that have eyes, light is seen by itself.

On the true test of the Scriptures. Oh! were it not for my manifold infirmities, whereby I am so all unlike the white-robed Leighton, I could almost conceit that my soul had been an emanation from his! So many and so remarkable are the coincidences, and these in parts of his works that I could not have seen—and so uniform the congruity of the whole. As I read, I seem to myself to be only thinking my own thoughts over again, now in the same and now in a different order.

[# 164]

> In all love, three things are necessary. (1) Some goodness in the object, either true and real, or apparent and seeming to be so; for the soul be it ever so evil, can affect nothing but what it takes some way to be good.

The lines on p. 107, noted by me [given above], are one of a myriad instances to prove, how rash it is to quote single sentences or assertions from the correctest Writers, without collating them with the known system or express convictions of the Author. It would be easy to cite 50 passages from Archbishop Leighton's Works in direct contradiction to the sentence in question—which he had learnt in the Schools when a Lad, and afterwards had heard and met with so often that he had never sifted its real purport.—

[# 165] This assertion [in the entry above] in these words has been so often made, from Plato's times to ours, that even wise men repeat it without perhaps much examination whether it be not equivocal—or rather (I suspect) true only in that sense in which it would amount to nothing—nothing to the purpose at least. This is to be regretted—for it is a mischievous equivoque, to make good a synonime of pleasant, or even the Genus of which Pleasure is a Species. It is a grievous mistake to say, that bad men seek pleasure because it is good—no! like children they call it good because it is pleasant.—Even the useful must derive its meaning from the good, not vice versâ.

Emanuel Swedenborg, *True Christian Religion*, trans. John Clowes, London 1819.

This book was probably a gift from Tulk, to whom Coleridge wrote about his own short "Essay on Faith" (which circulated in manuscript but was not published in Coleridge's lifetime) in July 1820.

[# 166]

> From the doctrine of faith we next proceed to that of charity, for faith and charity are conjoined like truth and good, or like light and heat in the time of

spring. . . . The case is the same with respect to charity and faith, as with good and truth, charity being the complex of all things belonging to the good which a man doeth to his neighbour, and faith the complex of all things belonging to the truth which he thinketh respecting God and things divine.

The point, I least like in Swedenborg, and which (I reluctantly confess) seems to me to detract considerably from the character of his mind as well as from the theological value and philosophical merit of his writings, is his evident disposition and constant effort to interpret the phrases of the Churches, to whose tenets he opposes his own, into meanings of the greatest possible difference that might be conveyed in those words, and then burthening them with consequences which they themselves disclaim, and which (as in the doctrine of Faith & Works common to the Lutheran and Calvinist) do not appear in their lives. Hence he often, nay, most often, misstates their opinions, which, in substance at least, he might have found reconcilable with his own, & with little other difference than arises almost inevitably when the same Object is contemplated by several persons from several different points of view; and probably would have found, had he imitated the mens conciliatrix [conciliatory mind] of Leibnitz, (herein most distinguishably a Philosopher for Philosophy is the Wisdom of Love no less than the Love of Wisdom, & must be both to be either) with as much fidelity as he has followed, or fallen in with, his metaphysics & metaphysical Theology.

Besides in this, as in most cases of this sort, mutual intolerance is the pledge of mutual ignorance. Swedenborg's definition of Faith is (to use his own phrase) *a falseness* of the first magnitude, too frequent indeed among the Calvinistic Clergy, but not *universal*: while it pervades Swedenborg's System & is the Queen Bee in the Hive of Rom. Cath. Errors.— Faith is *not* primarily or pre-eminently an intellectual Act—for the proof, & what Faith *is*, I refer to my Essay on Faith as used in Scripture.—

Lorenz Oken, *Lehrbuch der Naturgeschichte [Textbook of Natural History]*, Leipzig and Jena, 1813–26.

Joseph Henry Green, who gave lectures on the new subject of comparative anatomy, acquired these volumes as they came out and lent them to Coleridge for comment. Coleridge himself had written, for Gillman, part of a treatise on the "Theory of Life."

[# 167]

{The lung develops into the sense of the lung, the *nose*; flesh and bones develop into the sense of bones, the *ear*; the nerves develop into the sense of the nerves, the *eye*.}

Are then the Nerves of less necessity to the sense of Smelling and Hearing than to that of seeing? Are they not in all alike the primary and sole *proper* Agents: & to which the other parts are but the stands, joints, bolts, channels, tubes, &c. & sometimes little more than the protecting *Cases*? Is it not a presumption against Oken's Scheme, that the eye appears in almost the lowest & most Nerveless Animals? And why? Because (if we do not confound mere *Feeling* or *sensation* of Stimulus with the *Sense* of *Touch*) the Eye is of all the Senses the least *reflective*, the most superficial. Hence, the number of Eyes in Insects, whose Life is the life of Irritability, i.e. the electrical or *surface* Power, the *objective* selfless Sensibility ✳ [as opposed to] the *subjective* or proper Sensibility. But further. Insects have neither Lungs nor Gills; yet their Smell is almost miraculous. Mr R. Southey dipped some Beetles in oil. They remained to all appearance dead. He put aside 2 or 3 in another Room. To the rest he brought a female Beetle: in a few seconds the Males evinced signs of returning animation, & within a minute or two were pursuing the female briskly. The former, that were put aside, remained dead—died.

John Petvin, *Letters Concerning Mind*, London, 1750.

One of Charles Lamb's books. As the postscript indicates, Coleridge read it at a particularly anxious time, when he made the trip to Oxford to discuss his son Hartley's future with the provost of Oriel. The college ultimately decided not to renew Hartley's fellowship at the end of his probationary year, and he left the university.

"Heterozetesis" is the fallacy of "looking for something else," that is, proving something other than what is required to be proved.

[# 168] At the time, in which these Letters were written, the Haut Ton philosophique [high philosophic fashion] was ascendant, according to which Plato, Aristotle and the rest of the unfortunate Ante-Nati, who wrote before "John Locke had thrown the *first* ray of Light on the nature of the human mind and the true source of all our Ideas", were mere

Dreamers or word-splitters. Yet still there were many of a better mould, who retaining their love and veneration of the ancients were anxious to combine it with the new Orthodoxy by explaining Aristotle and even Plato *down* into John Locke. Such was that excellent man, and genuine *Classic* Scholar, the Poet Gray. Others there were, and Petvin appears to have been one of the number, who, if they did not *love* the Ancients more than the former class, *understood* them better; and yet wanted either will or courage to oppose the reigning Dynasty. These men attempted to reconcile the old with the new Authority by a double operation—now, like the former class, lowering down Pl. and Arist. to John Locke, & now pullying John Locke up to Plato and Aristotle. The result was, now a confusion in their own thoughts & an inconsistency in their several positions; now & more frequently, an expression of the Truth in lax, & inaccurate, & inappropriate Terms. But the general Effect, a nearly universal Neglect of Metaphysics altogether, & the substitution of a shallow semi-mechanical Psychology under the pretended Law of Association, which, however, is in fact no *Law* at all, but a mere vague general or *common* Term for causal connection as far as the same is seen in living & thinking, as distinguished from inanimate things, thus making one particular mode of causal connection the ground & cause and explanation of Causation itself.

But the whole scheme of Locke is an Heterozetesis—by which the Sun, Rain, Air, Soil &c are made to *constitute* the germs (as of Wheat, Oat, or Rye) of the *growth* & *manifestation* of which they are the efficient *Conditions*.—Instead of the words, "give, convey" and the like, write wherever they occur, "excite, awaken, bring into consciousness" or words equivalent—& little will remain in Locke's Essay to be complained of, but its dullness & superficiality, its putting up of Straw-men to knock them down again—in short, the making a fuss about nothing, & gravely confuting Nonsense, which no man ever *had* asserted & which indeed no man ever *could* believe—ex. gr. (as Des Cartes says to the Jesuit, Voetius, who had assailed him in the true Locke Style, tho' before Locke's Essay), that men saw before they saw, heard before they heard, & the like $2 + 2 = 5$, cross-readings!—

S. T. Coleridge

OXFORD, Oct. 14. 1820.—Saturday Afternoon. (Left Highgate, Friday— & London, by the three o'clock Shrewsbury Stage—arrived in Oxford, Friday Night, 11)—God grant me a safe return on Monday.—Sunday morning $\frac{1}{2}$ past 11. am to have my interview with Dr Coplestone.

[# 169]

But to return to the consideration of Νοῦς [Mind] and ἐπιστήμη [knowledge] above, after the Manner of *Aristotle*. And here it is plain, that *every self-evident Principle* must be a *general Idea*, because 'tis a *Medium* by which *general Conclusions* are drawn. I should hardly have made so obvious a Remark, but that, as obvious as it is, it seems to have escaped Mr. *Locke*, or not to have been considered by him in a right manner.

At length, Petvin dares *use* his own eyes. But what an instance of the effect of a *great Reputation* on an honest & even superior mind! For with this ground-falsity the *whole* of L[ocke]'s system as far it is System, sinks & is overturned.

1821

Emanuel Swedenborg, *Prodromus philosophiae ratiocinantis de infinito, et causa finali creationis [Outlines of a Philosophical Argument on the Infinite, and on the Final Cause of Creation]*, Dresden and Leipzig, 1734.

[# 170]

{This I believe is forbidden to all, and especially to Christian philosophers, who are bound to admit nothing in God but infinity, nothing in other spirits but finiteness; there being therefore no possible ratio or relation between the two. The difference between the infinite and the finite is so great, that the difference between heaven and earth is nothing to it. Actuality in the infinite must be considered as without mode, unless mode in an infinite sense; but the actuality in spirits, as involving mode; for in finite spirits nothing can be set in activity without a mode: and mode in finites there is none but what is immediately referable to substances, and proceeds from them.}

The Reasoning in these pages might be cited as an apt example of the inconvenience of the Dichotomic Logic: which acts in a contrary direction to the prime end and object of all reasoning, the reduction of the Many to One, and the restoration of Particulars to that Unity, by which alone they can participate of true Being—Omne Ens Unum [every being is singular]. Two terms in manifest correspondence to each other are yet opposed as contraries, without any middle term: the consequence of which is, that one of the two becomes a mere negation of the other—ex. gr. Real—/—Unreal but Unreal = 0. So Finite—Infinite. If the former be assumed as real, the latter merely expresses the absence of reality; but if the latter (i.e. the Infinite) be assumed as the Real, then the Finite expresses a negation of the Real, and quoad *finite* = 0.—Remove 0, and it becomes the Infinite/ i.e. the Finite can have only *subjective* existence—i.e. it is a mere act of the mind, arising from a defect of perception. Compare the Logic of Dichotomy with that of Trichotomy, or what is the same, the Pythagorean Tetractys—In this we seek first for the Unity, as the only source of Reality: and then for the two opposite yet correspondent forms, by which it manifests itself. For it is an Axiom of universal application, that

"Manifestatio non datur nisi per Alterum" [Manifestation occurs only by means of an Other]/ Instead therefore of the Affirmation and Contradiction, the tools of the dichotomic Logic, more truly Eristic—i.e. not of *Reasoning* but of Disputing, we have the *three* terms, Identity, Thesis and Antithesis—and consequently, as soon as it is *applied*, a 4th and 5th, viz. the Indifference, and the Synthesis, of Th. and Antithesis.—Example.

Identity
Real

Thesis	Antithesis
Actual	Potential

Thus too finite and infinite are the two necessary forms of Being Manifested—which can never be divided:—the instances, in which either is assumed singly, will be found mere abstractions, or else mere forms of Subjective imagination, such as an Atom, or Infinite Space/ and what is Space? a something with the attributes of Nothing!—But in real Science we must say

1. Being
or Identity of Finite & Infinite.

2. The Finite in the Infinite ✠ [as opposed to] The Infinite in the Finite. This is the proper answer to the argument in these pages. Finite & Infinite are not contrary things; but opposite correlative Forms of the same Reality—just as Attraction & Repulsion are the antagonist *forces* of one & the same *Power*.—And the same may be proved by the intolerable consequences of the contrary Scheme,

Application of the + and − of Real—
Real: = Identity
MAN

Thesis		Antithesis
+ Actual	Indifference	Potential −
Soul	Life	Body

Synthesis
Organization

That is: the Soul is the Actual Reality of Man, the Body the Potential Reality. Life is the Indifference of the Actual and Potential and the Organism the Synthesis.

Finally, the Error of this in so many important particulars truly excellent Work is grounded on the assumption of the Sensuous Intuitive, or the Sense, as the same with the Intellective, & as the only form of the Ratiocinative: whereas many things may be understood which cannot be imagined; and many truths apprehended which can neither be understood nor imagined.

1823

Pierre Jurieu, *The History of the Council of Trent*, London, 1684.

The letter Y, *with its thinner and thicker branches, is sometimes called the "Samian" letter because Pythagoras of Samos used it as an allegory of human life: the individual has to choose between the broad path to ruin and the narrow way of righteousness. The quotation "Shatters its waters abreast . . ." is from Coleridge's part of a poem,* Mahomet, *that he planned in 1799 to write in collaboration with Southey.*

[# 171]

> In the first place the Reformed decline the jurisdiction of this Council [of Trent], as a Judge incompetent, because a Party. I easily foresee I shall be stop'd short here, and that it will be returned upon me, that the Churches being a Party, is the ordinary refuge of Hereticks. Had not the *Arians* as much right to tell the Council of *Nice*, you are a Party, and therefore can be no Judge in the Cause?

A Beech rises in a columnal Trunk to the height of 20 feet from the Ground—and there it divides into two, diverging as the Samian Y. A River flows from its fountain in one widening stream over a vast track of Country and thro' various soils, till it reaches a bed of rocks, over & between which it twists, foams, roars, eddies, for a while,

> "Shatters its waters abreast, and in mazy tumult bewilder'd
> Rūshĕs dĭvīdŭŏus āll, āll rūshĭng ĭmpētŭŏŭs ōnwārds,"

till it is met by a vast compact breast-work of Rock, which divides the stream into two diverging Channels—and obtains the name of the Rock of Separation.—Which of the two Limbs shall call itself the Beech-tree & retain the name of Trunk? Which of the two Streams, the South West, or the South-East, shall call itself *the* River?—Is not the question palpably absurd?—What if the *Genie* or Naiad of the one Channel should with an angry sneer ask the Sister Naiad—Where were you & your Stream before Rock Separation?—Might not the latter—/ reply—Exactly where

you were, Sister—To be sure, I have deposited a good deal of the mud &
the filth which our waters had contracted during their long journey—I
wish, Sister! you would make use of my Filtring Machine!—In the same
purpose was the answer of ——— to his Catholic Neighbor who had
asked him—Where was your Religion before Luther?—"Where was
your Face before you washed it this morning?"

Heinrich Steffens, *Caricaturen des Heiligsten*
***[Caricatures of the Most Holy]*, Leipzig, 1819–21.**

*Coleridge annotated several works by Steffens, a pupil of Schelling's and
one of the leaders of the influential scientific movement known as* Naturphilosophie. *At the height of his enthusiasm he expressed a "restless wish
to place myself as a Pupil with H. Steffens." This book belonged to Green
and was probably part of his informal course of reading with Coleridge.*

*The Apocrypha are the books received by the early Christian Church
as part of the Old Testament, but later excluded from the canon; one is
Ecclesiasticus, also known as "The Wisdom of Jesus Son of Sirach" after
its author or compiler. In # 175, Coleridge casts up to Steffens his earlier
statement ("p. 217"), made in the context of a discussion of the importance of freedom for all citizens to develop and express their individual
natures, "If his vocation is to be someone powerful, no one else shall re-
strain him."*

[# 172]

{Critical questions have agitated all people—questions, whose prematurely
attempted answers have plunged a neighboring country into incalculable misery. The relation of the people to the sovereign has become the object of
scrutiny by the masses; the word freedom resounds again in all countries, in
all classes. Does anyone believe that this aroused spirit can be suppressed
through censorship and secret police?}

It vexes me to find Steffens condescending to make the 1000th echo of
this hackneyed piece of Declamation. Where is the proof, that the Population of France has been plunged into a misery deeper or more general
than what existed before the Revolution? *They* assert the contrary: and I
believe, with *truth* on the whole. Even during the first explosion and the
reign of the Terrorists, the Misery was more noisy, and that of individuals more prominent—but I would take a bet on the Quantum & Quale,

the Kind and the Degree, being less than under several periods of the preceding Despotism.—

[# 173]

{The development of the mind should of course not remain unknown to the peasant; but it should not remove the essential limitation of his existence; the futility of the endeavor to enlighten peasants in the wrong way has been recognized. Religion in its most profound form as holy <u>faith</u> is, however, the innermost principle of his life. . . .}

I have tried hard, and with sincere good will, to make some sense out of this; but I have not succeeded. An essential Contraction of an Agricultor's Existence, to which a proportional Negation of Knowlege & intellectual Development is to correspond—while Religion in its deepest holiest Form &c—ohe satis [Ho, enough]! Who told Steffens all this? Who authorized him to play such havoc with a human Soul, because it is a Farmer's? Not Nature—for it contradicts Nature, in her most evident tendencies? Not the God in Nature: for it shrinks up & mutilates his clearest Mouldings—not God in the *word*—unless Steffens holds the Apocrypha for Gospel & the dicta of the Epicurean Jesus the Son of Sirach for *the Words that are Spirit* of Jesus the Son of Man!—

[# 174]

{The scholar's peculiar activity in the state emerges in a two-fold manner, as bringing being to cognition—education in the widest sense of the word—and as bringing cognition to being—legislation.}

There is somewhat too much of these reductions of things to the primary Antithesis of Being and Knowing—besides that St. seems to forget, that this very antithesis is but a form of *thinking* of things, not of the things themselves. I might be made to understand das hineinbilden des Seyns in das Erkennen [the bringing of being to cognition] the better from being told that it meant Education: but that I should understand what education is better from being told that it is "das &c," I can not conceive—. How arbitrary too these abstract Universals are, may be proved from the fact that in the memory of this passage I had reversed the antithesis, applying to Law what St. had applied to Education, & vice versâ. Nay, I still prefer the reversed position. How much more intelligible & natural (if Abstractions muct be used on such occasions) would it have been to say, that by Education we give Knowlege to Power, & in Law Power to Knowlege!

[# 175]

{Thus that external equality which dominated during the Revolution and which even now appears in the background more frequently than is supposed as something desirable . . . is clearly a product of foreigners, hirelings, those who have no inner property; for it would tear down the beneficial limitations of an apparently limited nature; that is, it would destroy the true freedom.}

To hear Steffens talk, one would imagine that by some pre-established harmony, some new refinement of predestination, a boorly Soul was born a Boor—and that all calm and lofty souls entered into the foetuses of future Serene Highnesses.

O fie! fie! what other Equality but that which Steffens himself demands, p. 217, l. 15, do the German Patriots require—the equality of power to develope powers, subject to no other checks than the necessity of unequal possessions brings with it. These God knows! are numerous enough & powerful enough—without any wanton additions on the part of the Laws and Governments. In short, I do not know what or whom Steffens is combating. A Peasant does not wish to be a Lord—no, nor perhaps does he wish to be a Parson or a Doctor, but he would have the Soul of a Slave if he did not desire that there should be a *possibility* of his Children or Grand-children becoming such.

John Howie, *Biographia Scoticana*, Leith, 1816.

Coleridge borrowed this book from Allan Cunningham, a Scottish writer living in London, probably as a source for a projected volume of selections from Leighton with a biographical and historical introduction. That project turned into Aids to Reflection *(1825).*

"Pia-fraudish" is a word made up for the occasion, signifying a well-meant deception. "Our Lord's Prohibition" is recorded in Matt. 16.20; "Body of Death" alludes to the words of Saint Paul in Rom. 7.24: "What shall deliver me from the body of this death?" Antinomians hold believers to be above the moral law.

[# 176]

On a Tuesday morning, about day break, he [Mr. Simpson] went into his garden as private as possible, and one Helen Gardiner, wife to one of the bailies of the town, a godly woman, who had sat up that night with Mrs Simpson, being concerned at the melancholy condition he was in, climbed over the garden-wall, to observe him in this retirement; but, coming near the place where he was, she was terrified with a noise which she heard, as of the rushing of multitudes of people together, with a most melodious sound intermixed; she fell on her knees, and prayed, that the Lord would pardon her rashness, which her regard for his servant had caused. Afterwards she went forward and found him lying on the ground; she entreated him to tell her what had happened unto him, and, after many promises of secrecy, and an obligation, that she should not reveal it in his lifetime, but, if she survived him, she should be at liberty, he then said, "O! what am I! being but dust, and ashes, that holy ministering spirits should be sent with a message to me!" And then told her, that he had had a vision of Angels, who gave him an audible answer from the Lord, respecting his wife's condition: and then returning to the house, he said to the people who attended his wife, "Be of good comfort, for I am sure that ere ten hours of the day, that brand shall be plucked out of the fire."

God keep me from uncharitable Thoughts—It may have been a Posthumous Fancy, or a Prose Epic, of Mrs Helen Gardiner, suggested perhaps by the wind in a Scotch Fir at the moment she was peeping at her pious Pastor on his knees in his Garden—But it does look horribly like a pia-fraudish confabrication. If intended only for Mr Simpson's solace & as enabling him to predict with confidence, what need of the rushing of a Mob of Spirits or of the melodious Voice intermixed? And if intended for a bono publico Miracle [a miracle in the public interest] to the honor and glory of Misepiscopy [hatred of the system of church government by bishops] (no worse word than Misanthropy), why the injunction of Silence till after the Death of the only person who might have contradicted it & who alone could have confirmed it? At all events, this excuse for posthumous testimony (which is of frequent occurrence in Puritan Biography) is an injudicious, not to say, profane imitation of our Lord's Prohibition to his Disciples respecting his Messiahship, his Crucifixion, & Resurrection on the third day. For here the Motives for injoining Silence were evident & the suggestions of Mercy no less than of Wisdom—For to have proclaimed himself the Messiah i.e. King of the Jews, would have been High Treason to the Civil Government, i.e. the Roman Magistrates—& to have declared that the Messiah would be *hung* would have justified his apprehension for Blasphemy by the Sanhedrim, in the exertion of the privileges accorded to them by the Roman Emperor & Senate./
S. T. Coleridge.

who intreats & trusts in, Allan Cunningham's pardon for thus bescrawling a leaf of his Book. A. C. may be assured that S. T. C. is not so devoid

either of genial Taste, or of gratitude for pleasures enjoyed, as to have
treated a Book of A. Cunningham's own creation so irreverentially.

[# 177]

> One time, in conference concerning the sin in the godly, his father said to him,
> "I am sure you are not now troubled with corruption, being so near death." He
> answered, "Ye are altogether deceived, for as long as my foot remaineth on this
> earth, though the other were translated above the clouds, my mind would not
> be free of sinful motions."

I have at sundry times been disturbed and assaulted by the question—If
it pleased God to restore me to Health and Strength, have I any sufficient
ground of confidence, that the sense of the sinfulness of Sin, of the un-
worthiness and baseness of the sins, to which my constitutional softness,
sensibility, and craving for sympathy, render me most prone, would either
prevent or instantly suppress the workings of Sin on my members, or secure me against temptations, and opportunities of indulgence?—The inward Conviction of my weakness forces me to forego all hope of such a
result from the power or strength of any principle or habit of Will in myself—& to rest my only hope on the daily, hourly, nay, momently assistance of the free Grace of the Spirit of Christ. And yet according to Bishop
Jer. Taylor (Tract on Repentance) less than such a Victory over Sin is delusion, and even Archbp Leighton asserts the necessity of the same Holiness, which the Redeemed have in Heaven, as the indispensable condition of our ever getting thither. Of Taylor's Book I have elsewhere avowed
my opinion, that it partakes of the worst characters of Romanism, and the
Salvation by Works—But Leighton was a Divine of a better School: and
concerning his judgement I would remark—that if he means by Holiness,
the Righteousness of Christ, what disciple of John and Paul would hesitate to receive it? But if by Holiness while yet in the perishable Body he
means such a strength already united with the "*I*", with the whole Man,
as to exclude all danger, so that Temptations no longer act as Temptations—then he seems to me to make the Cross of Christ, his Blood shed
for us, and the mediatorial efficacy of his perfected Righteousness of no
effect—and the Redemption from the Body for which Paul prayed with
such fervent groans and taught us to pray for, no *deliverance* at all, or a
deliverance only from a few incommodities which to a Soul fearing Sin
& feeling the root of weakness in himself, must appear almost nothing.
Therefore, tho' this be not the only instance in which the ascetic Spirit of
Thomas a Kempis joined with a platonizing View of the Beauty of Virtue

has somewhat tinged and refracted the Rays of the Faith, as it shines thro' the Preaching of St Paul—I am inclined to interpret this sentence of the Archbishop's by its immediate purpose (the rousing of *loose*-living Believers from the lethargy of a false Conscience) rather than as a universal proposition, to be received without limit or qualification. And doubtless, there is a great need of guarding the Believer against turning the Grace of God into wantonness—or imagining that we can be saved without such a hatred of Sin as will make the Soul deliberately prefer any loss of temporal and bodily pleasure or advantage to a return under its tyranny. I trust that I sincerely & with my whole spirit pray to God thro' Christ, that he will preserve me in that state in which the temptations are not greater than my strength—the state, in which the portion of Grace, which he has bestowed, shall be sufficient for me—tho' it should be a continuance in weakness and languor of body and an incapacity of all the enjoyments of this world. Yet it would follow from Jer. Taylor's doctrine, that this very Prayer, supposing me to die immediately after, would be a presumption, that I had perished! But no! never never can I receive a doctrine which forbids me to believe, that there is any thing to be forgiven and supplied by and thro' Christ to my Soul, or that I shall leave behind in the deliverance from the *Body of Death* aught, that I had not in fact & completion, and not only in firm principle & sincere desire, already been detached from! Extremes generate each other. The truth lies between the Judaizing Pelagian and the presumptuous Antinomian—hard to be expressed in *words*, that may not be misunderstood, but easily found by a Soul that seeks a Saviour, in humility, and prays earnestly for the Spirit which is already given to whoever asks in faith by Christ.—

It seems to me as sufficient answer to the scheme of J. Taylor, that Christ has instructed us to pray—Lead us not into *Temptation*, but *deliver* us from the Evil one.—

John Milton, *Poems upon Several Occasions,* ed. Thomas Warton, London, 1791.

This edition by an eminent poet and critic (Warton was the author of a three-volume history of English poetry, among other things) was the gift of a young associate of Coleridge's, John Watson; Coleridge in turn bequeathed it to Anne Gillman. His notes touch on such important issues as the function of criticism, the nature of poetic genius, and literary indebtedness.

"Young's Night-thoughts" is Edward Young's long and once popular reflective poem The Complaint: or, Night-Thoughts on Life, Death, and Immortality *(1742–46); "Maister Tummas," a jocular name for "Thomas" Warton; "North's Plutarch," Thomas North's translation of* Plutarch's Lives, *a well-known source for Shakespeare's* Antony and Cleopatra. *"Bowle ... etc" are critics who had written about Milton's sources: Warton quotes them and also includes notes written by William Warburton and Richard Hurd, signed "W." and "H." In the note about Hurd, #183, the illegible word beginning "T" might be "Turd"—if so, it would be in keeping with the pun on* merder, *a homonym for "murder," following. Several of Coleridge's notes were prompted by Warton's editorial comments upon Milton's* Lycidas, *a great pastoral elegy in the classical tradition of Theocritus and Virgil, to whom Coleridge also refers.*

[# 178] Of Criticism we may perhaps say, that those divine Poets, Homer, Eschylus & the two Compeers, Dante, Shakespear, Spencer, Milton, who deserve to have Critics, κριται, are placed above Criticism in the vulgar sense, and move in the Sphere of Religion, while those, who are not such, scarcely deserve Criticism, in any sense.—But speaking generally, it is far far better to distinguish Poetry into different Classes: & instead of *fault*-finding to say, this belongs to such or such a class—thus noting inferiority in the *sort* rather than censure in the particular poem or poet. We may *outgrow* certain *sorts* of poetry (Young's Night-thoughts, for instance) without arraigning their excellence *proprio genere* [in their own kind]. In short, the wise is the genial: and the genial Judgement is to distinguish accurately the character & characteristics of each poem, praising them according to their force & vivacity in their own kind—& to reserve Reprehension for such as have no *character*—tho' the wisest reprehension would be not to speak of them at all.

[# 179]

[Warton's note:] *Yet once more,* &c. The best poets imperceptibly adopt phrases and formularies from the writings of their contemporaries or immediate predecessours. An Elegy on the death of the celebrated Countess of Pembroke, Sir Philip Sydney's sister, begins thus:

Yet once againe, my Muse.—

This, no doubt, is true; but the application to particular instances is exceedingly suspicious. Why, in Heaven's name! might not "once more" have as well occurred to Milton as to Sidney? On similar subjects or oc-

casions some similar Thoughts *must* occur to different Persons, especially
if men of resembling Genius, quite independent of each other. The proof
of this, if proof were needed, may be found in the works of Contemporaries of different Countries in books published at the very *same time*,
where neither *could* have seen the work of the other—perhaps ignorant
of the language. I gave my Lectures on Shakespear two years before
Schlegel *began* his at Vienna—& I was myself startled at the close even
verbal Parallelisms.

[# 180]

> [Warton's note:] *Mellowing year.* Here is an inaccuracy of the poet. The *Mel-*
> *lowing year* could not affect the leaves of the laurel, the myrtle and the ivy;
> which last is characterised before as *never sere.*

If this is not finding fault for fault-finding sake, Maister Tummas! I do not
know what it is. The young and diffident poet tells us, that the Duty to his
Friend's Memory compels him to produce a poem before his poetic Genius had attained its full developement, or had received the due culture &
nourishment from Learning and Study. The faculties appertaining to Poetic Genius he symbolizes beautifully & appropriately by the Laurel, the
Myrtle and the Ivy—all three berry-bearing Plants: and these Berries express here the *actual* state, degree and quality of his poetic Powers, as the
Plants themselves express the potential—the Leaves of the Ivy are "never
sere", both because this is the general character of Ivy and of Verse, and
by a natural and graceful Prolepsis in reference to his own future productions—Now if Warton had THOUGHT instead of criticized, he must
have seen that it was the Berries which were to be plucked, but that in consequence of their unripeness & the toughness of the pedicles he was in
danger of *shattering* the Leaves in the attempt. It was the *Berries*, I repeat, that the more advanced Season was to have *mellowed*: & who indeed ever dreamt of *mellowing* a Leaf?! The Autumn may be said to mel-
low the *tints* of the Foliage; but the word is never applied to the Leaves
themselves.

[# 181]

> But, O the heavy change, now thou art gone,
> Now thou art gone, and never must return!
> Thee, Shepherd, thee the woods, and desert caves
> With wild thyme and the gadding vine o'ergrown,
> And all their echoes mourn:

> The willows, and the hazel copses green,
> Shall now no more be seen
> Fanning their joyous leaves to thy soft lays.

There is a delicate beauty of Sound produced by the floating or oscillation of Assonance and consonance, in the rhymes gone, return, caves o'er-grown, mourn, green/ seen, lays. Substitute flown for gone, in the first line: & if you have a Poet's Ear, you will feel what you have lost & understand what I mean. I am bound, however, to confess that in the five last lines of this Stanza I find more of the fondness of a classical Scholar for his favorite Classics than of the self-subsistency of a Poet destined to be himself a Classic—more of the Copyist of Theocritus & *his* Copyist, Virgil than of the free Imitator, who seizes with a strong hand whatever he wants or wishes for his own purpose and justifies the seizure by the improvement of the material or the superiority of the purpose, to which it is applied.

[# 182]

[Warton's note:] *Fill'd her,* &c. Mr. Bowle is of opinion, that this passage is formed from GOWER'S SONG in the Play of PERICLES PRINCE of TYRE. A. i. S. i. . . .

> This king unto him took a phear,
> Who died, and left a female heir
> So BUCKSOME, BLITHE, and full of face,
> As heav'n had lent her all his grace.

Perhaps, no more convincing proof can be given that the power of poetry is from a *Genius*, i.e. not included in the faculties of the human mind common to all men, than these so frequent "opinions," that this & that passage was formed from, or borrowed, or stolen &c from this or that other passage, found in some other poet or poem, three or 300 years elder. In the name of common sense, if Gower could write the lines without having seen Milton, why might not Milton have done so tho' Gower had never existed? That Mr Bowle, or Bishop Newton, or Mr Gray etc should be unable to imagine the origination of a fine thought, is no way strange; but that *Warton* should fall into the same dull cant—!!—

[# 183]

[Warton's note:]

> *Or sweetest Shakespeare, fancy's child*
> *Warble his native wood-notes wild.*

Milton 157

. . . Milton shews his judgement here, in celebrating Shakespeare's *Comedies*, rather than his Tragedies. For models of the latter, he refers us rightly, in his PENSEROSO, to the Grecian scene, v. 97. H.

be damn'd! *An Owl!*—

H = Hurd: T = T[. . .]

H. thou Right Reverend Aspirate! what had'st thou to do with sweetest Shakespeare? Was it not enough to *merder* [beshit] the Prophets? But to be serious—if by Tragedies Hurd means "Songs of the Goat", and if there were any pagans that had to make such, they would have to look to the Ancient Greeks for Models. But what Shakespear proposed to realize was—an Imitation of human Actions in connection with sentiments, passions, characters, incidents and events for the purpose of pleasurable emotion; so that whether this be shewn by Tears of Laughter or Tears of Tenderness, they shall still be Tears of Delight, and united with intellectual Complacency. Call such a Work a Drama: and then I will tell the whole Herd of Hurdite Critics, that the Dramas of Shakespear, whether the lighter or the loftier emotions preponderate, are all, this one no less than the other, MODELS with which it would be cruel & most unjust to the manes either of Eschylus, Sophocles & Euripides, or of Aristophanes, to compare the TRAGEDIES of the former or the Comedies of the latter. Shakespere produced Dramatic Poems, not Tragedies nor Comedies.—If the Greek Tragedies, in as H. affectedly expresses it, "The Greek Scene" be a Model for any modern, it must be for the Opera House.

[# 184]

[In a note on the line "From her cabin'd loop-hole peep," Warton refers at length to Milton's use of the "loop-holes" in the Indian fig-tree in *Paradise Lost* 9.1110:] Milton was a student in botany. He took his description of this multifarious tree from the account of it in Gerard's HERBALL, many of whose expressions he literally repeats. [Warton quotes extensively from Gerard and then from *Paradise Lost*.]

If I wished to display the charm and *effect* of metre & the *art* of poetry, independent of the Thoughts & Images—the superiority, in short, of *poematic* over *prose* Composition, the poetry or no-poetry being the same in both—I question, whether a more apt and convincing instance could be found, than in these exquisite lines of Milton's compared with the passage in Gerald, of which they are the organized Version.—Shakespeare's Cleopatra on the Cydnus compared with the original in North's Plutarch is another almost equally striking example.

[# 185]

> My sliding chariot stays,
> Thick set with agat, and the azurn sheen
> Of turkis blue, and emrald green,
> That in the channel strays. . . .

[Warton supplies a long note arguing that Drayton's *Polyolbion* was a source for the description of the chariot.]

L. 895. the word "strays" *needed* a Note—and therefore it is the only part of the sentence left unnoticed. First of all, Turquoises & Emeralds are not much addicted to *straying* any where; and the last place, I should look for them, would be in channels; and secondly, the verb is in the singular number & belongs to Sheen, i.e. Lustre, Shininess, as its nominative Case. It may therefore bear a question, whether Milton did mean the wandering flitting tints and hues of the Water, in my opinion a more poetical as well as much more appropriate Imagery/. He particularizes one precious stone, the Agate, which often occurs in brooks & rivulets, and leaves the *substance* of the other ornaments as he had of the chariot itself undetermined, and describes them by the effect on the eye/ thick set with agate and that transparent, or humid, Shine of (turquoise-like) Blue, and (emeraldine) Green that strays in the channel—For it is in the water immediately above the pebbly Bed of the Brook, that one seems to see these lovely glancing Water-tints.—N.B. This note in the best style of Warburtonian perverted ingenuity.

Henry More, *Theological Works*, London, 1708.

This was Gillman's copy, hence the long introductory note appealing for patient indulgence for an out-of-date and unfashionable but rewarding author. "Physiogony," meaning "the generation or production of nature," found its way into English by means of Coleridge and Green. "Intentional colors" are such as exist in and for the mind. Sir Matthew Hale, Joseph Glanville, and Richard Baxter are eminent and estimable men of the seventeenth century who shared the then common belief in witches.

[# 186] There are/—Three principal causes to which the imperfections and errors in the theological schemes and works of our elder Divines, the Glories of our Church, Men of almost unparalleled Learning, Genius, the rich and robust Intellects from the reign of Elizabeth to the death of

Charles the Second, may, I think, be reasonably attributed. And striking, unusually striking instances of all three abound in this Volume—& in the works of no other Divine are they more worthy of being regretted. For hence has arisen a depreciation of Dr Henry More's theological Writings, which yet contain more original, enlarged and elevating views of the Christian Dispensation, than I have met with in any other single Volume. For More had both the philosophic and the poetic Genius, supported by immense erudition. But unfortunately, the two did not amalgamate. It was not his good fortune to discover, as in the preceding Generation William Shakspear discovered, a mordaunt or common Base of both; and in which both, viz. the poetic and philosophic Power blended into one.—

These Causes are

1st and foremost, the want of that logical προπαιδεια docimastica [examination preparatory to learning], that Critique of the human intellect, which previous to the weighing and measuring of this or that begins by assaying the weights, measures, and scales themselves—that fulfilment of the heaven-descended, *Nosce teipsum* [Know thyself], in respect to the intellective part of Man, which was commenced in a sort of tentative *broad-cast* way by Lord Bacon in his Novum Organum, and brought to a systematic Completion by Immanuel KANT in his Critik der rein. Vernunft, der Urtheilskraft, & die Metaphysische Anfangsgrunde der Naturwissenschafts [*Critique of Pure Reason, Critique of Judgment,* and *Metaphysical Foundations of Natural Science*]. From the want of this searching Logic there is a perpetual confusion of the Subjective with the Objective, in the Arguments of our Divines, together with a childish or anile over-rating of Human Testimony, and an ignorance in the art of sifting it, which necessarily engendered Credulity.

2. The ignorance of Natural Science, their Physiography scant in fact and stuffed out with fables, their Physiology embrangled with an inapplicable Logic and a misgrowth of Entia Rationalia [Entities of Reason], i.e. substantiated Abstractions; and their Physiogony a Blank, or Dreams of Tradition & such "intentional Colors" as occupy space but cannot fill it. Yet if Christianity is to be the Religion of the World, if Christ be that Logos or Word that was in the beginning, by whom all things *became*; if it was the same Christ, who said, Let there be *Light*; who in and by the Creation commenced the great redemptive Process, the history of LIFE which begins in its detachment from Nature and is to end in its union with God—if this be true, so true must it be, that the Book of Nature and the Book of Revelation with the whole history of Man as the intermediate Link must be the integral & coherent Parts of one great Work. And the

conclusion is: that a Scheme of the Christian Faith which does not arise out of and shoot its beams downward into, the Scheme of Nature, but stands aloof, as an insulated After-thought, must be false or distorted in all its particulars. In confirmation of this position, I may challenge any opponent to adduce a single instance in which the now exploded falsities of physical Science, thro' all its revolutions from the Second to the 17th Century of the Christian Aera did not produce some corresponding warps in the theological systems and dogmas of the several periods.

III.—The third and last cause, and especially operative in the writings of this Author, is the presence and *regnancy* of the false and fantastic Philosophy yet shot thro' with refracted Light from the not yet risen but rising Truth, a Scheme of Physics and Physiology compounded of Cartesian Mechanics, Empiricism (for it was the credulous Childhood of Experimentalism) and a corrupt mystical theurgical Pseudo-platonism, which infected the rarest minds under the Stewart Dynasty/ The only not universal Belief in Witchcraft and Apparitions, and the vindication of such Monster follies by such Men, as Sir M. Hales, Glanville, Baxter, Henry More, and a host of others, are melancholy proofs of my position. Hence in the first Chapters of this Volume the most idle & fantastic Inventions of the Ancients are sought to be made credible by the most fantastic hypotheses and analogies. See PAGE 67., first half of.

To the man who has habitually contemplated Christianity as interesting all rational finite Beings, as the very "Spirit of Truth", the application of the Prophecies, as so many *Fortune-tellings*, and Soothsayings, to particular Events & Persons, must needs be felt as childish—faces seen in the Moon, or the sediments of a Tea-cup/ But reverse this—and a Pope, and a Buonaparte can never be wanting—the Mole-hill becomes an Andes.—On the other hand, there are few Writers, whose works could be so easily defecated as More's. Mere Omission would suffice—& perhaps one Half* (an unusually large proportion) would come forth from the Furnace, pure Gold.

* If but a 4th, how great a Gain!

Eternal Punishment Proved to Be Not Suffering, But Privation, London, 1817.

In one of the marginal notes not printed here, Coleridge identifies the anonymous author of this religious tract as "a Tinman of Hornsey"—Hornsey being a village near Highgate, where Coleridge lived.

[# 187]

> . . . the author . . . has, as he best could, introduced himself to those most distinguished for rank, for talents, for zeal, in the Christian Ministry—he has solicited the objections of those who most warmly preach the doctrine he opposes, and—his conviction has been strengthened; to the word and to the sanctuary then he appeals, thinking he cannot better do his duty than by studying God's word, as in His presence.

Alas! but a previous step was wanting—viz. the calm and dauntless tho' humble attempt to ascertain what God's Word is: and on what Grounds He receives the 57 Books bound up in one or two Volumes, and called the Bible, as the Word of God or even as Words dictated by God. This is confessedly no self-evident Proposition—Nay, in the present day and since Biblical Criticism has been raised into a distinct Study, the most Convinced and orthodox Inquirers, even those who retain the hypothesis of an especial inspiration of the sacred Penmen, confine this super human influence to the *Substance*, and reject as not only untenable but as dangerous, the notion of a verbal dictation or infusion. If then the purpose and the truths intended to be conveyed are alone attributable to the Infallible Spirit, by what rules is our Search to be directed? What are the Canons of Interpretation? When I find four Wordings all in Greek of the same Saying of our Lord spoken in his vernacular language, viz. the Aramaic or Syro-Chaldaic, one only of which *can* be, and neither of which may be, a literal translation—which am I to take? Or rather is it not evident, that no logical deductions can be drawn from this or that word or phrase in either?—What is to be done?—Plainly, this! From the whole of the two Testaments draw forth all the passages, that are compatible & susceptible of being arranged in connection of dependency—and then seek from the Spirit of Truth that insight into the great Scheme of Revelation which will enable the Man of Faith to determine what the words mean by a previous knowlege of what the Writers must have meant. Every Book worthy of being read at all must be read in and by the same Spirit, as that by which it was written. Who does not do this, reads a Dial by Moonshine.

P.S. It is but justice to admit, that this method the writer of this work has in the main adopted.

1824

William Wordsworth, "Translation of Virgil's *Aeneid* Book 1," in manuscript.

At Wordsworth's request, Coleridge wrote a set of comments on this draft translation in April 1824. In the reference to Alfoxden and Grasmere, he appeals to shared recollections of the early years of their friendship, 1797–1804. Wordsworth's later revisions show him responding to Coleridge's line-by-line criticism, but the translation did not proceed beyond Book 3 and was not published in Wordsworth's lifetime.

[# 188]

> He, feeling not, or scorning what was due
> To a Wife's tender love, Sichaeus slew;
> Rush'd on him unawares, and laid him low
> Before the Altar, with an impious blow.
> His arts conceal'd the crime, and gave vain scope
> In Dido's bosom to a trembling hope.

You have convinced me of the *necessary* injury which Language must sustain by rhyme translations of narrative poems of great length.—What would you have said at Allfoxden or in Grasmere Cottage to giving vain *scope* to *trembling* hopes *in* a bosom?—Were it only for this reason, that it would interfere with your claim to a Regenerator & jealous Guardian of our Language, I should dissuade the publication. For to *you* I dare not be insincere—tho' I conjecture, from some of your original Poems (of the more recent, I mean) that our tastes & judgements differ a shade or two more than formerly—& I am unfeignedly disposed to believe, that the long habits of minute discrimination have over-subtilized my perceptions. I have composed about 200 verses within the last 18 months—& from the dissatisfaction if they *could* be read in the most newspaper flat reading other than strongly distinguishable verse, I found them polished almost to *sensual* effeminacy. You must therefore take my opinions for what they are—

George Herbert, *The Temple*, London, 1674.

[# 189]

> To *Egypt* first she came, where they did prove
> Wonders of anger once, but now of love.
> The ten Commandments there did flourish more
> Then the ten bitter Plagues had done before.
> Holy *Macarius* and great *Anthony*
> Made *Pharoah Moses*, changing th' history.

The Church—say rather, the Churchmen—of England under the two first Stuarts, has been charged with a yearning after the Romish Fopperies & even the papistic Usurpations/ but we shall decide more Correctly as well as more charitably if for Romish & Papistic we substitute the *patristic* leaven./ Their error was (natural enough from their distinguished Learning, & knowlege of ecclesiastical Antiquities) an over-rating of the Church & of the Fathers, for the first 5 or even 6 Centuries = These Lines on the Egyptian Monks, "Holy Macarius and *great* Anthony" supply a striking instance & illustration of this.

[# 190] G. Herbert is a true Poet; but a Poet sui generis [in a class of his own]; the merits of whose Poems will never be felt without a sympathy with the mind and character of the Man. To appreciate this volume it is not enough that the Reader possesses a cultivated judgement, classical Taste or even poetic sensibility—unless he be likewise a CHRISTIAN, and both a zealous and an orthodox, both a devout and a *devotional*, Christian. But even this will not quite suffice. He must be an affectionate and dutiful Child of the Church, and from Habit, Conviction and a constitutional Predisposition to Ceremoniousness, in piety as in manners, find her Forms and Ordinances Aids of Religion, not sources of Formality. For Religion is the Element in which he lives, and the Region in which he moves—./

1825

Daniel Waterland, *A Vindication of Christ's Divinity*, Cambridge, 1719.

The notes in this copy appear to have been written for Green. Since the great work of Epicurus On Nature *exists in only a few fragments, the understanding of his philosophy depends to a large extent on the account of it in Lucretius's poem* On the Nature of Things. *One of the innovations of Epicurus was the idea of there being a slight swerve in every atom. "La Place" and "La Grand" stand for expert French opinion in favor of an ordered universe, the astronomer Pierre-Simon Laplace and (probably) the mathematician J. L. Lagrange.*

[# 191] In all religious and moral use of the word, God, taken absolutely— (i.e. not *a* God or *the* God, but God), a *relativity*, a *distinction* in kind ab aliquo quod non est Deus [from anything that is not God], is so *essentially* implied, that it is matter of perfect indifference, whether we assert World without God, or make God the World. The one is as truly Atheism as the other. In fact, for all moral and practical purposes they are the same position, differently expressed—whether I say, God is the World, or the World is God, the inevitable conclusion, the Sense and *import*, is—there is no other God than the World, i.e. There is no other *meaning* to the term, God. Whatever you may mean by, or choose to believe of the WORLD, that and that alone you mean by or believe of *God*.—Now, I very much question whether in any other sense Atheism, i.e. speculative Atheism, is possible—for even in the Lucretian coarsest & crudest scheme of the Epicurean Doctrine a hylozoism, a *potential* life, is clearly implied, and in the celebrated "lene Clinamen" [slight swerve] becoming Actual.— Bravadoes articulating breath into a blasphemy of Nonsense, to which they themselves attach no connected meaning, and the wickedness of which is alone intelligible, there may be but a La Place, a La Grand would & with justice, resent and repel the imputation of a belief in Chance, or a denial of Law, Order, and Self-balancing Life and Power in the World. Their error is, that they make them the proper, underived Attributes *of* the World.—It follows then, that Pantheism = Atheism and that there is no other Atheism actually existing or speculatively conceivable, but Pantheism/ Now I hold demonstrable, that a consistent Socinianism following its own consequences must come to Pantheism, and in ungodding their Saviour goddify Cats, and Dogs, Fleas and Frogs, &c &c. There is, there can be no medium between the Catholic Faith (Trinitarianism) and *Atheism* disguised in the self-contradictory term, *Pan*theism: for every thing God, and no God are identical positions.

Wilhelm Martin Leberecht De Wette, *Theodor [Theodore]*, Berlin, 1822.

Carl Aders, a wealthy German businessman living in London, became a friend of Coleridge's after hearing him lecture in 1811; this was one of his books.

The reference to Kant's "reason-religion" perhaps means specifically his book Religion within the Bounds of Reason Alone. *The complaint about Wieland and Goethe has to do with the effect on the public of Wieland's light erotic poetry and of Goethe's fiction, especially* Werther.

[# 192]

{A God who, in order to know Himself, enters creatively into the world, and who time and again destroys Himself and gives birth to Himself anew in eternal transformations, seemed to him more vital and more substantial than the purely abstract God that Kantian philosophy had taught him, but also less holy and more worldly. . . .}

I can never without indignation read these most groundless attacks on Kant's System: which I distinguish from Kant's own personal opinions respecting Prayer & Miracles. But his System is most friendly to the Christian Faith—were it only, that it proves the utter worthlessness of all the Grounds against its doctrines. There is nothing (says Kant) in right Reason *against* it—tho' Reason has no means of demonstrating its truth/ for this plain reason, that Religion is not *Science* but Faith! And all the other Constituents of our proper Humanity plead for it and demand it— Our Conscience, our Love of the Good, our Love of the Beautiful, Hope and Affection and Reverence of the Enduring, and yearnings after a satisfying Object and an ultimate end, tho' Experience had shewn us neither the one nor the other.—But these Assailants of this genuine Philosopher overlook the fact, that Kant's Ethics & Vernunft-Religion [reason-religion] are to the practical Divine what Mathematics are to the Architect.

[# 193]

> {Is not every one of these dances, he thought, be it a waltz, a minuet, a quadrille, or an ecossaise, an allegory of sexual love? . . . It cannot be a good thing if the youth of both sexes approach each other in this heightened sensual mood. . . .}

Against this reasoning I protest. In England at least, our young Ladies think as little of the Dances representing the moods and manoeuvres of Sexual Passion as of the Man-in-the-Moon's whiskers: & woe be to the Girl, who should so dance as to provoke such an interpretation. Es mag anders getanzt seyn in Teutchland [Perhaps they dance differently in Germany]. My recollections of Germany in 1799 incline me to fear, that it is so. But still this is beginning at the wrong end. Bring about a revolution in the Books that the Girls read, and the conversation they hear: and the Dancing will be as harmless as the Dancers. But while Wieland, and Goethe are idolized; and even religious & philosophical popular works abound in discussions and psychologico-moral disquisitions on the sexual relations; the Reformation of Walzing & Ballets would but effect a quaker-like suppression of the Symptoms, while the Distemper would prey inwardly on the vital parts of their moral Being.

[# 194]

> {"The poetic significance of laughter lies still deeper. It arises from a contradiction, an absurdity. In order to grasp an incongruity, there must be a rule to compare it with. Such a rule is none other than the ideal of human life, with which the appearance of the laughable is contrasted; and insofar as we laugh at that, this ideal comes darkly into the consciousness; we raise ourselves above the incongruity into the free realm of the ideal. . . ."}

Laughter is a physical phaenomenon: and must be physically explained. The contrast of an act or image with our Ideal of Humanity may be the accompaniment of Laughter in particular instances; but when we laugh at a sweet Infant's droll looks? Where is the contradiction here? It is the Law of Pleasure to pass into Pain, and this is especially the case where from the unimportant nature of the incident the nerves are unprepared & withdrawn from the control of the Will: and Laughter is the nascent Convulsion by which Nature breaks off the train of sensations before they

Eikon Basilike

Eikon Basilike 167

reach a painful state. Hence it is, that the suppression of Laughter is always painful, and sometimes even dangerous.

[# 195]

{. . . in Christ, the pure and perfect man. . . .}

This is a favorite phrase, a fashionable point of view, with the sentimental Theologians of Herder's and Schleiermacher's School. But I want to know, when they assert that in Jesus the Human Character was realized in ideal perfection, by what standard they measure & appreciate? Before *I* can form any judgement of a person's Character, I must ascertain who and what he is, his rank, circumstances, aims, objects. If I thought of Christ, as the English Unitarians think, my opinions would not be the same respecting his moral excellence, as they would be if I denied or questioned his possession of miraculous powers & privileges with sundry German Divines. Still more, nay, altogether different will my appreciation be, if I regard him as Luther & the Catholic Church generally believe—viz. as the incarnate Word, the co-eternal Son of God who became Man. What I could not help deeming presumption, and fanatical arrogance on the former supposition strikes me with grateful awe as the most astonishing humility on the latter. And similarly in other points of character—sincerity, fortitude & so forth—In short, this fine sentimental Complimenting of our Lord seems to me a part of that scheme, which I utterly dislike—that of making Christ & the Christian Religion a lump of soft Wax, to play with & try fancies on.—

Εικων Βασιλικη [Eikon Basilike]. The Portraicture of His Sacred Majestie in His Solitude and Sufferings, **London, 1649.**

Coleridge read Eikon Basilike *in 1825 in the context of renewed debate about its authorship. Wordsworth's brother Christopher had recently published a book supporting the attribution to Charles I. Although Coleridge had earlier been inclined to accept John Gauden's claim to authorship, and although he thought Wordsworth's arguments weak, he came round to Wordsworth's view in the end. Present-day authorities support Gauden.*

The earl of Clarendon's History of the Rebellion *and other writings are a major source for seventeenth-century history. Robert Saunderson's work was translated as* Seven Lectures Concerning the Obligation of Promissory Oathes, *allegedly with revisions by Charles himself.*

[**# 196**] It is well worth a Christian's meditation, what important events are apparently linked to accidents of Nature & bodily Constitution. Such was timidity on any sudden danger, want of presence of mind, in the Stuart Family. They could suffer nobly: i.e. they could *act* in accordance with a previous meditation, *or a making up of their mind* on the proposed subject—but not when the Call came unexpected.

Charles's misfortunes may be traced with great probability to the undue terror, with which the mobs & tumults of the Apprentices & Rabble had stricken him—and his frequent reverting to this subject in the Εικων Βασιλικη [*Eikon Basilike*] may be placed foremost among the numerous internal evidences of its Authenticity—altogether inexplicable on the hypothesis of the Scoundrel Gauden's being the Antony of this Caesar's Will.

P.S. Clarendon has noticed that neither James I nor Charles I could stand the force of an eye fixed on their eyes. It was so painful, that they hastily granted even impudent requests, to get rid of the fascination. Hence Charles's total want of a commanding influence on his Followers, even after victory—the more striking, that his deportment was grave & his Countenance majestic. Hence too we may derive the explanation of the proximate cause of his troubles—that which his enemies interpreted as *lying*—in other words, the unsatisfying nature of his first determinations to him, & their frequent inconsistency with his after-thoughts—which almost forced him to seek relief in Casuistry. Saunderson de juramentis was one of his favorite Books. Alas! poor man! had he been more great or less good, Cromwell would have been a New England Elder & he an admired Monarch—

Sir Walter Scott, *Novels and Tales*, Edinburgh, 1823.

Although Coleridge had read many of Scott's novels as they appeared from 1814 onward, the annotated copies belong to a set of twenty-five volumes, issued in three groups under slightly different titles, which he appears to have acquired in 1825 and which he lent out freely: in one of the notes below he calls it his "ever circulating Copy."

"Strap" is the faithful companion of the hero in Smollett's Roderick Random; *another point of comparison with the fiction of a past age is Richardson's* Clarissa. *"Most believing mind" is Coleridge's own line, from "Frost at Midnight," but he shows that he is aware of analogues in*

Collins (on Tasso) and Shenstone (quoted, on Spenser). Ariosto is cited for his Orlando Furioso, *a prototype for romance. Ariel is the airy spirit who serves Prospero in Shakespeare's* Tempest.

[# 197]

[In *Guy Mannering*, Arthur Mervyn argues that dueling is justified by the natural right of self-defense. That right is surrendered to civil society on condition of legal protection; but the law does not protect one's honor.] If any man chuses to rob Arthur Mervyn of the contents of his purse, if he has not means of defence, or the skill and courage to use them, the assizes at Lancaster or Carlisle will do him justice by tucking up the robber:—Yet who will say I am bound to wait for this justice, and submit to being plundered in the first instance, if I have the means and spirit to protect my own property? . . . I suppose little distinction can be drawn between defence of person and goods, and defence of reputation.

This plausible Defence of Duelling *intra certos* limites [*within certain limits*] wants but two points to be more than *plausible*. The first is, a determination of what are & ought be regarded, as assaults on honor & reputation/ If not enumerated, yet let them at least be predefined and described. At present, it is notorious that in nine cases of ten, the offence is determined by the irascibility & pruriency ad pugnam [for a fight] of the Person who takes the Offence—The second point is—Admit the innocence and necessity of sending or accepting a challenge on any occasion, how is a sober minded Man to be protected from your hot Candidates for duellistic fame, who may take any the most absurd pretence for *beginning* a dispute?—In short, the Law of Duelling exposes my *honor* to every Bully or Fool.

[# 198]

[In *The Heart of Midlothian*, Robertson begs Jeanie to perjure herself to save her innocent sister's life.] "It is not man I fear," said Jeanie, looking upward; "the God, whose name I must call on to witness the truth of what I say, he will know the falsehood."

"And he will know the motive," said the stranger, eagerly; "he will know that you are doing this—not for lucre of gain, but to save the life of the innocent, and prevent the commission of a worse crime than that which the law seeks to avenge."

This is admirably wrought up: and I confess with deep awe that there has been a time when this sophistry would have weighed with me in a similar instance, but God be praised! I was not exposed to the Temptation.

[# 199]

> [In *A Legend of Montrose*, Dugald Dalgetty proposes a toast.] "Gentlemen Cavaliers," he said, "I drink these healths, *primo*, both out of respect to this honourable and hospitable roof-tree, and, *secundo*, because I hold it not good to be preceese in such matters, *inter pocula* [between drinks]; but I protest, agreeable to the warrandice granted by this honourable lord, that it shall be free to me, notwithstanding my present complaisance, to take service with the Convenanters to-morrow, providing I shall be so minded."

If Sir W. S. could on any fair ground be compared with Shakespear, I should select the character of Dalgetty as best supporting the Claim. Brave, enterprizing, intrepid, brisk to act, stubborn in endurance: these qualities, virtues in a Soldier, grounded on *low principles*, but yet *principles*; *low*, indeed, but clear, intelligible, and of pre-calculable influence, in all Circumstances co-ercive; & unbent by accident. I exceedingly admire Captn Dalgetty.

Sir Walter Scott, *Historical Romances*, Edinburgh, 1824.

[# 200] [At the end of *Ivanhoe*.] I do not myself know how to account for it—but so the fact is, that tho' I have read and again and again turned to, sundry Chapters of Ivanhoe with an untired interest, I have never read the whole—the pain or the perplexity or whatever it was always outweighed the Curiosity. Perhaps, the foreseen Hopelessness of Rebecca—the comparatively feeble interest excited by Rowena, the from the beginning foreknown Bride of Ivanhoe/ perhaps, the unmixed atrocity of the Norman Nobles, & our utter indifference to the feuds of Norman and Saxon (N.b. what a contrast to our interest in the Cavaliers & Jacobites and the Puritans, Commonwealthmen & Covenanters from Charles I to the Revolution!)—these may, or may not have been the cause—but Ivanhoe I never have been able to summon fortitude to read thro'—Doubtless, the want of any one predominant interest aggravated by the want of any one continuous thread of Events is a grievous defect in a Novel.—These form the charm of Scott's Guy Mannering, which I am far from admiring the most but yet read with the greatest delight—spite of the *falsetto* of Meg Merrilies, and the absurdity of the tale. But it contains an amiable character, tho' a very commonplace & easily manufactured Compound, Dandy Dinmont—and in all Walter Scott's Novels I know of no other. Cuddy in Old Mortality is the nearest to it, and certainly much more of a *Character* than Dinmont. But Cuddy's consenting not to see and recognize his old Master at his selfish Wife's instance, is quite inconsistent with what is meant by a *good heart*. No wife could have influenced *Strap* to such an act.—I have no doubt, however, that this very absence of *Heart* is one & not the least operative, among the causes of Scott's unprecedented favor with the higher Classes—

[# 201]

> [In *The Monastery*, the supernatural figure of the White Lady of Avenel appears to Halbert Glendinning and transports him to a grotto deep in the earth.]

This Chapter might be chosen by a philosophical Critic to point out and exemplify the difference of Fancy and Imagination. Here is abundance of the former with the blankest absence of the latter. Hence the "Incredulus odi" [I disbelieve and detest] which it leaves on the mind—the imperious sense of the *Absurdity* of the arbitrary *fiction*.

[# 202]

> ". . . the best of our feelings, when indulged to excess, may give pain to others. There is but one in which we may indulge to the utmost limit of vehemence of which our bosom is capable, secure that excess cannot exist in the greatest intensity to which it can be excited—I mean the love of our Maker."

This is a point of aweful importance, which I cannot handle without trembling. But surely our highest possible Love of God must in some measure differ from our Love of a Child, a Sister, or a Friend, in as much as the Affection does not partake of a passion—is more purely an Act of the Will confirmed by the dictate of the Reason.

Sir Walter Scott, *Novels and Romances,* Edinburgh, 1825 [1824].

[# 203]

> [From the author's "Advertisement" to *The Pirate*:] The purpose of the following Narrative is to give a detailed and accurate account of certain remark-

able incidents which took place in the Orkney Islands, concerning which the more imperfect traditions and mutilated records of the country only tell us the following erroneous particulars. . . . [A pirate named Gow, having terrorized the district and been betrothed to a local girl, was eventually seized with his crew, brought to trial, and executed.] It is said, that the lady whose affections Gow had engaged, went up to London to see him before his death, and that arriving too late, she had the courage to request a sight of his body; and then touching the hand of the corpse, she formally resumed the troth-plight which she had bestowed. Without going through this ceremony, she could not, according to the superstition of the country, have escaped a visit from the ghost of her departed lover, in the event of her bestowing upon any living suitor the faith which she had plighted to the dead.

Surely, nothing more injudicious than this Advertisement can well be conceived, as the introduction to a tale which imitates the tones of an historical Memoir!—But this is one of the distinguishing Characters of Sir W. S.'s Novels—best explained, perhaps, as the contrary to the *"most believing mind"* which Collins so happily attributes to Spenser, who

> Wept as he wrote and did in tears indite.

Sir W. relates Ghost-stories, Prophecies, Presentiments, all praeter-supernaturally fulfilled; but is most anxious to let his Readers know, that he himself is far too enlightened not to be assured of the folly & falsehood of all, that he yet relates as *truth*, & for the purpose of exciting the interest and the emotions attached to the belief of their truth—and all this, not with the free life & most happy judgement of Ariosto, as a neutral tint or shooting Light; but soberly, to save his own (Sir Walter's) character as an enlightened man.—

If Sir W. thought it necessary by this previous assurance of the falsehood of all the pretended facts, characters & incidents to prevent the pathos & interest of his tale from overpassing the bounds of pleasurable excitement, I can only say that in this Novel at least it was a needless alarm/ & that generally Sir Walter's merit does not lie in this quarter.

[# 204] The absence of the higher beauties & excellencies of Style, Character, and Plot has done more for Sir W. Scott's European, yea, *plusquam*-europaean [*more than* European] popularity, than ever the abundance of them effected for any former writer.—His age is an Age of *Anxiety*—from the Crown to the Hovel, from the Cradle to the Coffin, all is an anxious straining to maintain life, or *appearances*—to *rise*, as the only condition of not falling. Interest?—A few Girls may crave purity & weep over Clarissa Harlow, & the Old Novellists!—For the Public at large, every man (for every man is now a Reader) has too much of it in his own needs, and embarrassments. He reads, as he smokes, takes snuff, swings on a chair, goes to a Concert, or a Pantomime, to be *amused*, and forget himself—When the desire is to be *a* musis [away from the Muses], how can it be gratified *apud* musas [in the company of the muses]?—

The great felicity of Sir W. S. is, that his own Intellect supplies the place of all intellect & all character in his Heroes & Heroines; & *representing* the intellect of his readers, supersedes all motive for its exertion, by never appearing *alien*, whether as above or below.

[# 205]

[In this chapter of *Peveril of the Peak*, the villain Edward Christian talks to his accomplice Zarah about past and present plots, and it is revealed that she is the supposedly dumb girl Fenella.]

A man so pre-eminent in literary & contemporary reputation, as Sir W. Scott, ought not to have transferred a character from Goëthe, at all; a Man, of such accredited frankness of temper, as Sir W. S. ought still less to have transferred it *without* a*cknowlegement*—and lastly, so worldly-wise a man, a man of, among Authors, such unexampled strong shrewd Good Sense, as Sir W. S.—ought least of all to have appropriated Goethe's *Mignon* from the Wilhelm Meister's Lehr Jahre [*Wilhelm Meister's Apprenticeship*], & thus have placed himself in rivalry with Goethe in, perhaps, the only point in which he had no possible chance of succeeding—i.e. in the Imaginative, as contra-distinguished from the Fanciful. Hence Goethe's Mignon, an embodied, and impassioned Ariel, the most exquisite of all Goethe's Conceptions, becomes that repulsive nondescript Grotesque of a mechanical Fancy-casuistry, the *incredulus odi* [I disbelieve and detest], absurd and yet disgusting Ἑρμαφροδιτης [Hermaphrodite], Fenelia—Of all Scott's literary Sins this is the grossest.

[# 206]

[The narrator of *Quentin Durward* explains some of the advantages of a brief spell abroad.] Whatever, in short, I spend here, is missed at home; and the few sous gained by the *garçon perruquier* [hairdresser], nay, the very crust I give to his little bare-bottomed, red-eyed poodle, are *autant de perdu* [so much lost] to my old friend the barber, and honest Trusty, the mastiff-dog in the yard. So that I have the happiness of knowing at every turn, that my absence is both missed and moaned by those who would care little were I in my coffin, were they sure of the custom of my executors.

For the sake of young Readers of this, my ever circulating Copy of Scott's Novels I feel it a duty to say, that this is written in a *bad* spirit. Why *should* the Butcher, the Barber, &c feel any deeper regard for a Customer, than as a Customer? Esteem and Love are due only for Esteem and Love. If my Butcher behaves civilly and serves me honestly, he has fully balanced my doings toward him, in chusing him for my Butcher, in the belief that I should be better served by him than by an other.

Friedrich Daniel Ernst Schleiermacher, *A Critical Essay on the Gospel of St. Luke*, trans. Connop Thirlwall, London, 1825.

Close study of Eichhorn and the latest German commentators put Coleridge in the vanguard of contemporary biblical scholarship. The most influential of his own contributions to debate about the interpretation of Scripture are in Aids to Reflection *(1825) and the posthumously published* Confessions of an Inquiring Spirit *(1840).*

The "Essay on Method" in Coleridge's periodical The Friend *attempted to analyze the difference between patterns of thinking in educated and uneducated persons. The way in which legend infiltrates history is illustrated by the classical and Old Testament cases of Plato and Elijah. The* kathos *in the "Preface" of Luke 1.1–2, where eyewitness accounts of the life of Christ are described as being recorded "even as [*kathos*] they delivered them unto us." Ignatius, Justin Martyr, and Tertullian, writing in and about the early years of the Church, give some indication of the character of its leaders then. "After the flesh" is a quotation from 2 Cor. 5.16; the instruction to "Go into all the world" is from Mark 16.15. Klopstock's* Messiah *is an epic poem in German (completed in 1773 and translated promptly into English) about Redemption, following the example of Milton in* Paradise Lost *and* Paradise Regained.

[# 207]

[From Thirlwall's extensive preface:] One of the most interesting and valuable contributions to this inquiry is the Essay by Dr. Gieseler, to which Schleiermacher alludes in his preface, *On the Origin and Early History of the Written*

Gospels. It first appeared in a periodical work, and was afterwards published separately with considerable enlargements and additions. Gieseler conceives the only common source of our three first Gospels to have been oral tradition.

If I am right (and I am persuaded, that I am) in my premise, that the first Discourses of the Apostles, whether held in the ordinary Synagogues or to Assemblages of Jews & Jewish Converts consisted mainly in the Collation of Passages from the Old Testament which the Jewish Church had before the Birth of Christ agreed to interpret of the Messiah, with the gradual addition of other passages, in which the Apostles themselves discovered this prophetic Bearing—the collation of these with the Acts and incidents of the Life of Christ, each with each, yet so that all converged and found a focal fulfilment in Jesus, Schleiermacher's theory of a multitude of detached unconnected Narratives must appear alike improbable and unnecessary. Indeed, the very notion of Jewish or other Converts so shortly after the Death of Christ undertaking, each on his own impulse and each taking a different road, set pedestrian tours thro' Palestine for the purpose of collecting Anecdotes of Christ, strikes me as so grossly arbitrary and improbable that I scarcely know which most to wonder at, (i.e. in a writer of Schl^{rs} Learning and Genius) the strangeness of the hypothesis itself, or the slightness of the Grounds, on which it is rested.—the occasional presence, to wit, and the *conjectured* Omission, of *apparent* introductory Sentences to the various *supposed* separate Collections! Could no other account be given of the sentences of this kind, that actually do exist in Luke's Gospel, it would be enough to reply—that such is the character of inartificial Narration. See the Essay on Method, Friend, Vol. III. But in the way, in which I believe the Materials of the three Gospels to have originated, it could not have been otherwise. On this supposition too, we can at once understand the tendency to *increase*, and the insertion or addition of Traditions grounded on Mystic Hymns, or suggested by other verses of the Prophets, or by Legends of other extraordinary Men. (*Speusippus's* Story of the miraculous Conception of his Uncle Plato, preserved by Origen, and Elijah's Fast of Forty Days, are cases in point.—) Hence would arise the necessity of revision, and Selection: and those would of course be preferred, which the Writers declared to have heard from an Apostle or Apostolic Man—. The one was *according* to Matthew; another according to Mark, the Companion of St Peter & supposed to have been himself one of the Seventy. This "according" appears to me the same with the καθως in the Preface or Dedication of Luke. On this theory there can be no reason to doubt that the third Gospel is *authentic*, in the proper sense of the word—i.e. revised by Luke—and of these *Revisions*, I doubt not, the first in time.—But here it behoves us to remember, that the Revisors of our Matthew and Mark may, on the strongest grounds of internal evidence, be referred to a later date than Luke—they were not improbably revised by the Bishops of Jerusalem, or some other of the earliest Jewish Churches (το κατα Μαρκον [*to kata Markon*, The [Gospel] according to Mark] perhaps, by a Bishop of Alexandria)—and then we ought to take our Ignatius (if *any* parts be genuine), Justin Martyr, and above all Tertullian in hand, in order to form a correct notion, what sort of men these Bishops were—fervent, pious, and holy Men but neither Critics nor Philosophers, accustomed too to value the *question* of Fact by its bearings on Doctrine. The analogy of Faith was the Test, on which the primitive Church relied—& compared with which Documents, Autographs, & the et cetera of Historical Research stood in small honor.—Lastly, this View, ὡς εμοίγε δοκεῖ [as it seems to me, at least], is capable of suggesting the motives that impelled the Evangelist John to compose a Gospel κατα πνευμα [according to the spirit]; not so much to correct Matthew, Mark, and Luke, as to counteract the carnalizing passion for biographical anecdotes of Jesus—And what if the acquaintance with a number of these απομνημονευματα [memoranda], and a perception of the undue importance attached to them, had given an additional emphasis to St Paul's resolve not to know Christ himself *after the Flesh*. We cannot, however, be too thankful to Providence, that the Revisions of Matthew and Mark are such as they are—with so much of inestimable Worth, and with so little dross. And both this, and the Confinement of the Choice to these, may fairly be attributed to the priority and known authenticity of Luke.

[# 208]

[Thirlwall continues summarizing Gieseler's arguments.] In the meanwhile the apostles at Jerusalem, previous to their separation and departure for the purpose of propagating Christianity in foreign lands, exercised themselves in rendering the original cyclus [from Aramaic] into Greek, the language in which it was probable that they would have the most frequent occasion to deliver it, and with which their acquaintance was so imperfect that they must have stood in need of mutual assistance. They were by this means enabled to deliver even in Greek one and the same Gospel with scarcely greater variations than are presented by different copies of the same manuscript.

On what authority that deserves the name of historical are these Apostolical missionary Travels founded? And how are they to be reconciled with Sᵗ Paul's peculiar Title, and Privilege, the Apostle of the Gentiles? If such was the understood Office, Duty, and Intention of the Apostles, of each and all, must it not appear strange, that not even an incidental allusion to any one of the Twelve, as thus employed, should have escaped from Sᵗ Luke in the Acts of the Apostles? The last 12 verses of Mark the Translator gives up, and with good reason, as spurious. And the longer I examine the text, Go into all the world, or Go unto all nations, the firmer is my conviction, that the Aramaic words used by our Lord himself signified no more than the rescinding of his former Command which had confined the preaching of the 70 to the children of Israel. Henceforward they were to offer the Gospel to men of all Nations, indifferently. I do not by this mean to refuse all credit to the tradition, that Mark was at Alexandria, and John at Ephesus: & we learn from Peter's Letter, that he was at Babylon (for I see no reason, why Babylon should mean Rome). In all these Cities there were Jewish Communities & Synagogues: & nothing can be more probable, than that numerous Converts were made during the annual Conflux of Jews from all parts of the Roman Empire to Jerusalem—and these on their return to their homes would naturally be solicitous to receive a visit from their Spiritual Fathers, for the ordering of their Churches & the confirmation of their Faith. But this admission goes but a small way toward the vindication of the historic claims of Cave's Lives of the Apostles.

[# 209]

> . . . I cannot conceive that our Gospels represent in a literal sense the public preaching of the apostles. In their private intercourse with one another and their most confidential scholars, the scenes they had witnessed and the speeches they had heard, as they undoubtedly formed their most delightful recollections, might also be frequently the theme of conversation. . . . And that to these communications we are indebted for some passages of our Gospels is not improbable; though when we consider how fully the time of the apostles was occupied . . . we shall not be disposed to expect many such instances, and still less to assign this as the origin of a collection embracing the whole public life of Jesus.

This confutation of Gieseler is sensibly and pleasingly written—but it consists almost entirely of ὡς ἐμοὶ δοκεῖ [as it seems to me] declarations of the writer's *Opinion*. *He* imagines that the Apostles' Discourses were chiefly polemical or docential [instructional], and seldom narrative. I with equal right imagine, that the narrative part of their Preaching would follow the first and simplest articles of faith. Nay, I cannot imagine or conceive, that any number of Converts could have met together, without desiring to hear from the Companions of their Lord something like a connected Relation of Events and Actions, of which some had seen one or two only, some had seen at a distance, and others not at all. But in fact I do not see, how the Apostles could prove that Jesus was the Christ promised and predicted by the Prophets without first quoting the prophetic passage, and then relating the event or miracle that had fulfilled it. Suppose this done (and done it must have been) successively to each of the preadmitted "Marks of the Messiah"—& suppose only that some one "ready Writer" among the Auditors had *taken notes*—and we have the Proto-evangelium, for which Eichhorn contends. Now that the Jews were in the habit of using tablets, on which they took down the aphorisms or pointed SENTIMENTS of their Rabbis, may be shewn from the Talmud, even if the very existence of such Books, as "Proverbs" and "Ecclesiasticus" did not supersede all other proof. It is to this custom, common both to the Jews and the Romans, that we may probably attribute the coincidence of the Gospels in the Speeches of our Lord.—Finally, this is not merely hypothetical. S.t Peter's Harangue (Acts of the Ap. C. II.) is an instance:—first, a Prophecy quoted—then a miracle appealed to as the fulfilment.

[# 210]

> Can it at all lessen the credibility of the two evangelists [Matthew and Luke], that each admitted into his history some passages not purely historical? Certainly not with a candid judge, who reflects, in the first place, that all this serves still only as a prelude to the proper subject of the history, which was the public life of Jesus. . . .

I cannot repress the indignation which the perusal of this and the two preceding pages has excited. Better, a thousand times better, reject the three Gospels altogether as the spurious patchwork of the II.nd Century—The worst, that could happen *then*, would be, the want of any certain & authentic History of "Christ according to the Flesh." We should have the Faith & Religion of Christians without knowing the particular incidents which accompanied the Revelation—further than the Creed and unvarying Tradition had preserved for us—a great Loss indeed, but not a mortal injury. But these Imaginations of Schleiermacher poison the very sources of the Christian Religion while he represents the Eye-witnesses, the chosen Apostles & Preachers of the Faith, the only competent Recorders of the Actions and Doctrines of Christ, as men capable of blend-

ing Facts & Fictions, without leaving any clue to the Labyrinth. I dare affirm, that it is impossible/. One or the other of three cases must be supposed. Either all is fiction; or all is fact; or the former is not apostolic.
Even in reading the Par. Reg. of Milton, and most oppressively in reading the Messiah of Klopstock, tho' both are avowed Poems, the juxta-
position and immediate neighborhood of what we know to be fictitious
with facts, incidents and discourses which we had received as truths with
a deeper and more passionate Faith, than mere History, even the most authentic, can inspire, shocks our moral sense as well as offends our Taste
& Judgement—and by the violence of the contrast gives to poetic fiction
the character & quality of a Lie. The more than historic faith in the one
prevents us from yielding even a poetic faith to the other. How impossible then must it appear, that the chosen Companions of our Lord, Eye-
witnesses of his wonderful Acts, many of which were worked for *their*
sake, and in order that they might deliver them to all Nations, could for a
moment endure to *hear*, much less themselves to *relate*, to *record*, known
falsehoods, or truths magnified & fantastically refracted into falsehoods,
in close connection with and under the immediate impression of actions
and events, that *lived* on their very eyes, and filled their souls with Love,
Joy, Reverence, affectionate Grief and Devoted Loyalty even to Death!

Samuel Pepys, *Memoirs*, ed. Richard, Lord Braybrooke, London, 1825.

This handsome edition, the first publication of selections from Pepys's
Diary, *included about a quarter of the work as we now know it. Cole-
ridge's notes take up the old debate about what constitutes a poet, including the commonplace weighing of the respective merits of Dryden
and Pope, applying it to contemporary life and the prospects of Lord
Byron ("the Baron") and Sir Walter Scott ("the Baronet"). Abraham
Cowley (1618–67) is remembered chiefly for English Pindaric odes. Scott
had recently published an obituary tribute to Byron's "mighty genius."
Panurge is the crafty and utterly disreputable companion of the hero in
Rabelais's* Pantagruel. *By "Pollard Man" Coleridge means a man cut off
at the top, as trees are pollarded.*

[# 211]

. . . and we had a good dinner of plain meat, and good company at our table:
among others my good Mr. Evelyn, with whom after dinner I stepped aside

and talked upon the present posture of our affairs; which is, that the Dutch are
known to be abroad with eighty sail of ships of war, and twenty fire-ships, and
the French come into the Channell with twenty sail of men-of-war, and five
fire-ships, while we have not a ship at sea to do them any hurt with, but are
calling in all we can, while our Embassadors are treating at Bredah . . . and all
this through the negligence of our Prince, who had power, if he would, to master all these with the money and men that he hath had the command of, and
may now have, if he would mind his business.

There were good grounds for the belief, that more & yet worse causes
than sensuality and sensual sloth, were working in the King's mind &
heart—viz. the readiness to have the French King *his* Master & the Dis-
poser of his kingdom's power, as the means of becoming himself the un-
controlled Master of its Wealth. He would fain be a Despot, even at the
cost of being Another's Underling. Charles IInd was willing, nay anxious,
to reduce his Crown and Kingdom under the domination of the Grand
Monarque, provided he himself might have the power to shear & poll his
Subjects without leave, and unchecked by the interference of, a Parliament. I look on him, as one of the moral Monsters of History.

[# 212] To initiate a young Student into the mystery of appreciating the
value of modern History, or the books that have hitherto passed for
such.—First, let him carefully peruse this Diary; and then, while it is
fresh in his mind, take up & read Hume's History of England, Reign of
Charles the 2nd. Even of Hume's Reign of Elizabeth, generally rated as
the best & fullest of the work, I dare assert, that to supply the Omissions
alone would form an Appendix occupying twice the space allotted by him
to the whole Reign—and the necessary rectifications of his Statements
half as much. What with omissions, and what with perversions, of the
most important incidents, added to the false portraiture of the Characters,
the work from the Reign of Henry VIIth is a mischevous Romance. But
alike as Historian and as Philosopher, Hume has, meo saltem judicio [in
my opinion, at least], been extravagantly overrated.—Mercy on the Age,
& the People, for whom Lock is profound, and Hume subtle.

[# 213]

To my bookseller's, and did buy Scott's Discourse of Witches; and do hear Mr.
Cowly mightily lamented (his death) by Dr. Ward, the Bishop of Winchester,
and Dr. Bates, who were standing there, as the best poet of our nation, and as
good a man.

!!—Yet Cowley *was* a Poet, which with all my unfeigned admiration of his vigorous sense, his agile logical wit, and his high excellencies of diction and metre, is more than (in the *strict* use of the term, Poet) I can conscientiously say of DRYDEN. Only if Pope was a *Poet*, as Lord Byron swears—then Dryden, I admit, was a very *great* Poet. W. Wordsworth calls Lord Byron the Mocking Bird of our parnassian Ornithology—but the Mocking bird, they say, has a very sweet song of his own native Notes proper to himself. Now I cannot say, I have ever heard any such in his Lordship's Volumes of Warbles; & spite of Sir W. Scott I dare predict, that in less than a century, the Baronet's & the Baron's *Poems* will lie on the same Shelf of Oblivion—Scott will be read and remembered as a Novelist and the Founder of a new race of Novels—& Byron not remembered at all except as a wicked Lord who from morbid & restless vanity pretended to be ten times more wicked than he was.

[# 214]

To church, and heard a good sermon of Mr. Gifford's at our church, upon "Seek ye first the kingdom of Heaven and its righteousness, and all things shall be added to you." A very excellent and persuasive, good and moral sermon. He shewed, like a wise man, that righteousness is a surer moral way of being rich, than sin and villany.

Highly characteristic. Pepys's only ground of morality was Prudence—a shrewd Understanding in the service of Self-love,—his Conscience. He was a *Pollard* Man—without the *Top* (i.e. the Reason, as the source of *Ideas*, or immediate yet not sensuous truths, having their evidence in themselves; and the Imagination, or idealizing Power, by symbols mediating between the Reason & the Understanding) but on this account more broadly and luxuriantly branching out from the upper Trunk. For the sobriety and stedfastness of a worldly Self-interest substitute inventive Fancy, Will-wantonness (stat pro ratione voluntas [Let will take the place of reason]), and a humorous sense of the emptiness & dream-likeness of human pursuits—and Pepys could have been the *Panurge* of the incomparable Rabelais.—Mem. It is incomprehensible to me, that this great and general Philosopher should have been a Frenchman, except on my hypothesis of a continued dilution of the Gothic Blood from the reign of Henry IVth, Des Cartes, Malbranche, Pascal and Moliere being the ultimi Gothorum [last of the Goths] the last in whom the Gothic predominated over the Celtic.

Heinrich Steffens, *Ueber die Idee der Universitäten [On the Idea of the University]*, Berlin, 1809.

[# 215]

{The smaller circle is, however, not without inner depth and marvelous significance. . . . Therefore let us not regard as inferior or less worthy the man whose disposition originally fettered him to a mean occupation.}

All this is like a man talking in his Sleep. Steffens should at least have told us that his advice is addrest exclusively to the comparatively Few, who can give their children an independent fortune. How can the poor Cobler's Son help his being "fettered to a mean occupation"?? And if a rich man's Son, as is often the case, betrays the dispositions of a Groom or a Pedlar, is he to be apprenticed to the latter, or sent to service as a Stable-boy? In China indeed, where all are educated in National Schools, and their after rank determined by their talents & tendencies—And yet, does the Scheme answer? Is China the Utopia realized?

[# 216]

{Do not let fear of the future trouble your views; for seeking self-knowledge, you may calmly leave that to God's power. Poverty, external pressure, slander of silly fools . . . must not disturb you in the least.}

What *wild*, DELIRIOUS advice! Has the young man no Mother, no younger Brothers, no attachment of Love? and if he is not to be a mere metaphysician, how without means is he to pursue his investigations?—*My* advice is widely different. The more powerful & evident your genius, I say, the more incumbent is it on you to fix on a Profession as a means of honorable Livelihood, but let this not be your ultimate Object, and either choose an occupation, that will with vigor & industry on your part allow you a portion of time for the Studies & Labors of your free choice—or else choose a profession in which you may make it a worthy ultimate end to *raise* the profession, and not merely to rise in it./

[# 217]

{If in the life of appearances, which exists however only in circumstances, we seek to establish a deceitful existence by adhering to these relations, then hate and wild, passionate desire are born which would destroy everything in a senseless battle against external restraint. If we try to attach any fictitious value to the appearing thought, which arises from circumstances, through foolishly sacrificing the world of ideas for it, then the hollow lie springs forth—representing clearly the invalidity of the futile ambition.}

I have so often teized myself with the question—*What* does Steffens mean? that I now begin to ask—*Whether* Steffens means any What?—i.e. has any meaning. I am sure, that I as little understand what he is driving at in this ¶ph, as if it had been written in Sanscrit.

[# 218]

{All true cognition coincides with existence, and sacred truth with a sacred world. . . . This world is not strange to us; it is rooted in the soul of each and it is only dreams of external relations that keep it distant from us.}

I would give a trifle to hear Steffens—N.B. *not* define: but exemplify what he means by *Verhältnisse* [relations]. I suspect, that he confounds Reality, *Somewhatness*, with immutable Being./ The relation between Hunger and a Beefsteak, in the act of dining is not a Geometrical Truth; but is it therefore *nichtig* [null]? And after all, what use is there in calling names? Why not rather admit a scale of intensities in Reality? Even a Dream is while it *is*—

Item: if Pain and Pleasure were not, if there were no sensation: *then* there might perhaps be some *Sense* in this Declamation of an alone real eternal World!

[# 219]

{Thus a holy model is given to us, the only-begotten son of God, Jesus Christ, to whom we pray. All nature celebrates the blessing; and all things are holy where the blessed life conquers death. Don't you know how the earth rejoiced when man was born in the image of God? Don't you hear the continuous jubilation of the air, the exultation of the sea, and the hymns from the depths of the earth down to her deepest roots? Yearly she celebrates the eternal festival of the holy blessing in the rhythmic motion of her changes. The rough times have passed; what was once hostile now enjoys an eternal embrace: the rigid stone is enlivened in mobile limbs; fluidity itself finds the desired form, running through veins; and the heavens ring with melodious song.}

Assuredly, the gorgeous Clouds of Sun-rise are a delightful heart-stirring Vision; but if I repeated all the rapturous expressions, which this Object was so well fitted to evoke, of a particular Mist that I beheld skimming the breast of Skiddaw or Helvellin, *the reason* would be required of me for asserting the identity of the latter with the former./—Therefore, I ask:

what does Steffens mean by the word, CHRIST? Does he mean Jesus, the Son of Mary, the Contemporary of Augustus & Tiberius?—If he does, he ought then to solve the perplexing fact, that all these superbiloquies [grand phrases] would have whatever correspondence they now have in the state of Nature & of Mankind, tho' Jesus had not been born.—Now I believe all this and more of our Lord; but I would have taken a very different way of expressing my faith—that is: I would have followed St John's example, and have called the Ens Supremum [Supreme Being], or the absolutely Real, the co-Eternal Offspring of the Absolute Cause of Reality, THE WORD relatively to the Eternal Mind, the Reason, the living self-subsistent Reason; relatively to the Absolute Will & as its only adequate Exponent—& then have shewn its incorporation in the visible World—and lastly, its incarnation or personal Humanization in the son of Man, *the* CHRIST.—And then my Readers would at least know what I was talking about; & not merely stare and wonder.

[# 220] Almost every where I recognize the Truths and the Aims that for the last 20 years have been my meat and drink; but over all there is a dreaminess, a vibrating Haze, that takes away or bedims the sense of *Reality*—. The whole stands in contrast with the coolness and distinctness of *Good Sense*—the coincidence & as it were, collapse with which marks the moment of the Birth, of the atmospheric and common Life, of *the Ideas*—Then and not till then have the Objective and Subjective interpenetrated—and the Idea without changing its mental character, by which it is the correspondent opposite of Law, yet becomes a Law of Mind—

Thus I cannot see that Steffens has in any way answered the objections, at the conclusion of his first lecture—He makes assertions indeed (p. 46). But the want of Instances, & illustrations, is the common defect of German metaphysicians.—Does England act a subordinate part to Germany? Is Germany the ruling Influence of Europe?—

Richard Hooker, *Works*, London, 1682.

One of Gillman's books. "Scotch Solomon" is James VI of Scotland and I of England; "the Stagyrite" is Aristotle. Coleridge mentions the "Essay on Method" again because he had discussed Hooker's definition of a "law" there.

[# 221]

> As there could be in Natural Bodies no motion of any thing, unless there were
> some first which moved all things, and continued Unmoveable; even so in Pol-
> itick Societies, there must be some unpunishable, or else no Men shall suffer
> punishment. . . .

It is most painful to connect the venerable, almost sacred, name of R.
HOOKER with such a specimen of puerile sophistry—scarce worthy of a
Court-Bishop's Trencher-chaplain in the slavering times of our Scotch
Solomon!—It is, however, of some value, some *interest* at least, as a striking example of the Confusion of an *Idea* with a *Conception*. Every Conception has its sole reality in its being referable to a Thing or Class of
Things, of which or of the common characters of which it is a *reflection*.
An Idea is a POWER (δυναμις νοερα [intellectual power]) that constitutes
its own Reality—and is, in order of Thought, necessarily antecedent to
the Things, in which it is, more or less adequately, realized—while a Conception is as necessarily posterior.

[# 222]

> All things that are, have some operation not violent or casual: Neither doth any
> thing ever begin to exercise the same, without some fore-conceived end for
> which it worketh. And the end which it worketh for, is not obtained, unless the
> Work be also fit to obtain it by; for unto every end, every operation will not
> serve. That which doth assign unto each thing the kind, that which doth mod-
> erate the force and power, that which doth appoint the form and measure of
> working, the same we term a *Law*.

See the Essay on Method, FRIEND, Vol. III.—Hooker's words literally and
grammatically interpreted seem to assert the Antecedence of *the Thing* to
its *kind,* i.e. essential characters; & to its force together with its *form* and
measure of working, i.e. to its specific and distinctive Characters—in
short, the words assert the pre-existence of the Thing to all its constituent
powers, qualities and properties. Now this is either—I. equivalent to the
assertion of a prima et nuda Materia [first and naked Matter], so happily
ridiculed by the Author of Hudibras, and which under any scheme of Cos-
mogony is a mere phantom, having its whole and sole substance in an im-
potent effort of the Imagination or sensuous Fancy; but which is utterly
precluded by the doctrine of Creation, which it in like manner nega-
tives.—Or, II.ndly the words assert a self-destroying Absurdity—viz. the

antecedence of a thing to itself—as if having asserted that Water *consisted* of Hydrogen = 77 and Oxygen = 23, I should talk of Water as existing before the creation of Hydrogen and Oxygen—All *Laws* indeed are constitutive; and it would require a longer train of argument than a note can contain, to shew what *a Thing* is; but this at least is quite certain that in the order of *thought* it must be posterior to the Law that constitutes it. But such in fact was Hooker's meaning, and the word, Thing, is used prolepticè [proleptically; by anticipation], in favor of the imagination—as appears from the sentences that follow, in which the Creative Idea is declared to be the Law of the things thereby created. A productive Idea, manifesting itself and its reality in the Product, is a Law: and when the Product is phaenomenal (i.e. an object of outward Senses) a Law of Nature. The Law is Res *noumenon* [*noumenal* Thing]; the Thing is *Res phaenomenon* [*phaenomenal* Thing]. A physical LAW, in the right sense of the term, is the *sufficient* Cause of the Appearances/ causa *subfaciens*—

P.S. What a deeply interesting Volume might be written on the symbolic import of the primary relations and dimensions of Space—Long, broad, deep or depth; superficies; upper, under or above and below; right, left, horizontal, perpendicular, oblique. And then the order of Causation, or that which gives intelligibility, and the reverse order of Effects or that which gives the conditions of actual *existence*. Without the higher the lower would want its intelligibility, without the lower the higher could not have *existed*. The Infant is a riddle of which the Man is the Solution; but the Man could not exist but with the Infant as its antecedent.—

[# 223]

> It is no improbable opinion therefore which the Arch-Philosopher was of, That as the chiefest person in every houshold, was alwayes as it were a King, so when numbers of housholds joyned themselves in Civil Societies together, Kings were the first kind of Governours amongst them.

There are and can be only two Schools of Philosophy/ differing in kind and in Source. Differences in degree and in accident may be many; but these constitute Schools kept by different Teachers with different degrees of Genius, Talent &c—Auditories of Philosophizers, not different Philosophies.—Schools of Philopsophy (the love of empty noise) of Psilology [mere or empty talk], and Misosophy [hatred of wisdom] are out of the question. Schools of Philosophy there are but two—best named by the Arch-philosopher of each—viz. Plato and Aristotle. Every man capable of philosophy at all (& there are not many such) is a *born* Platonist or a *born* Aristotelean. Hooker, as might have been anticipated from the epithet of Arch-philosopher applied to the Stagyrite *sensu monarchico* [in the monarchic sense], was of the latter family—a comprehensive, rich, vigorous, *discreet* and discretive, CONCEPTUALIST—but not an *Ideist.*—

[# 224]

> Of this point therefore we are to note, that sith Men naturally have no full and perfect power to command whole Politick Multitudes of Men; therefore utterly without our consent, we could in such sort be at no Mans commandment living. And to be commanded, we do consent, when that Society whereof we are part hath at any time before consented, without revoking the same after by the like Universal Agreement. Wherefore, as any Mans Deed past is good as long as himself continueth; so the Act of a Publick Society of Men done Five hundred years sithence, standeth as theirs, who presently are of the same Societies, because Corporations are Immortal; we were then alive in our Predecessors, and they in their Successors do live still. Laws therefore Humane of what kind soever, are available by consent.

No nobler or clearer example could be given of what an IDEA is, as contradistinguished from a Conception of the Understanding, correspondent to some Fact or Facts, quorum Notae communes con-capiuntur—the common characters of which are taken together under one distinct Exponent, hence named a Conception—and Conceptions are internal subjective Words. Reflect on an original Social Contract, as an *incident,* or historical *fact*: and its gross improbability, not to say impossibility, will stare you in the Face. But an ever originating Social Contract *is* an Idea, which exists and works continually and efficaciously in the Moral Being of every free Citizen, tho' in the greater number unconsciously or with a dim & confused Consciousness. And what A POWER it is!—As the vital power compared with the mechanic, as a Father compared with a Moulder in wax or clay, such is the Power of Ideas compared with the influence of Conceptions and Notions!—

[# 225]

> Laws therefore concerning these things are Supernatural, both in respect of the manner of delivering them, which is Divine; and also in regard of the things delivered, which are such as have not in Nature any cause from which they flow, but were by the voluntary appointment of God ordained, besides the course of Nature, to rectifie Natures obliquity withal.

That all these Cognitions, together with the feälty or faithfulness in the Will whereby the mind of the flesh is brought under captivity to the Mind of the Spirit (the Sensuous Understanding to the Reason), are super*natural*, I not only freely grant but fervently contend. But why the very perfection of Reason, viz. those Ideas, or Truth-powers in which both the spiritual Light and the spiritual Life of the Soul are co-inherent and *one*, should be called super*rational*, I do not see. For Reason is practical as well as theoretical.—Or even tho' I should exclude the practical Reason, and confine the term Reason to the highest *intellective* power—still I should think it more correct to describe the mysteries of Faith as plusquam-rationalia [rational more than other things, supremely rational] than *super-rational* [above reason, more than rational]. But the Assertions, that provoke this remark, arose for the greater part and still arise out of the confounding of the Reason with the Understanding. In Hooker and the great Divines of his age it was merely an occasional carelessness in the use of the Terms, using Reason when they meant the Understanding, and when from other parts of their writings it is evidently that they knew and asserted the distinction, nay the diversity, of the things themselves—to wit, that there was in Man another and higher Light, than that of "the faculty judging according to Sense", i.e. our Understandings. But alas! since the Revolution it has ceased to be a mere error of language, and in too many amounts to a denial of Reason!—

The Holy Bible, containing the Old and New Testaments, **Oxford, 1822.**

This was Anne Gillman's book, lent to Coleridge in the late 1820s when he undertook a systematic study of the Bible.

[# 226] To exhibit the difficulties of the first Historians, in the absence of paper, ink &c—then in the extreme separate—then to consider that the knowlege of *facts* for their own sake, or for mere purposes of exact chronology, & to present succession without vacua, is a refinement of modern times—In the ancient the Moral purpose was ever predominant/ and History differed from Poesy in the *materials* rather than in the *forms* of putting them together.—His Jewels were all precious Stones—i.e. *real* facts—not factitious diamonds &c—but in the *Setting* he was determined by the Object, he had in view—The object of the first Evangelist (as the Gospels now stand) was evidently to bring the facts into a striking reference to & connection with, the Sacred Books of the Hebrews—that of

Luke, to inform the Italian Converts of the Facts themselves, in order of place & hour, as far as he had been able to ascertain—that of Mark, to combine the two purposes—his Gospel being written, like that attributed to Matthew, to Jews; but not, as Matthew's, to Palestine Jews, already acquainted with the facts more or less perfectly, but to Jews settled in foreign Lands—chiefly, it is probable, to the Jews in Egypt, especially, Alexandria.—John's alone for the Church Universal of all ages.—Under this view only can the 4 Gospels be intelligently studied./

[# 227] I cannot read the two first Gospels without a deep & (I trust) grateful sense of the goodness and wisdom of the Divine Providence, in that we know nothing of our Lord's History, as a Man, beyond what is necessary or profitable for us in reference to his office, as our Redeemer & as the Object so the Founder of the Church—& that as to these few facts our conviction of their truth rests chiefly—I should say wholly—on the *internal* evidence, on the Moral *impossibility* that they could have been invented or even conceived by the Compilers of these Memorabilia! How would it tarnish and unedge the beauty and pathos of many, almost of all, our Lord's Sayings (Λογοι του Κυριου [Words of the Lord]), were we under the necessity of supposing, that they were all delivered at one preaching on the side of a Hill, as represented in the first Gospel!—But to suppose this or to hold it necessary so to believe (tho' the contrary is implied in Luke's Gospel) argues gross ignorance of the nature & laws of historical Composition in Ancient Times/. The *Substance* is *fact*; but the *form* is the Historian's work as an *Artist*—his choice being determined by the particular purpose for which, or the View, in which he presented the facts. An Ancient Historian was a Jeweller—enough that he passed no false or paste Drops for precious Stones.

[# 228] It would greatly facilitate the understanding of St Paul's Writings and of this Epistle [to the Romans] in particular, if only they were *printed* as the Apostle himself, were he now on earth, would have prepared them for the Press—viz. subjoining or annexed in the margin or at the bottom of the Page as *Notes* what are now interworded, rather than inwoven as member Parentheses. I have in writing more than once found occasion to make a note on a note, a † to a * and something like this not seldom occurs in the long parenthetic passages of the Apostles. These with other marks and effects of a full and fervent Intellect distinguishes St Paul's Proper Epistles from the highly-finished Circular *Charge,* apostolico [in the apostolic manner] the Epistle to the Ephesians και απο των παυλοειδων [and from the Paul-like] pastoral charges to Timothy and Titus.

1827

Georg August Goldfuss, *Handbuch der Zoologie*, Nuremberg, 1820.

Despite his objections to Goldfuss's use of the notion of polarity here, Coleridge found this central tenet of Naturphilosophie *valuable for his own formulations about the created universe. Unlike traditional binary systems,* Naturphilosophie *worked with a conceptual model having four (sometimes five) cardinal points—North, South, East, West (and Central). Coleridge called this scheme the"compass of nature"; part of its appeal lay in its resemblance to the ancient tetractys and pentad.*

[# 229]

{The last branchings-out of the pulmonary arteries and of the bronchial tubes, and with them blood and air, dissolve into the substance of the lung, so that a momentary state of indifference results; this state, however, is at once transformed into the polarities of pulmonary veins and arteries, into red and dark blood, and simultaneously forms lung-substance on the one side and carbonated air on the other.}

The last ramifications of the Pulmonary Arteries and of the Air-pipes (Luftröhre? Air-tubes? What are they? What we call cells?) and with them Blood and Air dissolve or decompose into the *Substance* of the Lungs—
(What can this mean?)
and thus a momentary *Indifference* takes place—
(Why? how does this follow?)
The whole ¶ph is unintelligible to me—and I cannot help doubting whether Golden-foot [i.e. Goldfuss] attached any distinct conception to the term, Indifference.

Likewise I complain of the *Jack of all trades* use of the term, polarisch—. Where is the proof that red and dark-colored Blood are the polar opposites? What is the Identity, of which they are the Poles? Air and Air-vessels, Blood and Blood-vessels dissolved into the Substance of the Lungs?—But this Quartette are the Indifference—And Indifference supposes an Identity, no less than the Thesis and Antithesis

190

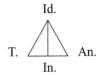

Polarisch [polarly]? Carbonated & decarbonated Blood! As well might you call Curds and Curds & Cream polarisch gestaltet [polarly patterned].

Samuel Noble, *An Appeal in Behalf of the Views of the Eternal World and State*, London, 1826.

Noble was writing to defend the Swedenborgians and particularly the "New Church" or "New Jerusalem Church" (in which he was a minister) against recent attacks. Captain Parry was commanding officer of one of the ships involved in an Arctic expedition led by John Ross in 1818. Their reports of red snow occasioned considerable scientific excitement and speculation; the color has since been attributed to algae. The "Vision of Mirza" and "Tablet" or "Picture of Cebes" were well-known allegories of human life.

[# 230]

[Footnote, quoting from an earlier address of Noble's:] "Some, probably, will say, 'What argument can induce us to believe a man in a concern of this nature who gives no visible credentials to his authority? . . .' But let us ask in return, Is it worthy of a being wearing the figure of a man to require such proofs as these to determine his judgment? Are we not endowed with rationality? . . . The beasts act from the impulse of their bodily senses, but are utterly incapable of seeing from reason why they should so act: and it might easily be shewn, that while a man thinks and acts under the influence of a miracle, he is as much incapable of perceiving from any rational ground why he should thus think and act, as a beast is.

"'What!' our opponents will perhaps reply . . . 'was it not by miracles that the prophets . . . testified their authority? Do you not believe these facts?'— Yes, my friends, I do most entirely believe them. . . ."

There is so much of Truth in all this Reasoning on Miracles that I feel pain in the thought that the *result* is false—because it was not the *whole* truth. But this is the *grounding* & at the same time *pervading* error of the

Swedenborgians—that they overlook the distinction between congruity with reason, truth of consistency, or internal possibility of this or that being *objectively* real, and the objective reality as fact. Miracles, quoad Miracles, can never supply the place of *subjective* evidence, i.e. of insight. But neither can subjective Insight supply the place of Objective Sight. The certainty of the truth of a mathematical Arch can never prove the *fact* of its *ex*istence.

P.S. I anticipate the answers; but know that they likewise proceed from the want of distinguishing between *Ideas*, such as, God, Eternity, the responsible Will, the Good, &c, whose actuality is *absolutely* subjective, & includes both the relatively subjective & the relatively objective as higher or transcendent Realities, which alone are the proper objects of FAITH, the great *Postulates* of Reason in order to its own admission of its own Being—the not distinguishing, I say, between these, and those positions which must be either matters of *fact* or fictions. For *such* positions it is that miracles are required in lieu of experience—i.e. A's testimony of Experience supplies the want of the same Experience for B. C. D &c. Ex. gr. how many thousands believe the existence of red snow on the testimony of Captn Parry.—But who can expect more than *Hints* in a marginal note?—

[# 231] I have often thought of writing a work, to be entitled, Vindiciae Heterodoxae, sive Celebrium Virorum παραδογματιζόντων Vindicatio —i.e. Vindication of great men unjustly branded—and at such times the 4 names prominent to my mind's Eye have been Giordano Bruno, Jacob Behmen, Benedict Spinoza and Emanuel Swedenborg. Of the last-mentioned especially nothing can be more unfair or more unthinking than the Language which our justly celebrated Poet, Historian and Critic, Robert Southey has permitted himself to use.

Grant, that the Origin of the Swedenborgian Theology is a Problem. Yet on whichever of the three possible Hypotheses (possible, I mean, for Gentlemen, Scholars and Christians) it may be solved—namely, 1. Swedenborg's own Assertion and constant Belief in the hypothesis of a supernatural Illumination: or 2. That the great and excellent Man was led into this belief by becoming the Subject of a very rare but not (it is said) altogether *unique*, conjunction of the somniative faculty (by which the products of the Understanding, viz. Words, Conceptions, &c are rendered instantaneously into forms of Sense) with the voluntary and other powers of the waking state: or 3. the modest suggestion, that the first and second may not be so incompatible as they appear—still it ought never to be forgotten that the merit and value of Swedenborg's System do only in a very secondary degree depend on either of the three.—For even tho' the first were adopted, the Conviction and Conversion of such a Believer must, according to a fundamental principle of the "NEW Church", have been wrought by an Insight into the intrinsic Truth and Goodness of the Doctrines, severally and collectively, and their entire Consonance with the Light of the Eternal and of the Written Word—i.e. with the Scriptures and with the sciential and the practical Reason.—Or say, that the second hypothesis were preferred, and that by some hitherto unexplained affection of Swedenborg's Brain and nervous System he from the year 1743 thought and reasoned thro' the medium and instrumentality of a series of appropriate and symbolic visual and auditual Images spontaneously rising before him, and these so clear and so distinct as at length to overpower perhaps his first suspicions of their *subjective* nature and to become *objective* for him—i.e. in *his own* belief of their kind and origin—still the Thoughts, the Reasonings, the Grounds, the Deductions, the Facts illustrative or in proof, and the Conclusions, remain the same! and the Reader might derive the same benefit from them as from the sublime and impressive truths conveyed in the Vision of Mirza or the Tablet of Cebes.— So much even from a very partial acquaintance with the works of Swedenborg I can venture to assert—that as a *moralist*, Swedenborg is above all praise; and that as a Naturalist, Psychologist, and Theologian he has strong and varied claims on the gratitude and admiration of the professional and philosophical Faculties.—

S. T. Coleridge
April 1827.
Grove, Highgate.

P.S. Notwithstanding all, that Mʳ Noble says in justification of his arrangement, it is greatly to be regretted that the Contents of this work are so confusedly tossed together. It is, however, a work of great merit.

Manuel Lacunza y Diaz, *The Coming of Messiah in Glory and Majesty*, trans. Edward Irving, London, 1827.

Coleridge's connection with Edward Irving, the translator and donor of this book, was becoming an embarrassment. A charismatic preacher and a great success when he first came to London from Scotland in 1822, Irving took Coleridge as his mentor and dedicated his first volume of "orations" to him in 1825. Coleridge reciprocated by praising his friend's

Luther-like reforming spirit in Aids to Reflection. *But Irving developed millenarian views, as this translation demonstrates, and Coleridge came to think he had gone too far in his desire to revive the spirit of the apostolic age.*

[# 232]

Christ the WORD.

The Scriptures—The Spirit—The Church.

The Preacher.

Such seemeth to me to be the scheme of the Faith in Christ. The written Word, the Spirit and the Church, are co-ordinate, the indispensable conditions and the working causes of the perpetuity and continued renascence and spiritual life of Christ still militant. The Eternal Word, Christ from everlasting, is the *prothesis* or identity;—the Scriptures and the Church are the two poles, or the *thesis* and *antithesis*; the Preacher in direct line under the Spirit, but likewise the point of junction of the written Word and the Church, being the *synthesis*. And here is another proof of a principle elsewhere by me asserted and exemplified, that divine truths are ever a *tetractys*, or a triad equal to a *tetractys*: $4 = 1$ or $3 = 4 = 1$. But the entire scheme is a pentad—God's hand in the world.

[# 233]

> Now, of these three, the office of Christ as our prophet is the means used by the Holy Spirit for working the redemption of the understanding of man; that faculty by which we acquire the knowledge on which proceed both our inward principles of conduct and our outward acts of power.

I cannot forbear expressing my regret that Mr. Irving has not adhered to the clear and distinct exposition of the understanding, *genere et gradu* [in kind and in degree], given in the Aids to Reflection. What can be plainer than to say: the understanding is the medial faculty or faculty of means, as reason on the other hand is the source of ideas or ultimate ends. By reason we determine the ultimate end: by the understanding we are enabled to select and adapt the appropriate means for the attainment of, or approximation to, this end, according to circumstances. But an ultimate end must of necessity be an idea, that is, that which is not representable by the sense, and has no entire correspondent in nature, or the world of the senses. For in nature there can be neither a first nor a last:—all that we can see, smell, taste, touch, are means, and only in a qualified sense, and by the defect of our language, entitled ends. They are only relatively ends in a chain of motives. B. is the end to A.; but it is itself a mean to C., and in like manner C. is a mean to D., and so on. Thus words are the means by which we reduce appearances, or things presented through the senses, to their several kinds, or *genera*; that is, we generalize, and thus think and judge. Hence the understanding, considered specially as an intellective power, is the source and faculty of words;—and on this account the understanding is justly defined, both by Archbishop Leighton, and by Immanuel Kant, the faculty that judges by, or according to, sense. However, practical or intellectual, it is one and the same understanding, and the definition, the medial faculty, expresses its true character in both directions alike. I am urgent on this point, because on the right conception of the same, namely, that understanding and sense (to which the sensibility supplies the material of outness, *materiam objectivam* [objective material],) constitute the natural mind of man, depends the comprehension of St. Paul's whole theological system. And this natural mind, which is named the mind of the flesh, φρόνημα σαρκός, as likewise φυσικὴ σύνεσις [natural intelligence], the intellectual power of the living or animal soul, St. Paul everywhere contradistinguishes from the spirit, that is, the power resulting from the union and co-inherence of the will and the reason;—and this spirit both the Christian and elder Jewish Church named, *sophia*, or wisdom.

[# 234]

> This which I read with my eyes, I said, taking into my hand the holy Bible, is certain, and of faith divine. GOD himself is he who speaketh herein. That which I read in other books, be they what they may, is neither of faith, nor can be. Because, verily, in them speaketh man, not God. Because, verily, some say to me one thing and some another. Why, in fine? Because, verily, they tell me things very wide, very foreign, and sometimes very adverse from that which is clearly and expressly told me in the holy Bible. Finding then between God and man, between God who speaks, and man who interprets, a great difference and even contradiction, to which of the two should I give credit? To man, and cease from God: or to God, and cease from man?

Language of this sort has been repeated by one good man after another so long that there must be one would think something in it. And yet what sad trifling it does seem *to me* to be! After all the *interpretation* of the

Scripture is that which passes into the mind, & is the proximate immediate object of our apprehension & consequently of our belief. But when
we *read* an interpretation given by another, say Lightfoot, Hammond, or
Cocceius under the name of a Comment we exclaim with J. J. Ben Ezra
alias Emanuel Lacunza, this is but a man that speaketh. But when we take
our own interpretation silently & without any visual or individual separation of the words from the Scriptures, words before our eyes.—O then
it *is* Scripture itself, the very utterance of the Holy Spirit; & it is God who
speaketh, tho' it is only Tim Titling in the one case & Jack Robinson in
the other—in the one all *my* eye, in the other it is another man's eyes &
we prefer the former to the latter & find an excuse for it perhaps in the
very circumstance that they had a learned Spectacles between them & the
printed text. Tis I says the fly with my little eye that *rightly* do spy!—
When then is the criterion? I know but one way, first to determine the true
character and purpose of the Sacred Scriptures collectively, & then to
draw up a code of canons of Interpretation *a priori* as abstracted from our
reading-experience collectively & established each canon by its evident
reasonableness & applying these with due consideration of the distinctive
character of the Sacred Book which is to be interpreted to abide by the
result. To conclude, It does not become me to use the minatory language,
in which my reverend Friend, as an ordained Minister of Christ, warns his
degenerate fellow servants, but I will dare make known the impression on
my mind, that the Wounds (If I may thus express my friends sense of the
dissent of his hearers from *his* view of the personal coming of the Son
of Man) will not granulate healthily or be closed smoothly, till he has
sloughed his diableries, & other like dead proud flesh of the popular
Mumpsimus from the living texture of his Theology. In plain English—
all parts of his belief must be homogeneous, either the very letter throughout, in the principle of plenary *dictation* of an Infallible informer—or the
letter every where subordinate to the *Spirit*, i.e. to the known general purpose of the Writer, with distinction of manifest argumenta ad hominem
[arguments directed against the person]; of sentences *in ordine* [in due
order] from those that contain the writers final object &c. the Supernatural light shining thro' the Human flesh-panes, but not removing the
waving lines or even every tiny speck, knot, or bulb of temporary &
individual

[# 235] I would not give a groat for a man, whose Heart does not sometimes betray his Judgement. The honest delight of finding a cöincidence
of Sentiment on a subject of grave concern to all and of keenest interest

to himself, in a quarter where it was least expected—this delight, characteristic of noble minds, whose passionate Love of Truth soars above all petty pride of original discovery, prevented my fervent Friend from *feeling* and a fortiori from seeing the prolixity και φυλλομανιαν [and running wildly to leaf] of the worthy Jesuit [Lacunza]. While embracing a powerful Coadjutor where he might rather have been prepared to meet the charge of a bigotted Adversary, there was no room in Mr Irving's Soul for Criticism.—Still however for the advantage of the Public it is matter of regret, that Lacunza's work had not been pruned down into a single Volume. To every fresh subject, almost to every Objection and to every Reply thereto, Lacunza has a garrulous* introductory ¶ph, not seldom a Chapter.—I hope, however, that Mr Irving will take muster of all his grounds, arguments and evidences, and reduce them to a systematic logical form— & thus supply the Religious Public with a check and circulable Synopsis of this great Pleading.

     * Nevertheless, a sound Logician and for a Theologian a remarkably clear-headed Man.

Gotthilf Heinrich von Schubert, *Allgemeine Naturgeschichte [General History of Nature]*, Erlangen, 1826.

This book was borrowed from Green. The "Microphone" to which Coleridge refers was an invention announced in 1827 not by Michael Faraday personally but by the journal of the Royal Institution where he worked at that time as director of the laboratory. (This device might now be called a hearing aid; the microphone as we know it was introduced in 1878.) "The walls of Jericho" is an allusion to Josh. 6.20.

[# 236] Next to that, to which there is no Near, the γυιλτ [guilt] and the avenging Daemon of my Life, I must place the neglect of Mathematics under the strongest motives, and the most favorable helps and opportunities for acquiring them. Not a week passes in which I do not regret this Oversight of my Youth with a sort of remorse that turns it to a Sin.—This day I read the account of Faraday's Microphone—& instantly recognized a fond and earnest dream-project of my own, of 30 years' standing—with sundry other imaginations respecting what might be effected in the only embryo Science of Acoustics. The Walls of Jericho were to fall before my Wartrumpets. But where were the *Hands*, where the Tools, of my Reason? I had not the *Organ* of all Science that respects Space and Quantity. My

Dreams were akin to Reason: but I could not awake out of my prophetic
Sleep, to effectuate their objectivization—for I was ignorant of the Mathematics!—

Jacob Rhenferd, *Opera philologica [Philological Works]*, Utrecht, 1722.

[# 237]

> [Rhenferd emends and interprets the two baptismal formulas of the Mar-
> cosians and the Heracleonites; in the teaching about redemption and the for-
> mulas in which it is expressed, he finds parallels between Jews, Christians, and
> these so-called heretics.]

Assuredly, it must to a candid mind appear a strong Presumption in favor
of a Scheme of Faith, that its principal articles are found in so many forms,
in so many different countries and ages—that a succession of Individuals, in many instances without knowlege of each other, should arrive at
the same truths, yet expressed in the greatest variety of terms and symbols, according to the presence or absence of a learned education, to the
different climates, different *positive* Religions &c of the individual Writers—a decisive proof, that they did not learn them by rote, in a line of
succession from a common source, but must have found them in themselves. In fact, no man *could* learn them from a Book who had not previously discovered the clue in himself: for in this system the first Idea contains the whole, and generates the Second. The second generates the third,
and by reflected Ray, lumine retrorso [by the light directed backward],
manifests the first—and so on thro' the whole descent and expansion. In
my own instance, I solemnly bear witness and declare that every Idea,
Law, or Principle, in which I coincide with the Cabbala, or the School of
Plotinus, or the Christian Gnostics, or the Mystics of the middle Ages
from Hugo de Sancto Victore to Tauler, or the Protestant Masters of the
interior way, as Behmen, Zinzendorf &c, I *recognized* in them, as truths
already known by me in my own meditation. Indeed, the language of the
greater number of the Mystics, from causes explained in my "Biog. Literaria", is so inadequate and arbitrary, & the Writers themselves are so
imperfectly Masters of the Ideas; (possessed by fragments of the Truth
rather than possessing even these) that it would have been impossible to
have decyphered the true import of their Strivings, without the hounding
Scent of Sympathy and without the Key of a previous and superior Insight.

Claude Fleury, *Ecclesiastical History*, trans. H. Herbert and G. Adams, London, 1727–28.

[# 238]

PAPIAS . . . taught, that after the resurrection of the dead, JESUS CHRIST would reign in the body, upon earth, for the space of a thousand years.

I am perfectly convinced that the Apocalypse does not sanction the fiction of the Millennium/ tho' it makes use of it, as of other Jewish Cabbalas, *symbolically,* in order to destroy the carnal hope by substituting the truth—i.e. the establishment of Christianity as the Religion of the Roman Empire for an *indefinitely long time*—i.e. in the symbolical language of the Jews, a thousand years—

[# 239]

[Origen's instruction of his disciples:] Having thus prepared and excited them to instruct themselves by a chain of agreeable discourse which they could not resist, he began to give them more solid instructions in true Philosophy, first in Logick. . . . He afterwards made them apply themselves to physics. . . . He besides taught them the Mathematicks, particularly Geometry and Astronomy, and last of all Ethicks. . . . After they had gone through their studies, he led them to Theology. . . . He made them read all the writings of the ancients, whether Poets or Philosophers, *Greeks* or *Barbarians*, excepting those only which professedly taught Atheism. . . . At last he explained the holy Scriptures to them, of which he was the most skilful instructor of his time.

A noble scheme of Education. 1. Belles Lettres. 2. Logic & Mathematics. 3. Natural History and Astronomy. 4. Ethics & Psychology. 5. Theology. 6. The whole exemplified, applied, & turned to their true ends & profit in the study and interpretation of the Scriptures—and an Origen for the Tutor!

Joannes Scotus Erigena, *De divisione naturae* *[On the Division of Nature]*, ed. Thomas Gale, Oxford, 1681.

[# 240]

{And again [Maximus makes clear] what is the nature of the return of this divine goodness, that is, that it is the gathering together, through the same stages, from the infinite and varied multiplicity of the things that exist to the most simple unity of all, which is in God and is God; so that while God is all things, yet all things are God.}

How is it to be explained that J. Erigena with so many other Christian Divines and Philosophers should not have perceived, that pious words and scriptural phrases may disguise but can not transsubstantiate Pantheism—a handsome Mask that does not alter a single feature of the ugly Face, it hides?—How is it to be explained that so comprehensive and subtle an Intellect, as Scotus Erigena, should not have seen, that his "Deus omnia et omnia Deus" [God is all things, and all things are God] was incompatible with moral responsibility, and subverted all essential difference of Good and Evil, Right and Wrong?—I can suggest no other solution, but the Innocence of his Heart and the Purity of his Life—for the same reason, that so many young men in the unresisted buoyance of their Freedom embrace without scruple the doctrine of Necessity, and only at a later and less genial Period learn, and learn to value, their free-agency by its struggles to maintain itself against the increasing incroachments of Nature and Society. It is a great Mercy of God that a good Heart is often so effective an antidote to the heresies of the Head. I could name more than one learned, godly and religious Clergyman, who is a Pantheist thro' his Zeal for the TRINITY—without suspecting what nevertheless is demonstrably true, that Pantheism is but a painted Atheism and that the Doctrine of the Trinity is the great and only sure Bulwark against it. But these good men take up the venomous thing, and it hurteth them not.

[# 241] The whole tremendous difficulty of a Creation e nihilo [from nothing]—and if ex aliquo [from something], how could it be Creation?—and not in all propriety of language—Formation or Construction?—this difficulty, I say, which appeared so gigantic to our Milton that he asserted the eternity of matter to escape from it, and then to get rid of the offensive consequences reduces this matter to an Attribute of God, and plunges head over heels into Spinosism—this difficulty, I repeat for the third time (the sad necessity of all Philo-parenthesists [lovers of parentheses]!) arises wholly out of that Slavery of the Mind to the Eye and the visual Imagination (or Fancy), under the influence of which the Reasoner must have a *picture* and mistakes surface for substance—Such men—and their name is LEGION—consequently *demand Matter*, as a *Datum*. As soon as this gross Prejudice is cured by the appropriate discipline, and the Mind is familiarized to the contemplation of Matter as a *product* in time, the resulting PHAENOMENON of the equilibrium of the two antagonist

Forces, Attraction and Repulsion, *that* the Negative and *this* the Positive Pole of Gravity* (or the Power of DEPTH) the difficulty disappears—and the Idea of CREATION alone remains.—For to will causatively with fore-knowlege is to *create*, in respect of all finite products.—An absolute and coeternal Product (improperly so called) is either an Offspring, and the productive Act a *Begetting*, or a Procession. The WORD begotten, the Spirit proceeding.

N.B. Attraction, Repulsion, and Gravity as the Root and Unity of both, are only a more special formula of the Dimensions, Length, Breadth and Depth considered as Powers, η δυναμικως [or dynamically].[†]

* Centrality, or Vis centrificus [Centrific force] would be the prefer-able term. It is the same with the Mosaic Darkness, in Hebrew, the with-holder or Holder-in, *Inhibitor*.—⚹ [as opposed to] Light, as the distinc-tive *exhibitive* Power.

[†] Several of the elder Logicians instead of the terms Length, Breadth and Depth use the far better terms, Linea, Superficies, Corpus [line, sur-face, body].

1828

Heinrich Steffens, *Anthropologie [Anthropology]*, Breslau, 1822.

Borrowed from Henry Crabb Robinson.

[# 242]

{People, especially old women, who have become addicted to drink or who, as in one of the most notorious cases, had the habit of rubbing their bodies with highly inflammable substances, e.g. spirits of camphor, suddenly burst into flame.} [Steffens proceeds to tell the story of Countess Cornelia Zangani, accustomed to rub her body with spirits of camphor, whose maids one morning found the grisly remains of her body in a heap of ashes.]

It is characteristic of H. Steffens to spoil and expose to ridicule deep psychological Hints and Possibilities by attempting to ground them on one or two questionable and anomalous facts—without reflecting that the exceeding rarity of such facts, even tho' they *should* have been accurately related, must be an incomparably stronger presumption against their having any connection with the imaginary Cause than the mere circumstance that the facts are capable of being accounted for by it, can be in favor of the supposition. The recently accredited Cases of spontaneous Conflagration of Dram Drinkers do not amount to half a dozen—during a period in which half a million inveterate Gin & Brandy Sots have gone in the dark to their Bed of Earth in the ordinary way of Dropsies, Schirrous Liver &c—

It is far more philosophic to suppose that the Conflagration took place after death, in consequence of rapid decomposition. The forcing the poor Countess Zangani's Camphor Frictions into an equivalent of Dram Drinking is too good a joke!!—

John Asgill, *A Collection of Tracts*, London, 1715.

A young admirer gave Coleridge this collection of religious and political tracts. Coleridge's note of 1828, with the 1832 afterthought here indi-

*cated in pointed brackets, conjures up memories of his childhood at a fa-
mous charity school, Christ's Hospital in London, known as "the Blue-
Coat School" from its blue uniforms.*

[# 243] Charm when one's foot is asleep—which I have tried 50 times
when a little Boy at the Blue-coat School, and always found efficacious—
It had been in the School time out of mind, possibly from the first foundation under Edward VI. ⟨Tho' now from "the march of intellect" perhaps
exploded and non-extant. S. T. C. 1832/⟩

> Foot! Foot! Foot! is fast asleep.
> Thumb, thumb, thumb, in Spittle we steep.
> Crosses three we'll make to ease us,
> Two for the Thieves and one for Christ Jesus.

And the same for a cramp in the Leg, only substituting for the first cou-
plet the following—

> The Devil is tying a knot in my Leg—
> Mark, Luke, and John, unloose it, I beg!
> Crosses three &c/

And getting out of bed, in which the Cramp most frequently occurred,
pressing the sole of the foot on the cold floor, and then repeating this
charm with the acts configurative therein prescribed, I can safely affirm,
that I do not remember an instance, in which the Cramp did not go away
after a few Seconds.

P.S. I should not wonder, if it were equally good for a Stitch in the Side;
but I cannot say, that I ever tried it for *that*.

S. T. Coleridge
1828

Grove, Highgate

Heinrich Eberhard Gottlob Paulus, *Das Leben Jesu [The Life of Jesus]*, Heidelberg, 1828.

*Coleridge started this new work of biblical criticism while on holiday in
Germany with Wordsworth and his daughter (the first note being dated
from an inn on the way). "Ev. Inf." (for "Evangelium Infantiae" or "Gospel of the Infancy") refers to the theory current among the German critics that accounts of the infancy of Christ in the first two chapters of*

Matthew and Luke were composed later than other parts of the Gospels; the "Magi Tradition" made the unnamed "wise men" of Matt. 2 into three named kings. In 1 Henry IV 2.4 Falstaff lies about having driven off a set of thieves, the number rising from two to eleven as he repeats the story. A "flatting machine" was a device like a clothes wringer or mangle used to reduce gold or silver ingots into ribbon or wire.

[# 244]

{Jehovah, it says, called to Moses from the mountain. Divinely inspired, the man confidently recognized as the true intent and voice of his God what would be of benefit to mankind. The ancient world, after its manner, has preserved this as an inspired statement or, as we are accustomed to say, as poetry. . . .}

Readily should I admit (what in fact for 30 years past I have acted on, on my own suggestion) the necessity of reducing the poesy of the old-hebrew Documents to their matter of fact import. But in the detailed account of the Delivery of the Law from Mount Sinai, the preparations, the series of Incidents and Appearances, the repeated and positive declarations of the Writer respecting their uniqueness and superhuman character are such, as leave no pretext for the resolution of the Statements into figurative language & poetic drapery (*Begeisterungsrede* [inspired statement])—and permit no alternative but *literal* matter-of-fact Truth, or intentional and deliberate Fiction meant to be received as truth.—S. T. C. 3 August 1828.—Antwerp, Le Grand Laboureur—Saturday.

[# 245]

{According to Luke's account of the rite of purification in the Temple at Jerusalem, it is not possible that the flight into Egypt had already occurred. This presentation in the Temple had to take place after 40 days. If they returned from Egypt later, it would no longer have been necessary. . . . Thus Luke, who had probably already read Matthew's gospel in Palestine but did not wish to review for his Theophilus the stories of the Magi and the flight into Egypt, events that he felt had no further consequences, links up two not immediately sequential events—namely, the Dedication at the Temple and the return to Nazareth—without indicating the omitted material, a frequent practice among historians.}

If Paulus's hypothesis of Oral Gospels be received, this previous acquaintance with a Gospel written by an Eye-witness and Apostle, a thing on all other accounts exceedingly improbable, would be in direct contradiction to Luke's own assurances. And as to Paulus's way of reconciling the absurd Magi Tradition with the narrative in the Ev. Inf. [Gospel of the Infancy] prefixed to Luke's Gospel, I would fain know what criterion of historic Truth or Falsehood would be left to us—for on the same privilege of inserting supposed spaces of Time ad libitum and against the plain sense of the Historian's Words, and at other times imaginary events, there would be no difficulty in harmonizing Sir John Falstaff's narrative of the Robbery on Gads-hill into a very consistent account. But Paulus's motive is evident. The Incidents of this symbolic Christopaedia [Boyhood of Christ], which in the 3rd Gospel still retain its poetic character, with the contents of some similar Poem or Hymn adopted as grave prosaic matter of fact by the far later compiler of the first Gospel duly blooded and purged by Paulus's psychological Process, &c would help him to account for our Lord's Self-persuasion &c without the necessity of any superhuman ministry, or of supposing Christ other than an hereditary Enthusiast, the Dupe of his Mother's, and two or three other *dreaming* Dotards' and Gossips', Enthusiasm. But all this is sadly foolish and mawkishly dishonest, on the part of the Heidelberg Professor of exegetic and hermeneutic Theology!

[# 246]

{And this rejection of evil shows him in an even more sublime light, when we consider that such determination, grounded in the Old Testament, was even maintained in a dreamlike state (for visions, it must be said, can only be imagined as a heightened dream state).}

There must be an original incurable Coarseness and Vulgarity in Paulus's mind—not to mention the psychological ignorance implied in this converted the beautiful Parable of the Temptation into a Dream! not one single character of which it possesses. In no one instance does "the Spirit"—"in the Spirit" "led by the Spirit" relate to a State of Sleep;—but on the contrary to the free exertion of the very faculties which Sleep suspends—viz. the contemplative and prospective. But putting this aside, the meanness and meagreness of Paulus's Interpretations are marvellous. He is a perfect *Flatting*-machine! But above all, the absurdity of treating with all the scrupulous respect due to the most authentic modern History Works that require or permit such interpretations!

[# 247]

{All the historical statements that follow converge on this one central point, on the purpose of proving that Jesus had become the true light of mankind, the kindler of soul-giving spiritual life and by this means establisher of the kingdom of God. In each one of these the conclusion is to be understood: he who was so acknowledged, so thought, spoke, behaved, and finally conquered the world by his endurance of crucifixion, yet by his resurrection raised the oppressed to the greatest heights of courage and inspiration, to the irresistible spreading of the history of his life as a teacher and his spiritual principles, this man was indeed everything that could be expected from the spiritual Messiah, the vice-regent of God.}

What I said 20 years ago, I say now—Sept. 1828. This Philosophy is true or false/ if true, why reject the faith *in* Christ grounded on it? If false, there can be no faith at all. Jesus must have been an enthusiast, and his Disciples Dupes.

[# 248]

[In regard to the miracle of the feeding of the five thousand (Matt. 14.13–22, John 6.5–14, etc.), Paulus points out that, despite the minute descriptions of detail, it is stated only that Jesus blessed the food and broke it, that he and his disciples had five loaves and two fishes, apparently for themselves. He argues that in all probability the others, the rich and the poor, had brought their own dinners from their camels.] {Nothing else is indicated by the four texts. For John glosses our German "blessing" (*eulogein*) with "giving of thanks" (*eucharistesas*). There is no mention of any multiplication. Rather, it is explicitly stated: "He broke the bread and had his disciples set it out, and in the same manner he divided the fish in parts for all."}

The same interpretation has occurred to me 5 and 20 years ago, as what an Infidel might suppose to have been the *origin* and *occasion* of the *Report* of Jesus having multiplied the Loaves and Fishes, but that *this* and *no more* was intended to be understood by the Writers or Compilers of the Gospels, above all, by the Author of the Gosp. according to St John— no! such an absurdity never could spring up in my Head!—

[#249]

[In commenting on the Gospels as historical documents for a reconstruction of the life of Christ, Paulus assumes that Matthew wrote the Gospel attributed to him:] {The Jewish publican Matthew, and Luke, who followed up the events that had recently occurred in Judaea, tended to retain only that which was more intelligible to the Jewish mind, the particular. . . .}

That there existed in early times a Syro-chaldaic Gospel, or memorabilia of Jesus, used by the Churches in Palestine: that this Gospel was compiled or revised by, or in some way received the Sanction of, Matthew; and that this was the Original or Groundwork of which our first Gospel was a free translation, with explanatory comments interwoven—I find no motive for denying—tho' as to any sound & convincing evidence from the Fathers and Ecclesiastic Historians, the attribution of the Gospels to the Apostles might very rationally be doubted, were there an adequate motive for the denial.—But that the Greek Gospel in its present form was written by Matthew and within 14 years after the death of Christ, I reject on what to me appears the clearest internal evidence.

Edward Irving, *Sermons, Lectures, and Occasional Discourses*, London, 1828.

Like the earlier translation of Lacunza, this work was a present from Irving, who inscribed it "To my Sage Counsellor & most honoured Friend." In his distress at Irving's increasingly unorthodox views (he was excommunicated in 1830 and set up his own "Irvingite" church in 1832), Coleridge publicly dissociated himself in his next book, On the Constitution of the Church and State *(1829).*

Katterfelto was a showman who claimed to be able to exhibit microscopic life-forms looking as large as birds by the use of a solar microscope. The words of Ps. 22 ("Why hast thou forsaken me?") are attributed to Christ on the Cross: Matt. 27.46, Mark 15.34. "Hades" Coleridge understood—on the authority of biblical scholars—to designate primal chaos, not hell. "Sky-scrapers" are sails set very high to take advantage of light winds. The "moat" (or "mote") in a brother's eye alludes to Matt. 7.3–5.

[# 250] I cannot help—notwithstanding the unfeigned and earnest respect, in which I hold Mr Irving, I yet cannot help at times comparing him in my fancy to a Hornet or Dragon-fly who having been caught and bound in the strongly-woven Spider-web of Calvinism had at length by vigorous efforts liberated himself, left the Web, rent and ruined but alas! carried off with him a portion of the Threads & viscous bonds that impede the free action of his Wings, and render his flight unsteady and bewildered—now soaring by his native vigor, now sinking by the weight of his still adhering bondage.—He writes like a fugitive from modern Calvinism, who has freed the chain from the Staple-ring, but not his ancles from the Chain. Mr Irving feels the grandeur and the moral necessity of that view of the redemptive Act which places it in the WILL and its holy causative yea creative and re-generative energies; but he cannot, rather he will not, leave hold of the old prison-mumpsimus of the Debtor and Creditor Account, so much pain & suffering for so much Sin, and of the accompanying contrariety of goodness and compassion in the self-substituted Debtor, or Debtors Proxy, the Son, to the enraged and (in strange contradiction to his asserted reasonless Sovereignty!) incapable-of-forgiving-Justice of the Father. And in order to reconcile this conception if not to his reason yet to his fancy and feelings he gives an exaggerated picture of physical and mental *Sufferings* of Jesus out of all warrant of the Gospel Record, which speaks of Temptations indeed, related doubtless by our Lord for the instruction of his Apostles (for they all refer to the great principles of their Conduct as Preachers of the Word endued with supernatural Powers)—but of Temptations calmly and triumphantly overcome—and in all else relates nothing that in intensity or continuity of *Suffering* exceeds what we read of as endured by the Martyrs and Missionaries of the first or even the latter ages. It is most observable, and most worthy of Observation, that in the statement of his higher views, the mysterious death-conquering energy of the sinless Will, and the *possibility* of re-union with Deity atchieved for the human race by the actual Union of Deity with that divine Humanity which is the *Ground* of the humanity or spiritual Personëity in every Person; he regularly repeats his sentiments in equivalent words cited from the Scriptures; while in the exhibition of his Calvinistic remnant he either refers to no scripture warrant, or presents it thro' the Katterfelto Glass of an extravagant Paraphrase.

[# 251]

> What, then, must the Son of Man's condition during three days and nights' abode in the heart of the earth have been! how abject, how dishonorable, how sorrowful! in order to stand between Jonah's misery and the misery of the Jewish people, the antitype of the former, and the prototype of the latter. It must indeed have been such as passeth all comprehension and belief: into the gulf whereof when he was passing downward, like Jonah into the open throat of that loathsome living sepulchre which widely opened its armed jaws upon the Prophet, he cried aloud, "My God, my God, why hast thou forsaken me! Father, into thy hands I commend my spirit."

I have more than once in Mr Irving's presence given the true interpretation of this most wildly perverted Text—have opened out the divine Wisdom & Goodness which our Lord here displayed: while at once to con-

sole the anguish and confirm the faith of Mary & John who were standing at some distance, he recited, with a loud voice a verse which must have
instantly reminded them of the 22nd Psalm—or as *we* should say, he *gave
out* the 22nd Psalm, which the Jews did not by mentioning the Book or
Number of the Chapter or Psalm but by citing the first Verse. He thus
flashed upon their recollection, that the very Scene at that moment before
their eyes with all its minute peculiarities were ever painted in this first
Half of this prophetic Hymn—But if in this the Prophecy had been accomplished to the uttermost point, how was it possible for them to doubt
the equal fulfilment of the latter half, announcing the triumph of the Saviour and the glorious establishment of his Kingdom, and the blessedness
of all that had received him. The Overcoming of his own Agonies, even
in the death-pangs occupied with lively compassion for others—the admirable appropriateness & the Godlike majesty of the consolation—Yes!
this was indeed a final Act worthy of him who in all things was to be our
Exemplar!—But what shall I say of the portentous and unhallowed Fancies, which Mr I. has conjured up without a single sentence of either
Gospel or Epistle for his Sanction or even for his pretext, out of an inter-
polation of the Apostles' Creed of the Sixth Century, & which even then
meant nothing more than verè mortuus est [he really died]! If such lawless Fictions as M^r I has here fabricated of our Lord's Torments in *Hell* (o
sad to meet in a discourse of the present day this vulgar mistranslation of
Hades) deserved a confutation, it would be enough to quote our Lord's
own words, It is finished!—No! (says Mr Irving) it had but just begun!
The worst was yet to come!! Alas! if Mr I. could see into my heart, he
would do justice to the pain & regret with which I have written these an-
imadversions!—

[# 252]

> [In his exposition of the relationship between Adam and Christ, the Fall and
> Redemption, Irving describes Adam as potentially "the perfect type of Christ"
> subjected only to a "test of obedience" coupled with a threat of death. God's
> "deeper purpose" reveals itself in the continuation of human life after Adam's
> lapse; it is "to permit the sin and to over-rule the Fall, to the destruction and
> extermination of sin" through Christ. The "one mighty plan" of God "is, to
> bring in the Christ through the avenues of sin and the jaws of death, and to es-
> tablish all things by the method not of first creation, but of restitution."]

N.B. The contents of this & the two preceding pages I neither grant nor
deny: for in truth I do not understand them. All I know is, that I cannot

express any article of my own faith, nor any opinion of mine, in these words. Nor can I recollect any thing, I have said or written, that could have suggested the matter of these pages. One thing, however, seems plain to me: viz. that after the assertion, l. 25 of p. 353, it is an inconsistency in Mr I. to ground his assertion of the actual infliction of everlasting torment on the fact of a Threat not half as clear & unmistakeable as this to Adam was. Strike out the Word, God, and substitute the name of an Individual, and I tremble to think what the Judgement of every upright man would be respecting the character of that Individual as measured by the schemes, stratagems, saying & unsaying, here described and asserted. I should despise myself for a Slanderer if I attributed to Mr Irving the indirect proceedings which he does not hesitate to attribute to God!

In short, in my conversations with Mr Irving I have repeatedly endeavored to fix his attention on that main *hinge* on which my whole System turns, & without which it is worse than senseless, a rank fomes [hotbed] of mischievous errors—viz. that what he calls Creation was the first Act of Redemption: which, of course, supposes an antecedent *fall* (antecedent in order of *Thought*, I mean, not in *Time*—For this Fall at least could not be in time, inasmuch as it was the origin of Time as *contra*-distinguished from Eternity.) But this was not stuff for the Pulpit: & on this account, tho' I fully believe not with his own consciousness, my friend always turned short off from my discourse on the Chaos, and the antecedents therein implied & presupposed, as so many hypertheological praeterscriptural Sky-scrapers, the mere puff and pride of the Vessel, which he was only too willing to suppose above his comprehension because he saw no motive and felt no impulse to make the attempt. From this one source all his errors & they have been most grievous errors, may be traced & have, in fact, been derived. Hence his ignorance respecting the Absolute, the abysmal Ground of the Trinity—his consequent utter misapprehension of the Trinity itself, neither apprehending aright the unity or the distinctities—hence his ignorance of the subsistences in the only-begotten WORD as the pleroma—and of the Father, as the I AM correlative to the Ὢν, or HE IS, the Son εν τῳ κολπῳ τοῦ πατρος [in the bosom of the Father]—hence his fantastic notions respecting an all powerful Personage or Individual whom he calls the Holy Ghost. But uninformed respecting the eternal Actualities & the eternal Realities, their Correlatives, he remains (if more *could* be) even more ignorant of the eternal Possibilities—& therefore of the *possibility* of a Fall, and of the necessary characters of a Fall actualized. Hence Matter, substantiated Matter (or Body in its physical sense as Matter filling a space) Body (in the narrower physiological sense, as Organ), Soul, Spirit—*every* thing! i.e. *systematically.* I begin to fear that I ought to regret my intercourse with Mr I. on his own account. For if he had never been tempted out of the popular way of thinking, & guided wholly & exclusively by his honest feelings & the letter of Scripture, treating each subject as an integer, standing on its own grounds, and exerting its appropriate influences within its own sphere, disregarding its connections with other truths, otherwise than as *one* among others, and thus regarding Theology as a bag of Coins, each of which had a value for itself & might be put out to interest on its own account—he might by his Zeal and exalted disinterestedness and extraordinary eloquence have been the Benefactor of Thousands & Ten Thousands—giving them the medicines, to each what the disease needed, without troubling either the Patients or himself with any SYSTEM of rational Pathology grounded on more general principles of Physiology; and at all events would have avoided the offensive Errors into which a supposed System has seduced him.

[# 253]

[Irving advocates paying attention to the history of the church as illustrated in the three discourses he has just given, for] until we study and understand, and can give some account of the Lord's dealings with his church, his choosing her of his own free grace, his leading and guiding her in righteousness, after she hath been fairly set out by his almighty power; his afterwards leading her into temptation . . . and after long, long ages, his returning to her with the warmth of his first love, that none of his promises to his chosen ones might fail;—I say, until all these his dealings with the outward visible church be understood . . . it will never happen that we shall be able to bear his dealings with us as individuals. . . .

If I know my own heart, I have every disposition to give the due weight to the arguments for the practical importance, or rather the indispensableness, of a lively watchful Attention to the political events of the World as successive fulfilments of this or that supposed Prediction of the same, now in this now in that text of this, or that, or third, 4th or 5th Prophet.— When an error in the Writings of a Man, whom I respect, flashes upon me, my first thought is to look about & into my own state of opinions, in order to discover if I can, whether it is not some Contrary error or defect in myself that has made me so quick in seeing the moat in my Brother's Eye. And truly in this instance, I think, that something of the kind has had place. My position, insulated as it were, & all my habits both of study and of life, have drawn my attention too exclusively to the invisible Church, to the communion of the Individual with the Spirit of Truth, in short, to Christianity as a Spiritual Light and at the same time an indwelling Energy from above. I have felt too little respecting the visible Church.—But still, while I earnestly ask for grace to fill up this chasm in my Christian Duties, I find myself wholly unable to reconcile my friend's Doctrines either with the to me palpable sense of the Scriptures, on which he grounds his Anticipations, or with our Lord's solemn declaration, that His Kingdom was not to be of this World. For if the Supreme Power in every Body Politic be bound to act as Vice-roys of Christ, to take the Old & New Testament for the practical Law-book, political, civil and criminal;—and this as a Book of Law & State-policy, and not merely as far as the Bible contains the fundamental *principles* of all Legality; and if (as Mr I. likewise asserts) the Kings and Rulers of the World are bound to receive the interpretations of this Book, and the applications of its Contents from the Pastors of the Church—it would be as rational to assert that George IVth is not King of Ireland because he governs by a Lord-Lieutenant, as to pretend that Christ's Kingdom is not a Kingdom of THE WORLD, i.e. of the Aggregate of civilized States.—My own System of Convictions on this point my honored Friend will find given at large in my, "Aids toward determining the right *Idea* of the Constitution in Church, and State, with the essential Characters of the three Churches, the National, the Christian, and the Church of Antichrist"—and will therefore have the opportunity of Ascertaining, wherein & how far my Convictions differ from his.

1829

The Quarterly Journal of Foreign Medicine and Surgery,
London, Nov. 1818–Aug. 1819.

This medical journal must have come to Coleridge's hands by way of either Gillman or Green. The notes could be of almost any date after 1819, but 1829 seems likely because of the way Coleridge was using the pentad in connection with color theory at that time.

[# 254]

[The author describes a class in a French school for the deaf and dumb.] The children . . . began by the alphabet both written and manual. They next proceeded to classified arrangements of substantives. To these they joined classified adjectives and next connected them by what is called absurdly the substantive verb . . . having no correspondence with anything in nature, serving merely to connect words in writing. . . . From adjectives to the class of substantives called abstract, the step is easy. The adverbs and prepositions, united with the substantives and adjectives already learned, are taught together, because it is obvious that, "with ease" and "easily" mean the same. The conjunctions follow, and are the most difficult, and though it is attempted here, as at Paris, to derive aid from grammatical philosophy, in teaching the conjunction, and indeed every other part of speech; yet, we are satisfied, that when the pupils have learned a great variety of prepositions and phrases, the difficulty of learning the conjunctions is in a great measure done away, and that it is practice alone which can surmount what remains of difficulty.

Prothesis—identity of Act and Being, or a Being essentially Act, an Act essentially Being: Noun = Verb + Verb = Noun. Verb Substantive, I AM.

Thesis	Mesothesis	Antithesis
Noun	Infinitive Mood	Verb
	Synthesis	
	Participle	

The modification of the noun by the verb is the ADNOUN or Adjective: the modification of the Verb by the Noun is the *Adverb*.

Every language must have five parts of speech: no language can have more than seven. Conjunctions and Prepositions are one or the other of the preceding, but most commonly the Verb in the imperative mood—as *But* i.e. divide, δε [but] corrupt imper. from Δαω divido [I divide], δη (= then) from δεω, connecto [I bind];—or the participle. The visual image, as expressing a *concrete*, is, by the frequent recurrence, made to express a *relation*, either of Time or Space—in the same way, in which Foot, Cubit, &c lose their visual image by abstraction of length. When such a word governs a whole sentence, we call it a conjunction; when only part of a sentence, a preposition: ex. gr. we encountered many obstacles; but we all went on but (i.e. except) James. An Interjection or Exclamation is no part of *Speech*, i.e. it does not express a thought, but a *sensation*, and is common to men and brutes.

This is the Logical Pentad; Prothesis, Thesis, Antithesis, Mesothesis (or the *Indifference* of Thesis and Antithesis, i.e. that which is both in either, but in different Relations; while the Prothesis is both as one in one and the same relation) and lastly the Synthesis. The modification of Thesis by Antithesis, and *vice versa*, constituting Adnoun & Adverb, convert the Pentad to an Heptad—analogous to the law of colours.

The Interpenetration of Light and Shade in the highest unity, or the Identity of Light and Shadow is RED, Color κατ᾽ εξοχην [pre-eminently], in positive energy. It is the Zenith, to which BLACK is the harmonious opposite, or Nadir—Color in negative energy.

Prothesis
Red

Thesis	Mesothesis	Antithesis
Yellow	Green indecomponible	Blue

Synthesis
Green—compon and decomponible.

But from the Prothesis, Red, to the Thesis an oblique line may be drawn, the bisecting point of which constitutes the Mesothesis of Red and Yellow, i.e. Orange, and in like manner a line from the Prothesis to the Antithesis, the bisecting point of which is the Mesothesis or Indifference of Red and Blue i.e. Violet or Indigo. And this is the Heptad of colours

The Infinitive mood is the Mesothesis or Indifference of Noun and Verb.

For not *to dip* the Hero in the Lake
Could save the son of Thetis from *to die*.
Spenser

Now here "to dip" is a Verb relative to "the Hero", as its objective or accusative case; but it is a *noun* and the Nominative, relatively to the Verb "could save." In the Greek and Italian languages this form is of perpetual occurrence—from to die, απο τοῦ θανεῖν, Could hinder him from to destroy brave Hector. Here "to destroy" is the Noun governed by the preposition (i.e. abbreviated Verb), from; and a Verb governing the Noun and Adnoun, brave Hector.

Thesis		Antithesis
Alkali	♓	Acid

Now hydrosulphurate is the *Mesothesis* i.e. an Acid relatively to an Alkali, an Alkali relatively to an Acid. Music (and Verse as its Articulate Analogon) is the Mesothesis of Order and Passion, or of Law and Life—of controlling, predetermining Will of Reason, and of Spontaneity, or lawless Will—*Will* of the Flesh, φρονημα σαρκος [mind of the flesh], Will surging up toward and against Reason as blind Life. Painting is the Mesothesis of Thing and Thought. A coloured wax Peach is one *thing* passed off for another thing—a practical lie, and not a work appertaining to the fine Fine Arts—a delusion, not an Imitation. Every Imitation, as contradistinguished from a Copy, is a Mesothesis, but which, according to the variable propiority [nearerness; comparative proximity] to the Thesis, or the Antithesis, may be called the *librating* Mesothesis. Thus, Real and Ideal are the two poles, the Thesis and Antithesis. The Sophoclean Drama, or the Samson Agonistes, is the Mesothesis in its propiority or comparative proximity to the Ideal—the tragedies of Heywood, Ford &c. (ex. gr. The Woman killed by kindness) is the Mesothesis in comparative proximity to the Real, while the Othello, Lear &c is the *Mesothesis* as truly as possible έν μεσῳ [in the middle], tho' with a *clinamen* [inclination] to the Ideal. The Tragic dance of the Horatii and Curiatii, to the Music of Cimarosa, such as I saw and heard at Leghorn, was the most perfect specimen of imitation, i.e. of a Mesothesis of Likeness and Difference, under the Maximum of the latter that I can even conceive. The proportions may vary manifoldly, but not lawlessly, and the proof of the legality is found in the *unity* resulting. Oil and Alcohol are both and equally *Units*, tho' their common components, Carbon and Hydrogen, are in almost reverse proportions, the one Hydrogen with predominance of Carbon, the other Carbon with predominance of Hydrogen: and the Atmospheric air as true a Unit as the nitrous oxyde, tho' the one gas be as 4 Nitrogen to 1 Oxygen, and the other as $2\frac{1}{3}$ N. to $2\frac{1}{2}$ Ox./ Hence the possible varieties in the fine arts, yet none *arbitrary*. The Arbitrary at once betrays itself, as a genus hybridum [hybrid genus], a *patch* work—like our modern inflated *prose* tragedies, Verse and Prose, Singing and Dialoguing Comic Operas, &c &c Chinese Mermaids, by stitching on the bust of monkeys to the tails of Seals.

Johann Gottfried Eichhorn, *Einleitung in das Neue Testament [Introduction to the New Testament]*, Leipzig, 1804–14.

This copy of Eichhorn on the New Testament belonged to Green. The account of the conversion of Paul in Acts 9 goes on to tell how God appeared to Ananias in a vision and sent him to restore Paul's sight.

[# 255]

> {But on the way, when Paul was already near Damascus, a bolt of lightning from clear skies struck and blinded him; in the manner of belief of the ancient world, he regarded this as an omen that would warn him against the continuation of his zeal for persecution, for which he had undertaken his journey to Damascus.}

Of the force or weakness of E's explanation of Sᵗ Paul's sudden Conversion, I say nothing.* But the Assertion, that Paul himself did not regard the incident, as miraculous and an actual presence of Jesus, when he grounds his apostleship and equality with the other Apostles, on the fact, that he no less than they had been in personal Communion with the Lord—this is too bad! Fair Play is a Jewel in all games. A psychological exposition of the *Causes* of a Man's Belief is one thing: an historical statement of the Belief is another. And how are we to account for the cöincident Vision of Ananias, and the instantaneous Restoration to Sight? From whom could Luke have received the Account but from his Friend and Comrade, Sᵗ Paul? or if from common report, is it credible that he should never have ascertained its truth and correctness from Paul himself?

N.B. Amaurosis and Blindness from nervous distemperature inter *casus*, in quibus Ζωο-μαγνητισμος multum valere creditur [among the *cases*, in which Zoo-magnetism is believed to have much virtue].

* I am bound to confess, that it would in my judgement strengthen and facilitate the evidence of Christianity, if it could be shewn, that *miracles* in the highest & specialist sense of the word were predicable of Christ alone.

1830

Daniel Defoe, *The Life and Adventures of Robinson Crusoe*, London, 1812.

This copy belonged to the Gillmans' younger son, Henry, born in 1814.

[# 256]

> But my ill fate pushed me on now with an obstinacy that nothing could resist; and though I had several times loud calls from my reason, and my more composed judgment, to go home, yet I had no power to do it. I know not what to call this, nor will I urge that it is a secret overruling decree that hurries us on to be the instruments of our own destruction, even though it be before us, and that we rush upon it with our eyes open.

Notice this ¶ph. "But my ill fate"—

When once the Mind in despite of the remonstrating Conscience has once abandoned its free power to a haunting Impulse or Idea—then whatever tends to give depth and vividness to this Idea, or indefinite Imagination, increases *its* despotism and in the same proportion renders the Reason and Free Will ineffectual. Now fearful Calamities, Sufferings, Horrors, & Hair breadth Escapes will have this effect, far more than even sensual pleasure & prosperous incidents/ Hence the evil consequences of Sin in such cases instead of retracting and deterring the sinner, goad him on to his Destruction. This is the moral of Shakespear's *Macbeth*: and this is the true solution of this ¶ph—not any over-ruling decree of Divine Wrath, but the tyranny of the Sinner's own evil Imagination which he has voluntarily chosen as his Master.

Robert Vaughan, *The Life and Opinions of John de Wycliffe*, London, 1828.

Coleridge's notes promote the idea of a "clerisy" or independent intellectual class that he had recently elaborated in On the Constitution of the Church and State. *He makes use of a topical analogy by referring to the*

*Bullion Controversy—the ongoing debate about the paper money intro-
duced in 1797 when the Bank of England had to suspend cash payments.
Coleridge's word "Ploutonomist" (an expert in the science of wealth) an-
ticipates the much later invention "Plutonomist."*

[# 257]

> [In 1209, as part of the crusade against the Albigenses:] The city of Beziers
> was first captured by the insurgents; and its inhabitants, amounting to many
> thousands, after a few hours were no more! [Footnote:] The numbers of the
> slain have been variously determined by catholic writers from 10,000 to
> 60,000. The half of the latter number is the more probable amount. . . .

This frightful massacre itself, under the circumstances of that dark and
ferocious age, is less shocking to the moral sense than the reiterated attempts of recent Catholic writers to defend or palliate the atrocity, by
keeping up anew the infamous calumnies on the innocent victims. The
great objects of our Church at present ought to be, first, the removal of
the wall of separation between them and the orthodox dissenters, by explaining the difference between the national clerisy, which ought to include all the three liberal professions as an *ordo civilis ad erudiendos
mores institutus* [a secular order instituted to improve morals], and the
Church, *i.e.* the Christian Church. 2. To promote throughout the continent, especially in France, Germany, and the north of Italy, the commencing reform *in*, not *from*, the Catholic Church, strictly confining their
exhortations to two points—the emancipation of the bishops and their
sees from all dependency on the Roman Pontiff,—and of the Clergy collectively from the obligation of celibacy. These points attained, all other
errors will die away gradually, or become harmless, or at worst, *ineptiae
tolerabiles* [tolerable fooleries].

[# 258]

> [Vaughan quotes Wycliffe:] "As the faith of the church is contained in the
> scriptures, the more these are known in an orthodox sense, the better. . . . the
> conclusion is abundantly plain, that believers should ascertain for themselves
> the matters of their faith, by having the scriptures in a language which they
> fully understand."

Note.—To *ascertain*, not for the first time to *learn* the truth. In order to
this, Christ had founded a *Church*, and by the first spiritually-gifted ministers of this Church, *some* of them instructed by Christ himself while in

the flesh, and all by the Spirit, with whom, and in whom, Christ returned to the faithful, as an indwelling Light and Life;—by the first ministers of the Church, I say, who were the fathers and founders of particular churches, the universal (Catholic) essential truths and doctrines of Christ were committed to writing, without withholding of any truth applicable to all times and countries, and binding on all Christians. Now these writings, collectively, form the New Testament, and whatever cannot be *recognised* there cannot be an essential article of faith. But the Scriptures, the great *charter* of the Church, does not supersede the Church; and till we have learnt the *whole scheme* of Christianity from the Church, by her creeds, catechisms, homilies, and according to the constitution of the apostles, the Bible could not but produce erring fancies, perplexities, jarring subjects;—and on the other hand, withdraw the Scriptures, and where is the check on the proceedings and pretensions of the certainly uninspired, and too probably ambitious Churchman? No! learn from the Church, and then in humility, yet freedom of spirit, test it by the Scripture. Note.—The Church doctrines are the bank-notes, the Scripture the bullion, which the notes represent, and which the Bank (*i.e.* the Church) must be always ready to bring forwards when fairly demanded.

Note to this note, by S. T. C.:—

> Nullum simile omnino quadrat—
> Quicquid *simile* est, non est *idem*.
> [No simile squares with everything—
> Whatever is *like* is not *the same*.]

No simile goes on all fours, or

> Every *simile* necessarily limps.

With this understanding, and so qualified, must the reader take my comparison of the Church doctrine relatively to Scripture as bank-notes to bullion. Now in this respect the simile halts,—that the bullion *may be* subdivided into doubloons, sovereigns, half-sovereigns, or to penny-pieces; and yet, notwithstanding this divisibility, we are assured, by the greater master of the science of trade, our most experienced Ploutono-mists, (Rothschild, Ricardo, Lloyd, &c. &c. &c.,) that the trade and commerce of this kingdom could not be carried on without ruinous stops and retardations, for a single week, by a metallic currency, however large! But be this as it may, the bullion of Scripture is not a bullion of this kind. It may be formally, I own, divided into bars = books; ingots = chapters; and coins, *i.e.* verses; but, alas! you might almost as well subdivide an organized body, and expect that the extracted eye would see, the insulated heart remain a heart, as attempt to interpret a text without its context, or that context without reference to the whole scheme. It is in the ὁμοπ-νευστια in the one and same divine spirit pervading and modifying all the differences, all the sundry workings of the *human* mind under different lights and different dispensations that the *divinity* of the Bible is manifested. The imperfect humanity must be there, in order, by its diversity and varying nature, to contrast with the *One* breathing in all, and giving to all one and the same direction.

John Bunyan, *The Pilgrim's Progress. With a Life of John Bunyan by Robert Southey*, London, 1830.

[# 259] I know of no Book—the Bible excepted as above all comparison—which I according to *my* judgment and experience could so safely recommend as teaching and enforcing the whole saving Truth according to the mind that was in Christ Jesus, as the Pilgrim's Progress. It is, in *my* conviction, incomparably the best SUMMA THEOLOGIAE *Evangelicae* [Compendium of *Evangelical* Theology] ever produced by a Writer not miraculously inspired—S. T. Coleridge. Grove, Highgate 14 June 1830.

P.S. It disappointed, nay surprized me, to find R. S. [Robert Southey] express himself so coldly respecting the Style & Diction of the Pilgrim's Progress. I can find nothing *homely* in it but a few phrases & single words. The Conversation between Faithful and Talkative is a model of unaffected correctness, dignity and rhythmical Flow.

Esaias Tegnér, *Die Frithiofs-Sage [The Story of Frithiof]*, trans. Amalie von Helvig, Stuttgart and Tübingen, 1826.

The German text has been preserved here since Coleridge reworks it in his note. "Burkes or Ciceros" stand for orators generally. Samuel Butler's Hudibras *(which Coleridge quotes) and Christopher Anstey's* New Bath Guide *were popular burlesque poems.*

[# 260]

> . . . Hoch war die erzgegossne Pforte, doch darin
> Trug mächt'ger Säulen Reih' auf starkem Schulterblatt

Empor der hohen Wölbung Rund, es hing so schön
Die Tempeldecke wie ein Riesenschild von Gold.

{ High was the cast-bronze portal, and within, a mighty row of pillars bore aloft
on their strong shoulders the round curve of the temple-dome, that hung there
as beautiful as a giant's shield in gold. }

I am in doubt whether for the German Language this hexameter Iambic,
or rhymeless Alexandrine, or the pentameter Iambic, i.e. our Blank Verse,
is the better. Two reasons plead for the former: first, that it is the Metre
for the narrative and colloquial portion of the Drama adapted by the *Greek*
Poets, and therefore doubtless best suited to the Greek Language, which
the German resembles in the three important points, that it is polysyllabic,
susceptible of compound words, and declines and conjugates the nouns
and verbs by cases, genders, and tenses. Second—that with the single exception of Lessing in his Nathan der Weise I remember no German Poet
who has written blank Verse, not even the dramatic, but still less the Epic,
that is endurable by an English Ear accustomed to the versification of
Shakespear and of Milton. The cause I believe to be that the Epic Blank
Verse is a compound of, or rather a *mid* thing, αμφοτερικον τὶ, between
Metre and *Rhythm*, as the two antagonist Powers, which the Ancients kept
separate, allotting the first to Poetry, the second to Eloquence—and the
Genius of the German Language is anti-rhythmical, but eminently metri-
cal. Hence, the Germans have a host of Poets, but very few Burkes or Ciceros. In epic blank Verse the Poet proposes to himself *Schemes* of harmonious sound, musical Paragraphs rather than sweet or strong single
lines—and where each line is a verse of itself, the effect of blank verse
is, that you feel yourself cheated of the rhymes. Now the Hexameter
Iambic is in fact a familiar lyrical metre, that of our ballads

$$\smile - \smile - \smile - \smile -$$
$$\smile - \smile -$$
$$\smile - \smile - \smile - \smile -$$
$$\smile - \smile -$$

Die Tempeldecke wie ein Rie—
—senschild von Gold
Empor der hohen Wölbung rund
Es hing so schön

For "von Gold" [of gold] substitute zu sehn [to see] or any better rhyme
to schön [beautiful], and it becomes the ballad metre.—And on the whole
I prefer it for grave and ornate yet not impassioned *Narration* to our blank
verse, even in our own language. The dactylo-spondaic Hexameter as

Gŏd cāme/ ūp wĭth ă̆/ shōut: ōur/ Lōrd wĭth thĕ/ Sōund ŏf ă /Trŭmpēt

preferable to either: but (to write it as it ought to be written, with due attention to the *quantity* as well as to the accent) it is far too difficult—even with the allowance of the frequent substitution of trochee for Spondee, – ◡ for – –, necessitated by the nature of our language. In fact, I am persuaded that even with the Ancients, the spondaic pronunciation of the Spondees in their recitation of Homer and Virgil was artificial, and peculiar to Verse—even as we now read Hudibras & the Bath Guide not as we talk but so as to humour the verse—

> ex. gr. With pulpit, drum ecclesiastic
> Tho' beat with Fist, instead of a stick—

where the Iambic ă̆ stĭck is humoured into the trochaically accented Spondee, ā ′stĭck.

1831

"Vindex," *The Conduct of the British Government towards the Church of England in the West India Colonies*, London, 1831.

This pamphlet was written in response to a comment made in the House of Commons that Christianity and slavery were "incompatible." "Vindex" protests that this opinion slanders Christ, who did not speak out against the slavery of his own time. Though he concedes that the tendency of Christianity is toward the eventual abolition of slavery, he disagrees with the program of direct political action advocated by T. F. Buxton and other members of the Anti-Slavery Society.

[# 261] A vigorous, eloquent, and for the far greater portion, wise and well-reasoned Remonstrance. My only objection, only important Objection, respects the ambiguity of the word "compatible" and "incompatible" in reference to Christianity. That it is and ever was compatible with the *co-existence* of the Christian Church, is fact of history—but so is ingratitude, gaming &c &c. But surely, what may co-exist with the Preaching, is not necessarily consistent with the precepts, and ultimate aims— i.e. with the Spirit, of Christianity. *War* is not forbidden, by the Gospel; but only the Passions, whence alone come Wars among men. Evils, the ultimate tho' perhaps slow & very gradual removal of which, are among the *Objects* of a Religion, cannot be incompatible with its *existence*. But let every remedy be applied according to its specific Powers—The Gospel is a remedy for Corruptions in the Will and darkness in the Reason (whence proceed the only dangerous errors in the Understanding) of Persons, of Individuals—It was not intended as a *direct* remedy for *Things*— and Institutions, *States* of Society, &c are *Things*—& therefore excluded from a *Spiritual* agency.—Indirectly indeed, and in as much as Causa Causae Causa Causati [the cause of a cause is the cause of the effect], the Gospel no doubt is an antidote to the evil of Slavery, as to the evil of War—of a bribed or a mob-managed Legislature—& what not?—In this one respect only I differ equally from Vindex & from Buxton & his Confreres.—Slavery is compatible with Christianity—& therefore Parliament may protect it, argues Vindex.—

223

Sl. is utterly incompatible with Christianity—screams B.—and therefore put it down by an Act of Parliament!—

Slavery—i.e. the perversion of a Person into a Thing—is contrary to the Spirit of Christianity (say I)—& therefore it is the duty of Christians to labor (as far as it is in their power & lies within the sphere of their immediate duties) for its ultimate removal from the Christian World—/ But that an Act of Parliament would be a fit or effectual Means toward this end, I not only do not believe; but I believe the very contrary/ and under these convictions give my conscientious vote for the measures recommended by Vindex as the right substitute for the fiery remedies prescribed by the Anti-slavery Society—

John Donne, *Eighty Sermons*, London, 1640.

Coleridge had annotated Wordsworth's copy of this book (with the first publication of Izaak Walton's life of Donne) twenty years earlier, but the notes in his own copy belong to his final years in Highgate.

[# 262]

And therefore our latter men of the Reformation, are not to be blamed, who for the most part, pursuing, S. *Cyrils* interpretation, interpret this universall light, *that lightneth every man,* to be the light of nature.

The error here—and it is a grievous error—consists in the word "Nature". There is, there can be no Light *of* Nature. There may be a Light *in* or *upon* it; but this is the Light, that shineth down into the Darkness—i.e. in Nature: and the Darkness comprehendeth it not. All Ideas, i.e. spiritual truths, are supernatural.

[# 263]

I remember one of the Panegyriques celebrates and magnifies one of the Romane Emperours for this, That he would marry when he was yong; that he would so soon confine and limit his pleasures, so soon determine his affections in one person.

It is surely some proof of the moral effect, Christianity has produced, that in all protestant countries at least, a writer would be ashamed to assign this, as a ground of *panegyric*: as if promiscuous intercourse with those of the other sex had been a natural Good, a privilege, which there was a great merit in foregoing! O! what do not *Women* owe to Christianity! As Christians only, do they or ordinarily *can* they, cease to be *Things* for men—instead of Co-persons in one spiritual I AM.

[# 264] When, after reading the biographies of Isaac Walton, and his Contemporaries I reflect on the crowded Congregations, on the thousands, who with intense interest came to these hour and two hour-long Sermons, I cannot but doubt the fact of any true progression, moral or intellectual, in the mind of the Many.—The tone, the matter, the anticipated sympathies, in the sermons of an Age form the best moral criterion of the character of the Age.—

[# 265] If our old Divines in their homiletic expositions of Scripture *wiredrew* their Text, in the anxiety to evolve out of the words the fulness of their meaning, expressed, involved or suggested, our modern Preachers have erred more dangerously in the opposite extreme, making their Text a mere *theme*, or *motto*, for their discourse. Both err in *degree*, the old Divines, especially the Puritan, by excess—the modern, by defect. But there is this difference to the disfavor of the latter—that the *defect* in *degree* alters the *kind*. It was ever God's holy Word, that our Donnes, Andrewses, Hookers preached, it was *Scripture* Bread, that they divided according to the needs & seasons—the Preacher of our Days expounds or appears to expound his own sentiments & conclusions—& thinks himself evangelic enough, if he can make the Scripture seem in conformity with them.—

Above all, there is something to my mind at once elevating & soothing in the idea of an order of learned Men reading the many works of the Wise & great in many languages for the purpose of making one book contain the life and virtue of all for their Brethren who have but that one to read—What then, if that one book be such, that the increase of Learning is shewn by more & more enabling the mind to *find* them all in it. But such, according to my experience, turned as I am of 3 score, the Bible is—as far as all moral, spiritual and prudential, private, domestic, or political, truths & interests are concerned. The Astronomer, Chemist, Mineralogist must go elsewhere; but the Bible is THE BOOK for the MAN—

1832

John James Park, *Dogmas of the Constitution*, London, 1832.

The Reform Bill, which redistributed seats in Parliament and significantly increased the number of men eligible to vote, was still under discussion when this work was published. Park acknowledges the influence of Coleridge's recent Church and State. This copy probably belonged to Coleridge's nephew and son-in-law Henry Nelson Coleridge, to whom the notes are directly addressed. "A liar from the beginning" is a quotation from John 8.44.

[# 266]

> Now either the theoretic right of the people to "a full and fair representation," in other words, to an exclusive occupation of the House of Commons by their own representatives, is a real right, or it is not; while Lord Erskine, in effect admitting it to be so, treats it in the same breath like the toy of a child, to be given out or withheld for the day, according as he is ill or well behaved. A Constitution which cannot weather an occasional fit of bad humour, must surely be a very faulty one!

Excellent! But the Whig principle like the Devil "a liar from the beginning". Even its essence is a contradiction under the form or notion of a compromise. And as the Devil is *per se* a mere *ens non verè ens* [a being not truly a being], that can *appear* only in coexistence with the product of the Logos [Word; Christ] or God-fiat—so Whiggism only by virtue of Toryism or republicanism with a symbol of unity.

John James Park, *Conservative Reform*, London, 1832.

[# 267] We are all, the best of us, imperfect Mortals, more or less laden with Sins, and sin-begotten infirmities. If we deemed no one worthy the name and duties of a Friend, but one who in no part of his conduct and character gave reasons for regret or for blame, Friendship could have no existence on earth, nor any occasion for displaying itself.

226

Now as a poor self-condemned Creature, who yet in any moment, in which I was myself, would hesitate at no sacrifice for the interest of those, I have professed to love, I require three things in the person who has asked me to call him my FRIEND.

First, a charitable if not a tender Consideration of the circumstances; a pitying allowance for the temptations, that have been resisted, in counterpoise of those, under which I have fallen.

Second—& notwithstanding the former, a prompt & unsparing Openness. To have seen or suspected should be instantly followed by the reproof or the question.

Thirdly, and the holiest office of Friendship, *Hope* even against Hope for the sustentation of Hope in our poor self-condemning Friend. O try to save him from despairing of himself. In the Duck-and-Drake projection across the stream of Error and Misery let the Friend be as the elastic force of the Water, giving a new bound to the Stone, & preventing its touch of the stream from being its submersion.—O how much can Hope & the Infusion of Hope from a kind Friend effect for a right-principled Soul, groaning under the sense even more bitterly than under the consequences of its error & frailty. My Disease is—Impatient Cowardice of Pain & the desperation of outwearied Hope.

1833

Samuel Johnson, *Works*, London, 1710.

Samuel Johnson "the Whig" (as opposed to the more celebrated Samuel Johnson the Tory) supported the Exclusion Bill which barred Roman Catholics—specifically, James II—from the throne. Some of the notes in Coleridge's copy of his works are addressed to Charles Lamb.

Considering Whiggishness in essence as a readiness to compromise and historically as arising from the conflicts of the Restoration, Coleridge traces a pattern from the first earl of Shaftesbury, who changed sides to the point of being imprisoned for treason, to Earl Grey, prime minister in the Whig administration that introduced the Reform Bill passed in 1832. "Highgate Oaths"—the phrase stemming from an old custom in Highgate pubs—are nonsensical oaths. Samuel Barrow wrote a Latin verse tribute published with Milton's Paradise Lost; *Samuel Clarke, a mathematician, wrote also on the Trinity.*

[# 268]

[From the biographical preface.] These several Propositions [in justification of "having abandon'd King *James,* and own'd King *William* and Queen *Mary*"] being maintain'd by Divines of Note, it is the less to be wonder'd that Mr. *Johnson* who oppos'd those Principles, and particularly in his Book about the Abrogation of King *James,* cou'd get no Church-Preferment, since he had such numerous and powerful Enemys among the Clergy, who represented him as a Republican, for maintaining that King *James* was dethron'd for Male-Administration, and that King *William* and Queen *Mary* were set up in his stead by Authority of Parliament.

Often have I had a wish whence my reason almost forbad a Hope, that God would yet grant me an interval of sufficing Health & Power to execute my long fostered purpose of writing the history of Whiggery, or the Principle (λογου αλογου [of illogical logic]) of Compromise of Principles, from the First Whig, Lord Shaftesbury (Cromwell's Ashley Cooper & Dryden's Achitophel) to Earl Grey—ultimum Whiggorum [the last of

the Whigs].—*Samuel Johnson, & Defoe.*—*S. T. C.* N.B. King William
(the Third) was no Whig; but an honest Man.

[# 269]

> . . . Magistrates themselves . . . when they turn Tyrants, do no less overthrow
> the Ordinance of God than the Seditious: and therefore their Consciences too
> are guilty, for not obeying the Ordinance of God, that is, the Laws which they
> ought to obey. So that the Threatenings in this place [Rom. 13] do also belong
> to them: wherefore let the severity of this Command deter all men from think-
> ing the Violation of the Political Constitution to be a light Sin.

Since the Reform Bill of 1832, following on the Bill for admitting Papists
to political Power under the inauspicious Auspices of the Duke of
Wellington & Sir Robert Peel, THE KING IS extinct—We have *Statutes* in
super-abundance—but no *Law*, no Constitution. They have perished by
the suicidal perjuries of George IVth & that precious *Plebs* personified,
William IV.[th]—

[# 270]

> Publick Laws are made by publick Consent; and they therefore bind every
> man, because every man's Consent is involv'd in them.

But to consent implies a moral responsible Person, and therefore a moral
obligation determining the consent, and therefore a Law antecedent to the
Consent, which therefore rather *declares* & actualizes the Law than constitutes it. The whole Scheme of a compact is a mere fiction, or shall I say,
an apologue, or allegory. If my Great-grandfather consented without or
against Right and right Reason, I am excused for following the bad example only as far as I cannot help myself—i.e. cannot do otherwise, without being hung or shot for it. But if he consented with good reason, the
same good reason independent of his example obliges me.

[# 271]

> Now I can tell him that Allegiance is so obstinate a thing, that neither De-
> sertion nor Conquest, nor any thing in the world but what is intrinsecal to it,
> (that is Breach of Covenant or consent of both Partys) can dissolve it: it is a
> Moral Duty, and Heaven and Earth may pass away before Allegiance can
> pass away.

An Oath of Allegiance to a Conqueror implies the qualification of, as long as no one conquers *you*. Louis 18th conquered Napoleon; & the French who had fought for Napoleon according to their Oath of Allegiance swore the same to Louis—but when Louis allowed Napoleon to reconquer *him*—why, then N. stood in the place of L. as L. had taken the place of N. The Light, the Oath, fell upon the *Place*, and on the *Figure* only *as*, and *while*, it occupied that Place.—I know no other Morality to suit such an Unmorality as Conquest.—Give me your money, or I'll blow out your Brains!—Swear that you will give me your money, or I'll blow out your Brains!—I confess, I see small difference between the two—& should scruple the latter as little or as much as the former. An oath extorted by violence is—the Air which the voice articulates, & all that a *Conqueror* has any right to demand.

[# 272]

> And again all *Englishmen* that have any tolerable knowledg of the Constitution are sensible, that the Office of a King depends wholly upon the Law, both in its making and in its being; and that a King as he is impower'd by Law must act by Law: and therefore they must needs know at first sight, that a King whose Authority is antecedent to the Law, independent of the Law, and superior to the Law, as Dr. *Sherlock* says ours is, is an invented and study'd King, whom the *English* Law knows not; but is of Dr. *Sherlock*'s own making, and is a King of Clouts.

Excellent! Much as I dislike Lord Grey & his Gang for their transferring the deliberative & determining functions from the Parliament to the Mob before the Hustings, & thus degrading Representatives of the Realm into Delegates of the Rabble, yet I dislike far more, yea, detest them for nullifying the kingly office, by reducing the Coronation Oaths to Highgate Oaths. For a genuine English King is the greatest possible Security for Freedom since the Agent without or against Law is ipso facto *not* the King but some punishable Subject. It is the King, only while it is the Law— and on the other hand, the King is bound by the most solemn Oaths before God & to the Nation, to make abortive every projected Law, destructive of Freedom.—I agree with S. J. that every *Subject* on reaching the age of discretion ought to take the Oath of Allegiance, the King's Coronation Oath having been first recited to him/ & the Subject answering—The King having thus bound himself, I on my part swear that I will *return* faithful allegiance to him—&c &c.

[# 273]

The Sea is our Element; where our Shipping was lately more numerous than any Nation's in the World, and better built being of *English* Oak, and our Seamen Heart of Oak. Such a Strength, well manag'd and well apply'd, is fit to give Laws to all the World. . . . We shou'd have scorn'd *Dutch* Help to fight the *French* Fleet, and to go to War upon Crutches. . . .

Another proof of my Assertion, that S. J. was *no Whig;* but a genuine old English *Nationalist*, and *Kings*man, as long as the King represented the Sovereignty of the Nation by being himself Liege and Loyal thereto.

S. T. Coleridge/*

* Nothing can *reconcile* me to my wobbling name, Samuel; but Dr Samuel Barrow, and the Rev^d Mr Samuel Johnson are Pound weights of palliative Consolation, to which sundry pennyweights are added by Dr Samuel Clark, and *D^r* Samuel Johnson. I suspect, that before the Puritan Times Samuel was no *Christian* Name, but confined to Jews.

Analysis of the Report of a Committee of the House of Commons on the Extinction of Slavery, London, 1833.

This Analysis, *produced by the Society for the Abolition of Slavery and edited probably by Coleridge's acquaintance Thomas Pringle, by whom it is inscribed, summarizes evidence given before a Commons committee in 1832.*

[# 274]

Inconveniences might possibly arise, both to master and slave, from any great and sudden change, like that of emancipation, as they arise more or less from all great changes. But it is Mr. Duncan's firm opinion, that, even if the Negroes were emancipated at a stroke, there would not be that loss or disturbance which must ensue if emancipation is long delayed. Emancipation might take place with perfect tranquillity, if a proper police were established. [Duncan then spoke of the possible transfer of land to freed Negroes in return for labor, of the superior character of the "religiously-instructed slaves," and of the violent opposition of most planters to religious instruction because it encouraged the slaves' desire for freedom.]

As to plans of emancipation, Mr. Duncan thought that all partial plans would fail of their effect. The best was that of emancipating all children born after a certain day, but even that was attended with great and perhaps insuperable difficulties. Still that would be better than nothing. The only plan not attended with very great, perhaps insuperable difficulties, is a general emancipation. Not that there are not great difficulties in the way of that measure, but they were more easily overcome.

Preparatives. 1. Stipendiary Magistracy. 2. Organized Police/ 3. Means of Instruction, Schools, Chapels/. *Then*, from Jany 1835, all Children, born in marriage, free by birth. 2. The Slave Population to be emancipated, each year, one tenth, for three days/ At the close of the year following, wholly emancipated—their places being then filled by the 10th of the following class, now half-emancipated—& so on, the priority being the premium of 1. moral good conduct & industry. 2. Progress in religious instruction. 3. Ability to read the Gospel—

At the end of the tenth year all would be free—or from incurable depravity under the control of Law. And from the very beginning all would be so far emancipated, that they would cease to be Mancipia = things, & become Persons, tho' not at first jure suo [their own masters], but sub tutelâ [under guardianship], as Wards & Clients of the Law./

Apocalypsis graece [The Apocalypse in Greek], ed. J. H. Heinrichs, Göttingen, 1821.

At a time when he was considering trying to write a verse translation of the Book of Revelation, Coleridge borrowed this edition with Heinrichs's commentary from the biblical scholar William Wright.

[# 275]

{These considerations . . . do not prevent the poet's words from being applied to a proconsul of Ephesus also [i.e., as well as to Nero], who seems to be being brought before us . . . and this suggestion will not be disproved because we have no knowledge of the existence of this proconsul nor of his good or bad fortune. . . .

But according to Herder's hypothesis, which refers everything to Judea and Jerusalem, all this points to Simon's crafty companion and accomplice, Joannes Levi of Gischala. . . . This false prophet is said below in numerous passages to have been with the Beast, so that a deadly duumvirate, and then on the arrival of the dragon of ch 12 a triumvirate (16.13 and elsewhere) rises to attack the Christians.}

O the sad historic prosaisms of the Proconsul of Ephesus, and Johannes Levi of Gischala!

I have too clearly before me the idea of the poet's genius to deem myself other than a very humble poet; but in the very possession of the idea, I know myself so far a poet as to feel assured that I can understand and interpret a poem in the spirit of poetry, and with the poet's spirit. Like the ostrich, I cannot fly, yet I have wings that give me the feeling of flight; and as I sweep along the plain, can look up toward the bird of Jove, and can follow him, and say—

"Sovereign of the air, who descendest on thy nest in the cleft of the inaccessible rock, who makest the mountain pinnacle thy perch and halting-place, and scanning with steady eye the orb of glory right above thee, imprintest thy lordly talons in the impassive snows that shoot back and scatter round his glittering shafts,—I pay thee homage. Thou art my king. I give honour due to the vulture, the falcon, and all thy noble baronage; and no less to the lowly bird, the sky-lark, whom thou permittest to visit thy court, and chaunt her matin song within its cloudy curtains; yea, the linnet, the thrush, the swallow, are my brethren:—but still I am a bird, though but a bird of the earth.

Monarch of our kind, I am a bird, even as thou; and I have shed plumes, which have added beauty to the Beautiful, grace to Terror, waving on the helmed head of the war-chief;—and majesty to Grief, drooping o'er the car of Death!"

1834

John Kenyon, *Rhymed Plea for Tolerance*, London, 1833.

A presentation copy from the author. The Athanasian Creed, which condemns nonbelievers to "perish everlastingly," had been proved in 1642 to have been erroneously attributed to Athanasius, bishop of Alexandria and firm defender of the doctrine of the divinity of Christ against the Arians in the fourth century. The English theologians George Bull and Daniel Waterland are cited as authorities on the Trinity; Waterland had also written a history of this Creed.

[# 276]

> . . . if the damnatory clauses of our Liturgy and of our Church articles be indeed not of general credence; then it requires small argument to show that they should no longer be suffered to remain.

If, as I suppose, the excellent Author refers to the Athanasian Creed, he might have called for its immediate expulsion from the Liturgy, it deforms, on many & more valid grounds—1. as pseudo-Athanasian, the work of a ignorant as well as bigotted Monk, half a century later than the Death of the truly good Athanasius; 2. as therefore without Church Authority. It is the Creed of no Council or Synod: 3. for its confusing Tautology: 4. because it is virtually *heretical* by omission of an absolutely essential Article, the subordination of the Filial Word, *as* God—& not *per accidens* [as an accidental], in the Incarnation.—5. because its determination in the Eutychean & Nestorian Controversy is controvertible, & of very doubtful accordance with the best Catholic Divines, & being without even the shadow of a Scripture Text to support its dogmas, is (as indeed the whole Creed is) most offensively presumptuous. Myself a zealous Athanasian, who hold the doctrine of the Tri-unity not only to be an important article of Christianity; but *to be* Christianity—not only not to contradict Reason or Religion; but to *be* the Reason & the Religion—denounce this Creed, as the great Dedecus, et Infortunium [Disgrace, and Misfortune] of the Established Church: and its continuance without a remonstrance the opprobrium of its Bishops, and Dignitaries, since the time

234

that Bull and Waterland *fixed* this Article for the whole Catholic Church, Romish & Protestant./

Robert Southey, *The Doctor*, London, 1834.

This first installment of The Doctor, *which was eventually finished in seven volumes in 1847, was a gift from Southey.*

[# 277]

> The Philosophers of whom you have read in the Dictionary possessed this wisdom [the "wisdom" that is celebrated in the Bible] only in part, because they were heathens, and therefore could see no farther than the light of mere reason sufficed to shew the way. The fear of the Lord is the beginning of wisdom, and they had not that to begin with. So the thoughts which ought to have made them humble produced pride, and so far their wisdom proved but folly.

Truth and Evidence are distinct terms; the latter implying the former, but not vice versâ. Truths, equal in *certainty*, may be of very unequal *Evidence*— ex. gr. Geometry and the Differential Calculus. Would that Southey could be induced to see, that the Light from Metaphysics, that lumen fatuum [misleading light], at which he so triumphantly scoffs, is better than the recollection of the Legends & technical Slang of Common-place Sermons! and then instead of "the light of mere Reason", he would have said—"the inferences of the sensual Understanding imperfectly enlightened by Reason." There is something shocking to a thoughtful Spirit in the very phrase "*mere* Reason".—I could almost as easily permit my tongue to say "mere God." I am a Christian of the School of John, Paul, Athanasius, Bull and Waterland, a Church of England Christian/ & therefore do not say, "God is the Supreme Reason"—but this I will and do say, that the Supreme Reason (ο Λογος, Jehova, ο ΩΝ [The Word, Jehovah, the One who Is]) is God—and are there two *Reasons*, a rational Reason, & an irrational?—

[# 278]

> The eighth had no male issue; he left two daughters, and daughters are said by Fuller to be "silent strings" sending no sound to posterity, but losing their own surnames in their matches.

This evil in genealogy the French and Germans endeavor, if not to prevent yet in part to remedy, by affixing the Maiden or paternal to the married Name—thus: *Frances Patteson*, NÉ *Coleridge.* Catherine *Pappen* heissen, *gebohrne* Von Axen [called Pappen, born Von Axen]—an heraldic usage worthy of adoption in England, where the disruption of the married Daughter from her parent Stock, and absorption into the name and family of the Husband, is not to be praised. It is a *discontinuity* in descent—and a Nothingizing of the Female.

Daniel Sandford, *Remains*, Edinburgh, 1830.

Said to be the last book Coleridge annotated, with notes addressed to Henry Nelson Coleridge. The two of them had also recently shared Francis Bond Head's book with its account of the paneidolon and illustrations made with its assistance. All the optical instruments mentioned brought a large scene into a small compass, making them convenient devices for artists.

[# 279] Pray, read at least the 1st 100 Pages of this volume & mark the book down for a 2nd reading—As far as I have read—for alas! thro weakness of the body & over-activity of the suggestive mind I now crawl thro' a book like a fly thro a milk splash on a Tea-tray! I who 20 years ago, used to read a volume, stereotype-wise by whole pages at a glance: as if my eyes & brain had been a claude Lorrain Mirror, or a Camera Obscura or Dr Woolaston's Camera Lucida or Mr Burton's new patent Paneidolon, specimens of the produce of which you have seen in Sir F Head's "Bubbles from the Brunnen".

INDEX

This index includes names and subjects in Coleridge's notes, and selected names and subjects in the passages quoted from the books he was reading. Proper names are given their standard modern spellings, e.g., "Shakespeare." Works are listed under the names of the authors where those are known; books of the Bible are listed under "Bible." An asterisk indicates a work annotated by Coleridge.